The
REVOLUTIONARY WAR
in the
SOUTHERN BACK COUNTRY

The
REVOLUTIONARY WAR
in the
SOUTHERN BACK COUNTRY

James K. Swisher

PELICAN PUBLISHING COMPANY
GRETNA 2008

LIBRARY OF CONGRESS CATALOGING-IN-PUBLICATION DATA

Swisher, James K., 1939-
  The Revolutionary War in the southern back country / James
K. Swisher.
     p. cm.
  Includes bibliographical references and index.
  ISBN 978-1-58980-503-3 (hardcover : alk. paper) 1. Southern
States—History—Revolution, 1775-1783—Campaigns. 2. United
States—History—Revolution, 1775-1783—British forces. 3. Great
Britain. Army—History—Revolution, 1775-1783. 4. South
Carolina—History—Revolution, 1775-1783—Campaigns. 5. North
Carolina—History—Revolution, 1775-1783—Campaigns.
6. Georgia—History—Revolution, 1775-1783—
Campaigns. 7. Virginia—History—Revolution, 1775-
1783—Campaigns. 8. United States—History—
Revolution, 1775-1783—Campaigns. I. Title.
  E230.5.S7S95 2007
  973.3'30975—dc22

                                        2007028064

Printed in the United States of America
Published by Pelican Publishing Company, Inc.
1000 Burmaster Street, Gretna, Louisiana 70053

For Dr. Raymond Warlick
Professor of History
Ferrum College, Ferrum, Virginia

A master teacher, historian, and storyteller whose drive and dedication to reveal the southern revolutionary struggle was only equaled by his passion to complete a definitive biography of his hero, Francis Marion. Tragically, both efforts were interrupted by his untimely death.

Contents

Introduction

"The Stream of Revolution, once started, could not be confined within narrow banks, but spread abroad upon the land."

J. Franklin Jameson, *The American Revolution Considered as a Social Movement*

Deep beneath the blue gray water of Lake Norman, thirty-five miles northwest of Charlotte, lies Cowan's Ford on the Catawba River. About 4 A.M. on February 1, 1781, Charles Cornwallis, lieutenant general in the armies of George III and member of the House of Lords, spurred a reluctant mount down a steep embankment and into the Catawba, swiftly running four hundred yards wide and four feet deep at full flood. He was closely followed by Colonel Hall of the Brigade of Guards with the light infantry of the Brigade of Guards, their bayonets fixed on uncharged muskets and cartouche bags of cartridges strung about their necks. A bold British striking force was quietly attempting to force a river crossing, striving to cut off Daniel Morgan's victorious Colonials, now retreating north across the North Carolina back country. In as bold a feat of arms as ever undertaken by a British army commander, Lord Cornwallis dispatched Col. James Webster leading a demonstration toward Beatties Ford and personally led the guards, the Royal Welsh Fusiliers, and the Hessian von Bose Regiment in an assault across the raging Catawba at night, low-lying fog masking the advance.

Slinging their Brown Bess muskets, the guardsmen cut eight-foot wooden staffs to maintain their balance on the rocky bottom and plunged forward four abreast behind a quartet of mounted officers, three generals and a colonel. Cornwallis entered first, flanked by General O'Hara of the guards, General Leslie, and the aforementioned Hall. Proceeding quietly in anticipation of rebel fire, the scarlet-coated soldiers completed almost half of their crossing before shouts and frantic movements signaled their discovery. Musket balls began to zing alongside the column as Colonial militia, stationed at the ford, fired blindly at the splashes of advancing troops. From upstream the boom of Webster's 3-pounders could be heard above the roar of rushing water. O'Hara's horse suddenly stumbled and rolled, throwing its rider under, while Leslie was swept from his saddle to be saved by a guardsman's extended staff. Standing to wave his guardsmen on, Hall was struck and killed by a musket ball just as Cornwallis's horse was hit for a second time. A contingent of light infantrymen sprinted past Cornwallis, sweeping up the steep bank on the Colonial side with bayonets, paused to load, and formed ranks. Cornwallis dismounted as his horse fell dead on the rebel bank. A musket ball struck Gen. William Lee Davidson, the capable American militia commander, setting off a confused and precipitous Colonial retreat. The desperate river crossing was complete.

Nearly a month earlier, in the damp, cold fog of early

morning on January 17, 1781, a ragged American force composed of militia battalions, Continental regiments, and a few cavalrymen huddled about campfires on the gentle slopes of a broom-straw field interspersed with oaks and chestnuts. A tall, rawboned, forty-four-year-old brigadier general, identified only by his uniform and wearing a battered old sword, stalked arthritically from fire to fire, joking, laughing boisterously, and patiently explaining his plans for first light. "Bany" was coming at a gallop, but if they listened to the Old Waggoner, Banastre Tarleton and his regulars would be running by noon.

A child of the frontier, his back scarred with 499 lashes of a British whip, this veteran of Braddock's inglorious defeat and a hundred Indian fights was a born backwoods leader. He could neither read nor write until taught to do so by his sixteen-year-old bride. With a lack of education, ignorance of the military arts, and a loud and profane method of expression, Daniel Morgan would never have attained leadership of a single file in the caste-defined British system of officer selection. But on the American frontier leadership was attained by merit and here on the dew-covered slopes of Cowpens, South Carolina, he brilliantly placed his followers in progressively stronger lines, constructing a tactical trap for Tarleton's aggressive and impatient nature. In doing so Morgan achieved one of the most outstanding American tactical victories of the revolution.

Astride a broken-down old nag, his leggings soaked with dew, the scar-faced Morgan anxiously viewed the Mill Gap Road from which he knew British outriders would appear. He was exactly what he appeared: a barroom brawler of fearless reputation. He led by example and demanded equal effort from those who followed him. Physically, despite his infirmities, he could and would whip any man

Mill Gap Road. On January 17, 1781, Daniel Morgan observed green-coated dragoons followed by the scarlet of British infantry emerge from the mists on the Mill Gap Road. (*Photo by Penny Swisher*)

on the field, friend or foe. Beneath that coarse exterior lurked a heaping of common sense and the patience to integrate a ragtag force of militia and Continentals and outgeneral, outmaneuver, and outfight a combined arms strike force of professional soldiers. As Morgan swung his arms from side to side to keep warm while vapor trails issued from his lips he spied what he sought. Through the pine limbs, green coats of the British Legion appeared, followed by the scarlet and white of the infantry. Morgan wheeled his horse and galloped for his first line of militiamen.

These vignettes, and a hundred similar others, illustrate the stellar individual contributions that characterize this final and decisive campaign of the revolution. Many of these individuals so intimately involved in the war can be recalled only by their fading pictures hung on the walls of county courthouses or schools. Occasionally they find mention in dated old history texts. Numerous counties and villages in the southern back country of North America are named for patriot heroes, but their actual deeds are often forgotten in the mythology of a dusty past. British and Hessian participants met an even more inglorious end. Buried where they fell, alongside roads or in plowed fields, these brave men disappeared even from the memories of families and friends far away, forgotten like the cause for which they fought.

But in the spring of 1775, these men were creating history. Numerous protests, boycotts, and acts of civil disobedience coalesced into open conflict between Great Britain and her North American colonies. Strangely, those provinces most like the mother country revolted just as an era of expected imperial glory emerged as a result of France's concession of her American colonies. During the almost eight years of warfare that followed, a nation was birthed, one that has exerted more impact upon modern world history than any other and now stands alone as a global superpower. The ensuing revolution was contested over a vast territory extending from Canada south to Florida and stretching inland from the Atlantic Ocean to the Appalachians and beyond.

Prior to 1775, American protests led to some quartering of redcoat infantry in the Colonies, particularly in Boston, Massachusetts, a major seaport, economic hub, and center of protest and defiance. In April, when Gen. Thomas Gage detached grenadiers and light infantrymen toward Lexington in search of a powder cache, he inadvertently touched off a powder keg. An exchange of gunfire on the triangular village green triggered a fighting retreat from Concord by 1,800 British troops who absorbed 73 killed and 174 wounded from swarms of rebel militia firing from every stone wall or copse of trees. As a result Boston was soon besieged by an armed mob of floppy-hat-wearing musket bearers. In January an attempt to break the rebel lines saw a blood bath on Breed's Hill, where another 226 British soldiers were slain, including many prominent officers.

George Washington, a Virginia planter, was appointed by the Continental Congress to organize an army from the almost fifteen thousand volunteers about Boston. He quickly approved an invasion of Canada by Generals Phillip Schuyler and Benedict Arnold, an endeavor that failed abjectly. On March 27, 1776, Gen. Robert Howe, who had replaced the unenthusiastic Gen. Thomas Gage, temporarily evacuated Boston, moving the army to Halifax, Nova Scotia. The Colonies were free of British troops.

This action was only preparatory to an actual campaign, and on June 25 Howe landed an overwhelming army on

Staten Island near New York City. Thirty-two thousand British regulars and Hessian allies stormed ashore, the largest expeditionary force ever dispatched from England. Desirous of awing the American Congress into a negotiated settlement, he launched a traditional campaign intended to clear New York and New Jersey of Colonials and defeat Washington's rebel army. But Washington, after serious setbacks around New York, realized that the odds dictated his adoption of a policy of preservation and avoided confrontation with the main Hessian and British army.

A subsequent action saw British commanders launch a selected army down the Lake Champlain route from Canada in an attempt to cut off New England from the remaining Colonies. Gen. John Burgoyne led the grandiose invasion but was surrounded and forced to surrender near Saratoga, New York. This mini-disaster has often been called the turning point of the war. French intervention was forthcoming and fighting in the northern theater soon largely was stalemated. Sir Henry Clinton replaced Howe as commander, but his troops were generally confined to the New York area without the ability to fight Washington, save on the American choice of terms. Since this initial campaign to recapture the Colonies had miscarried, reconsideration of a further strategy was necessary.

With the active entrance of France into a war rapidly spreading to worldwide significance and an ever hardening impasse in the northern combat zone, the British ministry was forced to reduce the resources it employed to defeat the American rebels. In addition, control of all-important sea lanes was now subject to interruption by the French fleet. But the king and his ministry refused to concede freedom to the Colonies, instead determining to increase reliance on American Loyalists. British strategists considered instituting a southern campaign to break the northern stalemate. Clinton and others were convinced that Loyalists were more prevalent in the southern provinces and that these Tories would openly declare their support when a British army appeared. Additionally, weather in the southern states permitted year-round campaigning, while in northern climes armies were inactive during winter. Too, the British foothold in Savannah, strengthened by the repulse of a French attack, encouraged their expansion of power from that base.

Based, therefore, on unsupported evidence of a groundswell of Loyalist support and under continuous pressure from the home office, Clinton launched the second strategic phase of the American Revolution, an invasion of the American southern provinces. In September 1779, when thirty-eight hundred reinforcements arrived in New York, Clinton withdrew troops from Rhode Island and initiated an expedition to the southern provinces utilizing eighty-seven hundred soldiers. The basic plan was to chop off one state at a time, beginning with Georgia and moving north to South Carolina, then North Carolina, and finally, Virginia. One by one, the southern colonies would return to British control and the northern provinces, isolated, blockaded, and besieged, would not long be able to resist. The consolidation of these provinces into the empire would bring with it the economic advantages of holding Charles Town and Savannah. With patience and a slow, deliberate approach, the strategists could see a slow demise of rebel solidarity. This decision would bring about a second turning point in the revolution, a juncture more definitive than the surrender at Saratoga.

This second phase of the revolution was initiated with high hopes of success. The major shift in British strategy and the expected consolidation of the southern provinces would discourage their northern sisters from continued resistance. Historically, the campaign to recapture America from the south has been underestimated in its critical importance and almost forgotten in its military significance. As the campaign was extended and moved inland the nature of revolution evolved into partisan, guerilla, or even civil war, and the viciousness of action increased dramatically. Colonial armies developed tactics to combat invasion while tough professional British forces faced some of the most daunting expeditions of their history as they forged into the back country.

On the eve of the revolution the southern back country encompassed an area from Maryland through the Piedmont, or the western portions of four British colonies: Virginia, North Carolina, South Carolina, and Georgia. Heavily wooded and well watered, this tract was bound on the west by the crest of the Appalachian Mountains and on the east by the fall lines of the many rivers that drained from these mountains to the Atlantic Ocean. This elongated, peninsular-shaped region stretched from the Potomac River to mid-Georgia and had been sparsely populated by Europeans until the migrations after 1725. Its green, rugged land stretched endlessly into folding mountain crests. A region of striking contrasts, the back country was so heavily forested in places that foliage overlapped and prevented any view of the sky, making travel difficult. Contrasting areas, however, were parklike and open, awarding the observer with superlative vistas.

Oak, hickory, and chestnut trees thrived in the valleys and alongside streams, while the higher elevations were clothed in birch, maple, spruce, and pine. In the fall a myriad of colors—rust, yellow, red, and brown—filled the hillsides in profusion. The beauty of mountain laurel, flowering dogwood, and wild azaleas was breathtaking in spring. Game was plentiful. Deer, elk, and woodland buffalo roamed the valley while turkeys gobbled in the thickets. Rattlesnakes and moccasins were numerous, presenting a constant danger. Panthers and wolves prowled the ridges; overhead, eagles spiraled and hawks dived in swift stoops.

As streams of land seekers poured south down the Great Wagon Road in the years prior to the revolution, population rates soared. Eager immigrants attempted to carve out a home in the tough environment. Subsistence farming dominated the decent soil as fields of corn, potatoes, and vegetables were scattered about and rangy cattle and half-wild pigs roamed the fields and woods. Labor was family produced, the large numbers of children working the cornrows and gardens. A few indentured servants joined the hardworking pioneers, but slavery was almost nonexistent. The predominant cash crop of future years, tobacco, had not yet appeared as a part of the area's agriculture. The southern back country was a hardscrabble existence, available for freedom seekers, but only to the rough and persistent. It was these determined survivors who would come face to face with the invading British and who, unexpectedly and unbelievably, would change the course of America's war.

This book will attempt to analyze the sequence of battles that occurred as a result of this basic British strategic change and the modification of that strategy, which pushed the fight into the Carolina back country. From the two Indian wars of earlier eras that reduced the threat of Indian allied participation in the revolution to the defense and capture of the great southern seaports, the sequence of events favored Crown armies. But active partisan groups from the back country were destroying the myth of Loyalism in the south. In an attempt to conclude the revolt, an impatient Lord Cornwallis moved inland, intent on the destruction of American armies. Through a series of three critical battles in the winter of 1780-81, British superiority was seriously challenged and with accompanying French naval assistance the opposing armies set upon a path that led to Yorktown. After the surrender of a second major British army at that small Virginia fishing village, British will to continue the fight eroded much as American will to persevere in Vietnam would disappear some 200 years hence, and the British Admiralty conceded a war it was no longer willing to contest.

CHAPTER 1

Clash at Point Pleasant

"As Israel mourned and her daughters did weep for Saul and his hosts on the mount of Gilbo, Virginia will mourn for her heroes who sleep in tombs on the bank of the O-hi-O."

Unknown

In the fall of 1774 the royal governor of Virginia, John Murray, Lord Dunmore, in violation of British policy and most likely for personal land acquisition, committed the backwoods militia of that province to a short, violent war with the Shawnee Indians and allied tribes, an action historically connoted as Dunmore's War. The Boston Tea Party, so famously enacted in December 1773, had signaled the resolution of some Americans to assume control of their own affairs, particularly economic endeavors. But in the west, along the frontier, equally important were the implications of the royal proclamation of 1763, establishing demarcation boundaries along the crest of the Appalachian Mountain, separating Indian Territory from land available for colonial settlement. This attempt to separate two quarreling parties was not, however, backed by redcoat garrisons and was largely ignored by the hordes of white immigrants flocking to the frontier.

In 1768, when a treaty negotiated at Fort Stanwix realigned the 1763 demarcation boundaries between settlers and Native Americans, colonial migration westward dramatically increased, as, correspondingly, did Indian aggression. The newly aligned boundary permitted white settlers to advance adjacent to the banks of the Ohio River, further compressing the eastern Indian tribes into a region north and west of that river's great curving arc. As early as 1768, Kentucky was full of long rifle hunters who spent months obtaining deer and buffalo hides. Daniel and Squire Boone, Casper Manskat, Abraham Bledsoe, and others were attempting to homestead the area by 1773.

As British Crown officials replaced French troops in the forts of the Northwest, Indian protests of white invasion found sympathetic ears, but no military support. Displeased with this constant encroachment, several tribes formed an alliance under the leadership of the intrepid Shawnee war chief, Cornstalk, determined to resist all further white trespassing. The Miamis, Ottawas, Delawares, Wyandots, and Mingos demurred to Cornstalk's leadership, a rare coalition for tribally conscious Indians, and together they prepared to defend their bountiful Kentucky hunting grounds.

As the two implacable enemies drew closer in physical proximity, the collision of their cultural values initiated an undeclared yet open warfare, a merciless exchange of raids, assaults, and reprisals pursued by both parties to the death. Scores of Shawnee raids into the Valley of Virginia created widespread panic, initiating vociferous demands for retaliation among the immigrants. Among the most serious was an attack on the Kerr's Creek settlement in Rockbridge County led by Cornstalk himself, where dozens of settlers were slain and scores of others taken captive. A second onslaught witnessed the slaying of John Rhodes, a respected Mennonite minister, and his ten children near present-day Harrisonburg, Virginia.

Atrocities were not, however, limited to one faction. A gruesome encounter instigated by frontier scout Daniel Greathouse and a party of white hunters occurred near Yellow Creek on April 30, 1774. Chief Logan's family was lured across the Ohio River with offers of rum, and the waiting hunters slew all who accepted, including several women. Governor Dunmore, reacting to the protestations of Indian raids while additionally acting to support Virginia's territorial rights—as well as protecting his personal land claims—called out the back country militia in July 1774. Secure in the support of frightened frontier settlers and the tacit approval of the Virginia House of Burgesses, his Lordship initiated a full-scale military campaign against the Shawnee.

The imperious, slightly overbearing, and overweight Dunmore, son of William Murray, had been appointed in 1770 governor of New York through the political auspices of Lord Gower, his wealthy brother-in-law. When Governor Berkeley of Virginia died in office that October, Dunmore was transferred to Williamsburg and appointed Virginia's royal executive, despite his initial protestations. An experienced soldier, Dunmore held the rank of captain in the Third Foot Guards and was an avid proponent of horseback racing, parties, and dancing. He and his attractive wife, Lady Charlotte Stewart, immediately became extremely popular with the socially conscious Virginians. The auburn-haired, brown-eyed Scotsman, who often donned traditional kilts, possessed all the Scotch charm and willfulness.

Enrolling his three sons at the College of William and

Mary, Murray purchased a large estate not far from the colonial capital. He, like most Crown appointees, undertook this important colonial assignment in order to augment his personal financial fortunes by acquiring valuable wilderness land tracts. Allying himself with experienced Virginia land speculators, he enlisted in several schemes designed to acquire Indian tracts quite cheaply. This nefarious participation surely influenced his decision to launch a campaign designed to break the power of the tribes along the Ohio. Dunmore justified these actions to the colonial office by suggesting that unruly frontier settlers would be easier to control—and therefore less likely to rebel against the Crown—if they were permitted to freely expand their land acquisitions at Indian expense. His approval of the restless nature, wanderlust, and greed of frontier settlers contributed to the development of a trait of frontier advancement that would reign unabated for one hundred years. But Dunmore's position would also soon relax control of the Crown on its colonial citizens, for his expansionism coexisted with increased freedom and independence.

When the British army evacuated Fort Pitt at the Forks of the Ohio River, Dunmore quietly and quickly garrisoned the critical post with Virginia militia, placing his confidant, Maj. John Connolly, in control. Connolly became the driving force in a series of adept manipulations that triggered the Indian war. He circulated a series of letters to settlers in which he warned them of expected Indian raids and advised them to "fort up" in defensible positions. These repeated alarmist announcements reinforced the general outcry for retaliation against the tribes, for settlers needed to work their fields in spring and summer rather than defend themselves in hastily constructed forts. Dunmore approved the employment of numerous survey parties sponsored by large land companies, allowing their penetration into the tracts alongside the Ohio River. He appointed Col. William Preston, a rabid expansionist, as official surveyor for Augusta County. These surveyors, precursors of homesteading, redoubled their activity across the Ohio River in the early spring of 1774, marking tracts for future settlement, while the Shawnee watched and seethed, for they well knew the intrusion of survey parties was preparatory to an influx of migrants.

As Dunmore prepared his military campaign, he first dispatched militia major Angus MacDonald to raise a company and probe across the Ohio to measure Shawnee preparedness. MacDonald marshaled almost four hundred men under able militia captains such as Daniel Morgan and George Rogers Clark and advanced cautiously and methodically. He skirmished with a few Indians, burned several villages on the Muskingum River, and then returned without a major encounter. Most of the participating frontiersmen condemned MacDonald's incursion as ineffectual, feeling that his campaign actually strengthened the resolve of the Shawnee. Fortunately, as Dunmore continued preparations, the British Indian Department, led by the efforts of William Johnson, the northern commissioner, and John Stuart in the south, succeeded in preventing alliances between the Shawnee and the Iroquois or the Cherokee, thus preventing a general Indian war.

The cocky Virginia governor followed MacDonald's sortie with a massive two-pronged offensive utilizing almost twenty-five hundred Virginia militiamen. He ordered Col. Andrew Lewis of Big Lick (Roanoke), Virginia, to raise one thousand men from the militia of Augusta, Botetourt, and Fincastle Counties and to advance overland through some of the most rugged country on the frontier, uniting with a second column led by Dunmore himself at the junction of the Kanawha and Ohio Rivers. The governor's contingent of fifteen hundred volunteers would be recruited from Berkeley, Frederick, Hampshire, and Dunmore Counties. His column would float down the Ohio from Fort Pitt or march along the riverbank to the proposed junction with Lewis. Once united they would cross the Ohio and advance on the Indian villages north of the river, over-whelming the tribes with numbers and destroying their fighting ability. To the amazement of the militiamen the doughty, kilted Dunmore marched alongside the ranks, shouldering his own knapsack.

In the lengthening shadows of a late October afternoon, a column of tired marchers attired in dusty, fringed hunting dress emerged from the trees along the north bank of the Kanawha River, raising an exhilarating shout upon sighting the glimmer of the Ohio River. Moving to the beat of an awkward drummer and the high, shrill squeal of fifes, which caused the birds to scattered wildly across the sky, the flower of Virginia's upland militia filed into a triangular meadow formed by the coalescence of the two rivers. Despite the undercurrent of growing dissatisfaction with Crown policies, these volunteer frontiersmen were on campaign in response to an appeal by the royal governor of Virginia.

As they settled about twinkling campfires in the chilly, moon-washed night, the marchers carefully surveyed their surroundings. A more attractive camping location could scarcely be found. Large trees, scattered parklike about the site, provided shade, while springs of cold, pure water were plentiful. The multihued leaves turning red and ochre displayed the eye-filling beauty so characteristic of an

Appalachian upland autumn. European army officers would scarcely have recognized the assemblage as a military force, for few uniforms were in evidence and discipline seemed voluntary when present at all. Most of the marchers wore long hunting shirts or frocks of heavy linen dyed to various hues with leather or woolen stockings stretched almost to the thigh over woolen shirts, pants, and moccasins. Headgear was made effectively from animal skins or knitted from wool. The firearms they so carefully protected were flintlocks, primarily the recently developed American long rifles, with a scattering of English-style muskets. From broad, beaded belts hung leather shot bags and elaborately carved powder horns. Tomahawks and scalping knives completed their armament. They moved with a carefree shuffle that was almost a swagger. So cocksure and confident were these young militiamen that commissary officer William Ingles remarked: "We looked on ourselves as in safe possession of a fine encampment and thought ourselves a terror to all the Indians on the Ohio."

This hastily organized militia army of slightly more than one thousand Virginians was led by the stout, brown-eyed Andrew Lewis, descended from Presbyterian Scotch-Irish stock. He was born in Ireland in 1720 and brought to the Valley of Virginia as a child in 1731. An experienced colonial military commander, he was one of those brave, intrepid souls who accompanied George Washington to the Forks of the Ohio and was wounded in the futile defense of Fort Necessity in 1754. Promoted to major of militia, Lewis followed dying British general Thomas Forbes on his 1758 road-building expedition, earning the thanks and appreciation of Col. Henri Bouquet, Forbes' successor. Dispatched with two hundred select riflemen to reconnoiter Fort

Duquesne with Maj. James Grant and his Highlanders, Lewis feuded constantly with Grant. He was again wounded and captured by the French when Grant's tactics fell apart, initiating a spiteful dispute between the two soldiers. Reportedly slain, Lewis was conveyed by his captors to Montreal, then on to Quebec, but proved such an intractable prisoner that he was exchanged in November 1759. Andrew Lewis was described by most who knew him well as "of reserved manners and great dignity of character, vigorous intellect, unquestionable courage, and apt to inspire confidence in those about him." His reputation as a frontier militia officer progressed as he set about the defense of isolated settlements and doggedly pursued hostile raiders. Highly authoritarian, he was respected and usually obeyed by his followers for his obvious military abilities, but his personality forbade true closeness.

Lewis's militia force was composed of landholding farmers from the back country Shenandoah Valley. These spacious yet thinly populated counties provided their citizens with freedom from the bonds of authority, encouraging the true development of Mr. Jefferson's ideal "republic of farmers; the bedrock upon which the republic should be based." Provincially absorbed in their local and personal affairs, these stout backwoodsmen were only a few generations removed from Celtic or Germanic roots, yet already they were expert hunters, skilled in the use of their long rifles and accustomed to living on the disordered borderlands of civilization where boldness and readiness to defend oneself was a way of life. Most developed a rural individualistic lifestyle supported by belief in a strong evangelical Protestant God and an equally intense distrust of any authority figure. They were almost impossible to discipline, but could prove terrible, violent, and effective soldiers if properly motivated. Uninhibited, they replied to the war whoop of the Shawnee with the long-drawn hallo of the hunter—a precursor to the bone-chilling scream of the gray-clad followers of Jackson, Lee, and Forrest eighty-five years hence.

Col. Charles Lewis, the thirty-eight-year-old brother of Andrew, led the Augusta County Regiment, composed of fourteen companies, while Col. William Fleming, who replaced Andrew as the commander of the Botetourt Regiment, directed the contingent from Botetourt County. Col. John Field commanded an independent company from Culpeper County to which the independent companies of Captains Evan Shelby and William Russell from the Holston River were attached.

Marching in the fringed ranks were scores to whom fame and fortune would appear in the eventful days to come. Seven members of the unit would rise to the rank of general in revolutionary armies. Pvt. Samuel Barton, Capt. Thomas Posey, and dozens of others would form the backbone of Capt. Daniel Morgan's riflemen, fated to be recognized as one of the finest fighting units produced by American revolutionary armies and critical to the American defeat of Gen. John Burgoyne at Saratoga. Colonel Fleming would serve briefly as governor of Virginia and four additional state chief executives were in attendance. Young Isaac Shelby, marching in a company commanded by his father, Evan, would become the first governor of Kentucky, while John Sevier would serve Tennessee as both governor and U.S. senator. Likewise Capt. George Matthews would become chief executive of Georgia, and Capt. John Steele would hold the identical position in Mississippi. Posey would serve as governor of the Indiana Territory. Six years hence, William Campbell,

Isaac Shelby, and John Sevier, all serving as colonels, would lead the sudden gathering of mountain men who surrounded and destroyed the Loyalist legion of Patrick Ferguson atop Kings Mountain.

On August 12, Colonel Lewis conferred with his principal lieutenants, reviewed their recruiting efforts, and announced a rendezvous for September 1 at the Great Levels on the Greenbrier River, an area that Lewis had surveyed in 1754. Lewis called the meeting site (presently Lewisburg, West Virginia) Camp Union, and when he arrived several days prior to the first, he discovered an eager Augusta County Regiment already snuggly encamped. Having set up lean-to shelters along the small streams, the frontiersmen smoked their pipes, swapped yarns, and impatiently awaited orders to march. Large packhorse herds, assembled under the supervision of Major Ingles, grazed peacefully in the lush savannahs along the Greenbrier River. Supplies were dispatched by wagon over Warm Springs Mountain from Staunton, Virginia, to the end of the trail. From that point all ammunition, powder, and supplies were loaded on packhorses, of which three were allotted to each company. A small herd of cattle accompanied the column, rations on the hoof. On September 6 the vanguard, the Augusta Regiment of Col. Charles Lewis, departed Camp Union accompanied by five hundred packhorses burdened with fifty-four thousand pounds of flour.

The frontiersmen, led by local expert tracker Capt. Matthew Arbuckle, slashed a wide path through the forest to Elk Creek, where they made camp and began constructing canoes. Lewis's marching orders instructed the unit to move with horses, cattle, and the main body of troops in the middle of the column while an advance guard and a rear guard, each of two hundred men, were charged with security. A screen of individual flankers, all experienced woodsmen, encircled the entire expedition. To the amusement of the frontiersmen, fifers and drummers accompanied each regiment to relay commands, a reminder of Lewis's British military roots. If attacked, the column was to form a circle, stand fast, and await further orders. Such tactics should prevent the panic that often followed an Indian ambush.

Hacking through dense forest, the Augusta volunteers scaled steep defiles, forded fast-flowing streams, and encountered more rattlesnakes than most had previously seen. Upon reaching the bottomland at Elk Creek, the column turned downstream to a junction with the Kanawha River, near present-day Charleston, West Virginia. The exhausted Augusta riflemen paused there to rest for several days and erected a stout little blockhouse to shelter their provisions. Canoe manufacturing was hastened, for these backwoods crafts were necessary to transport heavy supplies down the wide, swiftly flowing Kanawha while the packhorses returned to Camp Union for a second load of provisions.

On September 12, Col. Andrew Lewis departed Camp Union with the second contingent of troops, composed of Colonel Fleming's Botetourt Regiment and Colonel Field's combined regiment. The bulk of Col. William Christian's Fincastle Regiment remained at Camp Union, guarding the remaining provisions until the packhorses at Elk River returned. This second column moved by a slightly different route. Unencumbered with large numbers of horses, they followed a buffalo trail for some distance, then climbed directly over the mountains to the Gauley River, moving down to the Kanawha and then continuing downstream. On

September 21 they filed, open-mouthed, past burning springs where subterranean natural gas leaked to the surface and was periodically ignited by lightning. By the twenty-third the column met Charles Lewis and his regiment at the encampment on the Elk. The soldiers completed the bark canoes as Lewis dispatched scouts to search for signs of Indians. Lewis's woodsmen found little evidence of hostiles, but Shawnees lurked nearby, shadowing the line of march and reporting each move of the "long knives" to Cornstalk.

A muster or military review was conducted on September 30 amid much shouting, culminating with the

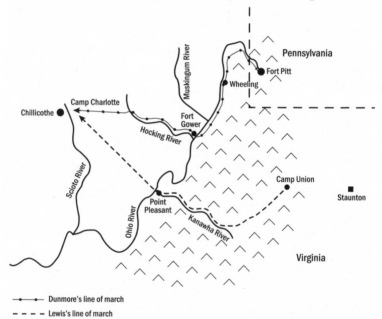

Advance of the Virginia militia, September-October 1774. Andrew Lewis led the southern wing of the Virginia army from Camp Union (Lewisburg) to Point Pleasant, while Lord Dunmore advanced down the Ohio River from Fort Pitt with the northern wing to a planned union at Point Pleasant.

discharge of one thousand rifles, gunfire echoing from the surrounding mountainsides. In high spirits on the following day, the long files moved out of Elk Creek camp, bound for the Ohio. They followed a narrow footpath along the northeast bank of the Kanawha as the heavily laden canoes kept pace midstream. Lewis dispatched an advance company led by his son, John, and covered his right flank with another hundred-man unit. At length on October 6 the signifying shout of arrival arose as the head of the column filed from the tree line and sighted the Ohio, four hundred yards wide and flowing with a current as quiet as night. At the junction of the two streams, a meadow-like park provided an extensive view up both rivers, hence the name, reportedly endowed by frontier scout Simon Kenton, "Point Pleasant."

As the marchers prepared their mess fires on the triangular point, the stars hung so low over the Ohio River that a man seemingly could touch them. A feeling of melancholy isolation prevailed throughout the army that first night, for although their exhausting, 160-mile march was complete, their future was shrouded in mystery. Dunmore's division, expected to arrive first, was nowhere in sight and despite deep confidence in their own prowess these hardy militiamen realized they were encamped in the land of their enemies.

Dunmore had stoutly supported Virginia's claims to these western lands, arguing with representatives from Pennsylvania over the Forks area and ownership of Fort Pitt. He insisted on departing with his arm of the militia force from Fort Pitt to demonstrate Virginia's possession of this important base. Eventually the Pennsylvanians backed down before the militant Virginians, as the Indian threat brought on an uneasy truce between parties. The governor changed his strategy regularly as the campaign progressed, often based on information of dubious value.

Dunmore's indecisiveness can partially be attributed to a lack of confidence in his scouts, but Chief Cornstalk's mysterious ability to conceal his force and his true purposes amplified Dunmore's information deficiency. By late September, the governor decided to abort a direct advance to Point Pleasant, abandoning the Ohio River route in favor of striking out westward from a point higher upriver. He thus desired Lewis to proceed across the Ohio at Point Pleasant and initiate a drive west to unite with his forces.

At this juncture coordination between the two men, according to the testimony of those present in both army divisions, became extremely clouded. Just how much Dunmore's alterations of plan were actually communicated to Lewis is not determined. Statements vary, some sources claiming that notes for Lewis were left in a hollow tree while others testified to a message from Dunmore delivered by Simon Girty that so enraged Lewis he beat the messenger about the head with his walking stick. Years later a number of officers with Lewis's expedition, including his son, John, avowed that absolutely no exchange of information took place between the two men. But it seems logical to conclude that Lewis either knew of Dunmore's tactical alterations or that he deduced that some change in plan had occurred for he did not prepare to fight at Point Pleasant and seemed ready to cross the Ohio to proceed west. It's virtually impossible to further decipher the level of communication between the two, except to determine it was far less than required and almost proved fateful.

Upon his arrival at Point Pleasant, Lewis ordered William Sharp and William Mason to proceed upriver toward Fort Pitt on October 7, seeking contact with Dunmore. At first light all hands turned to work. Canoes, heavily laden with supplies and ammunition, were unloaded, necessary houses were

constructed for each company, and rude shelters of pine
boughs erected. A large log pen was built to contain the cattle at night. On October 9 the Reverend Mr. Terry presented
a lengthy, fire-breathing sermon that was attended by all.
Resting in the afternoon, the soldiers listened to the tales of
traders, who described the savage appearance and extraordi-
nary fighting abilities of the Shawnee. Few seemed concerned, for the enemy was believed to be far away. However,
the little army was in for a surprise. A long-remembered
mountain ballad describes the morning to come:

> Brave Lewis our Colonel, an officer bold,
> At the mouth of the Kanawha did the Shawnees behold
> On the tenth of October, at the rising sun,
> The armies did meet and the battle begun.

During the early-morning hours of October 10,
Cornstalk, war chief of the Shawnees, stealthily crossed the
Ohio with an allied Indian force of between eight hundred
and eleven hundred warriors, grounding their canoes and
rafts in Old Town Creek, less than five miles upriver.
Camping within two miles of Lewis's force, the hostiles prepared to attack the Point Pleasant camp at dawn. Painted
for war, the Indians slipped quietly through the forest
toward the glow of campfires, barely seen through an
increasing ground fog. Armed with lightweight, smoothbore
flintlocks obtained from French traders, the Indian warriors were well prepared for close combat. These inaccurate
trade guns became formidable weapons at close range when
loaded with between three and ten pieces of buckshot and
a musket ball. A quick rush of the sentries, and the warriors
could explode from the fog onto the sleeping militiamen.

Andrew Lewis, frustrated at every turn by Dunmore's
silence, for once experienced some good fortune. Tired of

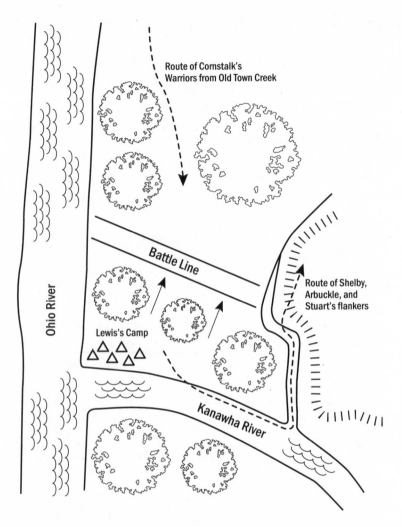

Battle of Point Pleasant, October 10, 1774.

stringy beef, two Virginia soldiers had risen early and slipped unobserved out of camp. James Mooney and Joseph Hughey moved furtively up the Ohio, scanning the riverbank for turkey or deer. Emerging from a pocket of dense fog, the duo confronted "five acres of Indians." Hughey fell under an initial volley, shot down by Tavender Ross, a white renegade, but Mooney was more fortunate, ducking back into the fog and sprinting toward camp screaming a warning. Almost concurrently, two hunters from Shelby's company, Sergeants James Robertson and Valentine Sevier, also out early, reported the sighting of hostiles. Immediately the militia soldiers rolled out of their blankets, checked their flints, and fell into company formations. Lewis, believing the enemy force to be only a scouting force, sent forward two detachments of 150 men each under Colonel Lewis and Colonel Fleming to confront the advancing hostiles. Fleming's Botetourt men probed forward along the Ohio River bank while Lewis's Augusta force advanced parallel and farther inland abreast of the Kanawha. After moving forward almost a half mile, the columns were abruptly checked at sunrise by a hail of enemy gunfire.

Col. Charles Lewis forged to the front, conspicuous in his bright red officer's waistcoat. Such a target could not long be ignored and he was soon down, a musket ball in the lower abdomen. Reportedly, Lewis exclaimed, "I am wounded but go on and be brave" as he was carried rearward to his tent by Capt. John Murray, his brother-in-law (of no relation to Lord Dunmore), and William Bailey. His detachment wavered and began to fall back slowly. The pressure of the Indian fire then fell primarily upon Fleming's unit. Within minutes Colonel Fleming, who was attempting to realign his force, received a serious wound in the breast, then was hit twice in the left arm. Coolly, Fleming walked to the rear. Colonel Field, who bravely rallied forward with two hundred colonial reinforcements, stabilized the wavering colonial line. As the Indian onslaught crested, Field was struck in the head and slain despite sheltering behind a tree. A fellow officer stated, "Field was shot at a great tree by two Indians on his right as he was endeavoring to get a shot at a hostile on his left." Capt. Evan Shelby assumed command of the entire hard-pressed colonial line, gradually configuring a continual line of resistance that stretched from the Ohio on the left flank to the Kanawha on the army's right. Although restrictive to rapid maneuvering, this line was unflankable. Individual soldiers from the encampment, responding to the gunfire, began arriving, filling in the line wherever gaps appeared. Each soldier found cover behind a rock, tree, or stump and fought his individual war. In the heavy fog and thick, hanging gun smoke the Indian warriors pushed in close. Neither party could drive the other nor would either retreat. Rifles and muskets were used as clubs, as were tomahawks, knives, hands, and feet. No quarter was asked and none given.

The voice of Cornstalk, whose real name was Hokolesque, could be heard above the ear-splitting din as he shouted, "Be strong, be strong." Taller than his followers and easily recognizable, Cornstalk's form appeared everywhere, first striking down a colonial then racing to bury his tomahawk in the skull of an Indian shirker. Numerous colonial riflemen snapped rifle shots at the fast-moving Indian leader, but without success. The struggle continued hour after hour with first one side rushing forward then the other. Capt. James Ward, who fell, shot cleanly through the head, was unaware that a son, John, who had been captured by the Shawnee at age three and renamed White Wolf, was firing his rifle with uncommon effect from directly across the battle line.

Warriors shouted, "Why don't you whistle now?" to deride the colonial fifers who mustered the rifle companies. The Virginians, their backs to the river, were unable to retreat. The anchored line, however, prevented the favored tactic of the Shawnees, turning a flank and gaining an enemy's rear. Surprisingly on this occasion, the Indian warriors came on frontally in brave rushes led by their chiefs, Red Hawk, Blue Jacket, Black Hoof, Chiksikah, Hokolesque, and his son, Elinipsico. Colonel Fleming later wrote, "Never did Indians stick closer to it [European tactics], nor behave bolder."

The bottomland along the river was filled with driftwood from seasonal floods and scattered rock outcroppings and about 1 p.m. a concerted push by the colonials gained a long ridge where abundant logs and rocks offered excellent cover. Slowly the Indians retreated to an opposing ridge that stretched from the Ohio to a swamp on their left, and the firing gradually slackened. As the ground fog lifted, the rifle fire of the colonials increased in effectiveness, for long rifles were decidedly superior to the Indian weapons at that greater range. The fierce hand-to-hand combat that characterized the morning fight could be sustained for only so long, and the afternoon's fighting slowed to intermittent long-range sniping. Still, exposure of one's person could bring rapid death.

Col. Andrew Lewis, who had thus far not meddled with the largely individual fighting, decided in the late afternoon to conduct a maneuver that could turn the battle in his favor. Coolly lighting his pipe, Lewis detailed Captains Evan Shelby, Matthew Arbuckle, George Matthews, and John Stuart to form their companies and find a method to flank the enemy line. The young officers withdrew their men from the colonial line and led them on a circular route up the Kanawha, wading under cover of the riverbank. Turning up Crooked Creek they emerged from the stream on a slight ridge to the enemy's left rear and suddenly opened a scalding fire that shocked and surprised the Indian warriors. Cornstalk was aware from active scouts that Col. William Christian was moving toward Point Pleasant with the remainder of the Fincastle Regiment. The flanking force was undoubtedly mistaken for the arrival of that column and Cornstalk began to withdraw his forces. He selected the best of his warriors to remain and continue the fight until all the Indian wounded were carried across the Ohio. His sister, Nonhelema, whose great size and strength had earned her the title Grenadier Squaw, conveyed their severely wounded brother, Silverheels, back across the river. Many of the Indian dead were committed to the river and, skillfully, the Indian chief withdrew, his rear guard fading sullenly back into the forest. The engagement had lasted from before sunrise to almost an hour before sunset.

When Christian's regiment arrived about midnight, they found the colonial camp in chaos. The colonial soldiers had begun fortifying their camp by constructing log breastworks, but many were so tired they simply fell asleep. Casualties among the militia troops had been severe. The wounded were suffering horribly, with only minimal medical assistance available. There was little hope of recovery for a large number of them, as many had been shot numerous times. Colonel Fleming, the most noted surgeon, was so badly injured that his very survival was doubtful. Eventually the casualty totals would include seventy-five killed and one hundred forty wounded, almost 20 percent of the force engaged. Col. Charles Lewis and Col. John Field would die of their injuries while Col. William Fleming would be disabled for life. Equally high were losses among the militia captains.

Casualties among the Indians were difficult to ascertain. Thirty-three bodies were recovered, but many of the slain were carried from the field. Colonists felt the enemy loss at least equaled their own, but most sources feel Indian losses of thirty-five to seventy-five are more appropriate. There were no prisoners. The tenor of the colonial survivors can be measured by their bloodthirstiness in erecting a huge pole on the Ohio River bank, which they adorned with eighteen Indian scalps.

Colonel Lewis buried his dead in long rows underneath the trees, where they still lie today. Completion of the fortifications and care of the wounded occupied the army for several days, until on October 17, Lewis crossed the Ohio, leaving a guard to protect the wounded. He advanced toward the Shawnee towns on the Scioto River with each man carrying 1½ pounds of lead and four days' rations, vengeance on the mind of each soldier. A messenger arrived as the force neared the Scioto, informing Lewis that Dunmore was currently drawing up a treaty with the Shawnee and that Lewis should advance no further. Angry and frustrated, Lewis continued to move forward across the Pickaway Plains. He had lost a brother, and his soldiers, many friends and kinsmen.

During the interval following the October 10 clash and Lewis's crossing of the Ohio, Cornstalk's actions were purposeful and decisive. First he attempted to rally his followers to continue their resistance. At council in Yellow Hawk's town on the Scioto he stated, "We must fight no matter how many may fall or we are undone." But when he received no affirmation from his allies, Cornstalk realized that the Shawnee could not fight alone. Burying his tomahawk in the ground, he angrily shouted, "Since you will not fight I go and make peace." Wisely, the Indian chief opened negotiations with Dunmore at Camp Charlotte. So smoothly did he present his case that Dunmore intercepted Lewis and ordered his lieutenant to countermarch. Cornstalk promised to surrender all white prisoners held by the assorted tribes and vowed that the Indians would cease hunting south of the Ohio and discontinue harassing boats on the river. Dunmore followed with a promise that no more whites would enter Kentucky and that no settler should ever set foot north of the Ohio River.

At a formal little ceremony, Dunmore met Lewis's officers, and shaking hands, complimented them profusely on their victory. But Lewis posted guards around the governor's marquee, for the mood of his soldiers was abusive toward Dunmore, several frontiersmen having made direct threats. Reluctantly Lewis began to march back toward Point Pleasant, arriving there on October 28. Dunmore's extravagant claims of saving the frontier allocated little credit to Andrew Lewis and his men, but Lewis knew well how close the contest had actually been. He was aware that if the scales of victory had tipped to the enemy, then he and each of his men would lie dead on the battlefield or be bound over as captives to grace the fires of the very villages he was forbidden to destroy.

Leaving Captain Arbuckle and fifty volunteers to garrison newly erected Fort Blair at Point Pleasant, Lewis dismissed his army by companies to return to Camp Union. Officially, his entire command was disbanded on November 4, 1774. Lord Dunmore's little war was over.

The governor received an extravagantly complimentary resolution from the Virginia House of Burgesses for his rapid redress of the Indian threat, but the controversy of his leadership and suspicion of his purposes was only beginning. Many Virginia families suffered grievously as a result of the brief campaign. Samuel Crawley of Pittsylvania County enlisted in the Botetourt Regiment and marched off, never to return. His widow, Elizabeth, and her many children consequently were reduced to a life of absolute poverty, unaided by pension or state compensation. Col. Charles Lewis's wife, Rachael, grieved so long and hard for her slain husband that many grew to believe her demented. Numbers of other Virginia frontiersmen, wounded seriously, would evermore exist on the care of their families. John McKenney, who had two bullet holes and a tomahawk blow to his back, would remain an invalid for life. So too would Col. William Fleming remain physically handicapped, although his active mind would gain political employment.

As details emerged and the ideological conflict with Great Britain grew imminent, Dunmore's status among the populace diminished rapidly amid extreme bias. The royal governor's actions in the Indian war were critiqued and questioned, even to the point that some claimed he had contrived to bring on the war for personal reasons. Many Virginians openly accused Lord Dunmore of duplicity in his dealings with the enemy. Col. John Stuart, who marched with the force, stated, "Dunmore acted as a party to British politicians who wished to incite an Indian War which might prevent or distract the Virginia colony from the growing grievances with England." While the serious nature of that charge is evident, some went even further, avowing that Dunmore had actually connived with or attempted to manipulate the Indians into annihilating Lewis and his army. This action, which Andrew Lewis personally came to believe, could have benefited Great Britain in the approaching conflict by stripping the Virginia frontier of defenders. But such a broad-based charge of contrived plotting seems to endow Lord Dunmore with skills of prognostication even beyond the scope of a royal governor.

A more likely accusation lodged by historian Archibald Henderson places Dunmore as party to a conspiracy with the nefarious Dr. John Connolly. The two reportedly initiated a complicated scheme to secure vast tracts of land from the Indians and found an expansive colony in the area between the Ohio and Mississippi Rivers. This scheme resembled and rivaled Lord Dartmouth's 1769 project of founding Vandalia in the American forests with a capital at the mouth of the Great Kanawha, a plan that may have been more con than reality. While Dunmore surely coveted western acreage, so did George Washington, Patrick Henry, and even Andrew Lewis. Possession of cheap western land was the surest route to power and prestige in America. Dunmore was surely willing to use the patronage appointments attached to his office for that purpose. While he attempted to extend Virginia lands over the mountains and into the Ohio Valley, as evidenced by his efforts to acquire Fort Pitt and its environs from Pennsylvania, could he and his associates not enjoy some personal advantage?

A realistic appraisal of Lord Dunmore's talents perhaps can be ascertained by comparing his military and political exertions with the individual with whom he competed and consistently underestimated, Cornstalk. This handsome, charismatic war chief maintained a diplomatic presence several strides in advance of his colonial adversary. Through an excellent cadre of scouts, Cornstalk shadowed each movement of both advancing colonial columns. He opened long-distance negotiations with Dunmore as the governor's force moved downriver, while the crafty

Shawnee leader concurrently planned the isolation and destruction of Lewis's column at the rendezvous point. It can be postulated that Cornstalk's messages to Dunmore were merely premeditated ruses to delay, stall, and pacify the governor with promises of peace while he destroyed Lewis. If Lewis and his men were removed from the military chessboard, Cornstalk could then possibly bluff, intimidate, or defeat the inexperienced Dunmore.

Fearless in combat, Cornstalk almost achieved the military victory, for in truth, his advancing forces were discovered by accident. When Lewis's army narrowly survived, and Cornstalk's allies deserted, the war chief quickly journeyed to Dunmore's camp and reopened his overtures, settling for a favorable peace before Lewis's vengeful column could unite with the governor. Dunmore only caught a single glimpse of Cornstalk's range of character, intellect, and ability, though as he later discussed the agreement of Camp Charlotte, Dunmore conceded, "I have heard the first orators of Virginia . . . but never heard one whose powers of delivery surpassed those of Cornstalk on that occasion."

The brief little war that history would label "Lord Dunmore's War" was but another chapter in the violent struggle to control the Ohio. From the close of the French and Indian War in 1763 until Anthony Wayne's victory at Fallen Timbers in 1794 the cruel, violent clash of cultures persisted. The last bastion of defense for the eastern Indian tribes was the Ohio River Valley. Both whites and Indians believed their cause was right and as warfare persisted they both came to believe that continued existence of the other party threatened their future. The colonists' obsession with land, to be held and passed on in perpetuity, gave them the individual freedom and self-determination that they so avidly desired. But this fundamental concept could never be understood, save as avarice by an Indian culture to which land, streams, and rivers were a communal possession. War, disease, and settlement—the three horsemen of the Indian apocalypse—gradually pushed the Indian population into extinction.

Dunmore's War quieted the ongoing conflict, at least for several years. It was 1777, three years later, before Indian tribes began to ally themselves with the British who replaced the French in the forts along the Great Lakes. This interlude freed the experienced frontiersmen of Virginia to provide needed leadership and spirit to the American Revolutionary army. The victory of Lewis's small army was the first purely American military effort, undertaken and executed totally by frontier militia, a valuable prognosticator for military organization in the Colonies.

Turning Against the British

Within twenty-four hours of her husband's triumphant return to the Williamsburg governor's mansion, Lady Dunmore gave birth to a daughter whom the rejoicing couple named Virginia. Honored by the edicts of both the House of Burgesses and the College of William and Mary, John Murray's status in the colony seemed unassailable as winter approached. But the progression of events about Boston and the congressional discussions in Philadelphia strained the governor's relationships with the Burgesses and the populace. Dunmore sternly condemned all colonial protestors and identified most as traitors, leaving little opportunity for mediation with his Virginia subjects. John Murray was never a commanding presence in the New World; however, he was at best a competent administrator in the British tradition. When revolution erupted, Dunmore's zeal in seeking to retain the colony within his majesty's realm of influence earned the earl the burning hatred of his former subjects.

In April 1775 he dispatched sailors from the HMS *Magdalen* on a midnight raid to remove more than fifteen barrels of powder from the octagonal brick powder magazine in the capital. Mob protests developed with conditions so tense that Dunmore sent his wife and children aboard the HMS *Fowey*, anchored near Yorktown. While a settlement of payment was negotiated with Patrick Henry concerning the powder, Dunmore's position deteriorated as he alternately offered conciliatory terms then issued threats of a slave insurrection. Finally on June 5, 1775, Dunmore joined his family aboard the *Fowey*. Sailing down the York River into the Chesapeake Bay, Dunmore's small flotilla anchored in the Elizabeth River near Norfolk, and he attempted to rule the colony from his floating town.

Immediately his Lordship began efforts to assemble a military force sufficient to coerce the Virginia colony's continued loyalty to George III. In February, the HMS *Roebuck*, a ship of forty-four guns commanded by Capt. Andrew Hammond, arrived in the Chesapeake, augmenting Dunmore's military power markedly, despite the fact that Captain Hammond and Lord Dunmore were continually at contrasting purposes. Dunmore next landed troops and entrenched on Tucker's Mill Point, a peninsula in the Elizabeth River from which he could obtain water and livestock by raiding nearby plantations. By March his flotilla, now grown to almost eighty vessels, was forced to evacuate Tucker's by several well-sited rebel artillery batteries emplaced by American general Charles Lee.

Sailing up the bay to the mouth of the Piankatank, Dunmore began unloading his forces at Gwynn's Island, a secure site that he considered unassailable. Fortifications were begun, including two stockades, several batteries, and an entrenchment encircling the tented camp. Here his former reluctant ally, Andrew Lewis, now an American brigadier general, would challenge Dunmore.

As Lewis prepared to attack the royal governor, his well-placed scouts reported scurvy and bilious fever raging amid the British with scores of burials conducted daily on Gwynn's Island. A company of the Seventh Virginia led by Thomas Posey crept to the water's edge and observed as additional soldiers landed off the island in a pelting rainstorm. On July 8, Lewis arrived with two additional regiments and an artillery train to find Posey's frontiersmen employed in digging trenches into the riverbank that opened on to the waterfront, whereupon a battery of two 18-pounders was emplaced in concealment. Also masked was a second battery of 6- and 9-pounders.

On July 9 at 10 A.M., only five days after the Declaration of Independence was ratified by the Continental Congress, the batteries opened on Dunmore's unsuspecting and carelessly anchored ships with significant effect. The first shot, touched off by Lewis, holed the *Dunmore,* creating panic. Soon the *Otter, William,* and *Fowey* were struck by American balls. John Buchanan, a valley soldier, remarked, "We could hear our 18 pound balls hit the sides of the ships as if one was throwing stones against a tobacco barn." As Dunmore's ships fled, Lewis's gunners directed their fire on the British camp and fortifications. Soon the scene was one of disjointed and frightened British troops attempting to board the remaining ships of the fleet.

Lewis had collected rowboats and skiffs preparatory to a proposed dawn attack by Capt. Robert McClanahan's unit of selected frontiersmen. However, when Posey's company, which led the sea-born assault via these small craft, landed on Gwynn's Island no fighting ensued. Only the dead and dying remained. Unburied bodies were scattered among the breastworks interspaced with others crying for assistance. Almost five hundred casualties were discovered, including a majority of Dunmore's ill-fated Royal Ethiopian Regiment, a black unit led by white officers, abandoned by the governor. Vulnerable to disease, the ex-slaves had been decimated by smallpox, their bodies burned beyond recognition in an attempt to minimize contagion. Only one American casualty was recorded; a Captain Arundel of the artillery was slain by the premature explosion of his own hand-constructed wooden mortar.

A final refuge on St. George's Island in the bay permitted Dunmore to prepare his vessels for an Atlantic crossing and on August 6, 1776, he cleared the Virginia Capes for England. Doubtless, Andrew Lewis enjoyed driving Dunmore from Virginia, despite the absence of a real military confrontation. But the skirmish at Gwynn's Island would prove the final military effort of the old soldier. His health declined and he suffered a stroke at a friend's house near Montvale, Virginia, dying at age sixty-one, mere weeks prior to the American victory at Yorktown.

The third individual so conspicuous in the Point Pleasant fight was Cornstalk, the Shawnee chief who suffered an even more ignominious fate. An expert at the cut, slash, and burn raids that characterized Indian warfare, Cornstalk deployed and fought his warriors on the Kanawha banks in the style of the long knives. He was surely the most famous and feared Indian leader of the border wars preceding the revolution. His very name evoked terror and fear among the frontier settlers.

By the spring of 1777 the Camp Charlotte agreement, never formally adopted, was in a state of dissolution. At last

Cornstalk concluded that the "treaty was no longer" and he set out for Fort Randolph at Point Pleasant to nullify his personal oath. When he explained his inability to honor his former promise to Commander Arbuckle, the militia captain placed him in confinement while awaiting higher orders. His companions, including Red Hawk and the chief's own son, Elinipsico, were also retained. On November 9, gunfire erupted across the Kanawha. Two young hunters, Hamilton and Gilmore, had crossed the stream in search of deer. Indian warriors concealed on the riverbank fired on the duo, killing and scalping Gilmore. When a rescue party returned with Gilmore's body, a cry was raised to kill the Shawnee imprisoned at the fort. Soon a mob of twenty-five men charged the gates, brushing aside Arbuckle's objections.

The wife of an interpreter ran to warn Cornstalk, advising him to flee, but he turned to his son and companion stating, "The Great Spirit had determined we shall die together! Let us submit." Stepping into the doorway, Cornstalk received a rifle volley and fell dead on the threshold. His son and companion were also slain. A sudden exodus of the perpetrators followed the violent massacre. Although a Rockbridge court made inquiries, inspired by the anger of Patrick Henry, a formal trial was never convened. No justice ensued for the death of even so famous a Shawnee. The only vengeance for the act was that exacted by the Shawnee in the war to follow—and no man ever bragged of his part in the dishonorable affair.

At Tu-Endie-Wei Park (Shawnee for "mingling of the waters") near the bridge to Gallipolis, Ohio, lie the dead of Point Pleasant. For nearly seventy years they lay in silence and neglect, despite their valor and sacrifice. They rest now in long rows beneath a bronze tablet recording their names. A statue of a Virginia frontier rifleman guards their final bivouac. Close by in a simple grave rests the remains of the Indian warrior and statesman Cornstalk. Near these gravesites rises an eighty-four-foot granite shaft, the tallest battle monument west of the Alleghenies, honoring a battle stoutly contested and long forgotten. The revolutionary conflict, with its wide-reaching implications, swallowed the survivors of Point Pleasant, and the scope and ferocity of open warfare overshadowed the sacrifice of the men who fought and died there.

The campaign that culminated at Point Pleasant has often been styled "the first battle of the American Revolution." This is, of course, an exaggeration of facts, but the campaign did serve as an important training ground for Continental soldiers and officers. There were no British regulars involved; the operation and initiative were entirely colonial, and in fact, British home authorities expressed their disapproval of Dunmore's martial enterprise. The logistics, transportation, and tactics of the campaign were militia based, all areas that had previously—in other campaigns—been led by redcoat professionals. The training and experience obtained proved of great value in the organization of Continental forces in the southern provinces. The men in the columns of both Dunmore and Lewis participated in the revolution in large numbers, many becoming Continental officers of merit.

This first purely American victory additionally provided a window of opportunity whereby Virginia Continental regiments for a time could be recruited uninhibited by Indian raids. The exposed flank of the Virginia colony was temporarily protected and by the influx of settlers into Kentucky and the Ohio Valley, the Indian warfare that sputtered all during the revolution did not warrant state participation.

CHAPTER 2

The Cherokee War of 1776

"None of the previous Indian wars, even when aided by British regulars was as successful as this, the first warfare of our young republic."

Joseph Johnson

Prior to Euro-American encroachment on the shores of North America, the Cherokee had long maintained a well-ordered and sophisticated culture within the southern Appalachian Mountains. The Cherokee were inheritors of the mysterious Mississippian mound builders, a culture that flourished in the river valleys of eastern North America between 1000 and 1500 A.D. They relied on corn, beans, and squash supplemented by a steady diet of venison for sustenance, gradually abandoning the nomadic lifestyle.

At its peak, this Cherokee culture occupied between eighty and ninety snug mountain villages grouped into four distinct geographic areas. The so-called Lower Cherokee villages were located on the Tugaloo and Keowee Rivers in western South Carolina or northern Georgia, while the Middle towns were astride the headwaters of the Tuskasegee and Little Tennessee Rivers in the deep valleys of western North Carolina. The Valley towns controlled the

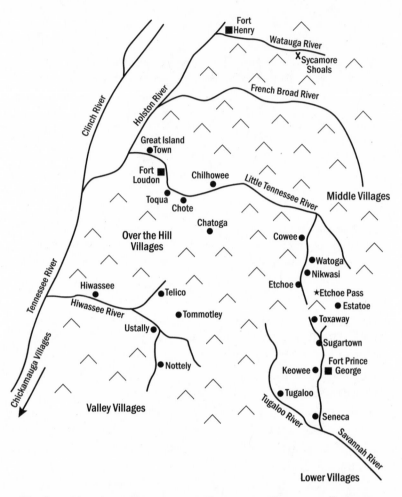

The four Cherokee village groups. The Lower villages were located on tributaries of the Savannah River, the Middle villages were astride the headwaters of the Little Tennessee, the Valley towns controlled the Hiawassee, while the Over-the-Hill villages were located west of the mountains in eastern Tennessee.

Nottely and upper Hiawassee Rivers, tributaries of the Tennessee, while the Over-the-Hill villages were west of the continental divide in present east Tennessee, scattered upon the Tellico and lower Little Tennessee Rivers. A network of well-beaten footpaths connected the villages, winding tightly among abysmal defiles, around escarpments, and alongside swift-flowing mountain streams.

Each village was arrayed about a central civic building, a dome-roofed edifice that served as council house and temple. This seven-sided structure was configured to accommodate the seven clans or kinship groups into which all Cherokee were assigned along matrilineal lines. The council house contained tiers of benches encircling its interior perimeter with an altar and seats for chiefs and notables located in the center. The atmosphere was dark and gloomy, as little light penetrated from the single entrance, and smoke from a perpetual altar fire hung heavily in the ceiling dome. Lt. Henry Timberlake, a British officer who spent considerable time among the Cherokee, described with wonder the massive council house at Cowee. He remarked that it was so large as to "resemble a small mountain and capable of containing hundreds of Cherokee." Items sacred to a village were often stored in the council house and on occasion a distinguished chief might be buried beneath the earthen floor. Individual and family residences were constructed about the central square, usually facing the council house. Constructed of upright logs or tree trunks with branches stripped of bark woven to create walls, these flimsy abodes were plastered with dry grass or clay and topped with domed roofs of chestnut bark. Each dwelling contained a central fireplace with a hearthstone for baking the dietary staple, corn cakes. Political authority was vested in a chief elected by the village council while all eligible warriors chose a war chief. These leadership positions were earned, never inherited, and their possession fragile. Each village served its own laws and formed its own alliances, a trait that caused political decisions to proceed at a snail's pace and made negotiations with outsiders difficult and cumbersome.

The initial contact between Cherokees and Euro-Americans occurred as early as 1513 when Spanish soldiers led by the indomitable Ponce de Leon came ashore in Florida to explore into the southeastern mountains. The subsequent efforts of Lucas de Ayllon to establish a colony on the Waccamaw River and the attempts of both French and Spanish adventurers to occupy St. Elena Island were noted by but did not greatly affect the Cherokee, safely protected in their mountainous citadels. But in 1540, Hernando de Soto, a persistent and brutal adventurer, disembarked some 570 soldiers with 240 warhorses in present Tampa Bay and marched north on his exhaustive and elusive search for gold. Following an erratic track through the Appalachian Mountains, de Soto's entourage halted periodically, enticed to explore the old mound sites, seeking riches but finding only further mystery. Ultimately three years of marching, looting, and killing culminated in de Soto's death of disease and subsequent "burial" in the Mississippi in 1542. A further probe into the mountains in 1566 was initiated from Fort San Felipe on Port Royal Sound as Capt. Juan Pardo led 125 soldiers northward on an exploratory mission. Attempting to establish a base in the foothills, Pardo erected Fort San Juan near Salisbury, North Carolina, and Fort San Pablo on the French Broad River. Sgt. Hernando Morales, one of Pardo's energetic subalterns, became obsessed in his own search for gold mines, moving over the mountains into east Tennessee. While these entrees resulted in limited effect on Cherokee life and culture, the epidemics that followed decimated the native tribes residing in the Piedmont.

In 1670, Englishmen from Barbados landed at Albemarle Point near what would become Charles Town, South Carolina, in search of land to farm, initiating a new era of European contact. Soon a trade relationship was established founded on the acquisition of deerskins from the Cherokee, a product highly valued in Europe. In the years between 1731 and 1765 more than 150,000 pounds of deer hides were shipped from Charles Town each year with another 50,000 pounds leaving the wharves of Savannah. In return the Cherokee acquired trade guns, cloth, and rum as well as various items such as mirrors, beads, and cooking vessels. An unsavory trade in humans flourished for a time as captives of Cherokee war parties from tribes located south and west were exchanged with slave traders for disposition to plantation owners. But male Indian captives made recalcitrant field hands and were particularly adept at escape, thus they were often shipped to the West Indies. Female captives, however, became highly prized for their skills at both agricultural production and food preparation and gradually provided the core of a cooking style famed today as Low-Country cuisine.

The growing trade relationships with English settlers, coupled with the constant clashes and raids of nearby tribes into their villages, convinced the Cherokee to invite the construction of English forts near their villages. Envisioning that these posts would serve as trade centers conveniently located within the Cherokee spheres of influence, village headmen gladly awarded land for colonial construction. But the South Carolinians and Virginians who responded considered these posts as initial steps in solidifying their power over the Cherokee nation, hopefully to the exclusion of French or Spanish competition. The first such outpost was erected on the Keowee River in western South Carolina, opposite the Indian village of the same name. Named Fort Prince George in honor of the Prince of Wales, this stout fortification dominated access to the wealthy Cherokee Lower villages. About one hundred feet square, with four large corner bastions, Fort Prince George was surrounded by a deep ditch and earthen walls topped by a palisade of yellow pine logs. Barracks and additional facilities were erected to sustain a garrison of several hundred.

In 1757 a second Carolina outpost was completed on the Little Tennessee River near Tommotley amid the Over-the-Hill Cherokee towns. Fort Loudon was isolated and vulnerable, being more than 150 miles from Fort Prince George and reachable only by a footpath through some of the most formidable terrain in the east. Diamond shaped and bastioned, Fort Loudon was girded by a fifteen-foot wooden palisade and a hedge of honey locust. Twelve light cannon or swivel guns were packed over the mountains and installed on the bastions; these weapons, however, would prove of little value, save to signal the king's birthday. Both forts were garrisoned by troops of South Carolina Provincials, units of red-coated colonials who were permitted to have their wives and children accompany them on garrison duty.

No sooner was Fort Loudon completed than the Cherokee-British partnership began to show signs of dissolution. Henry Timberlake felt that the arrogance and disrespect shown to the Cherokee by English officers and traders eventually caused the onset of hostility. In agreement, John Stuart, an officer at Fort Loudon, remarked, "No people are more offended by contemptuous treatment than the Cherokee." Significant numbers of homesteaders, flowing down the Great Wagon Road, had begun construction of homes in the river valleys that were long deemed Cherokee land, and the constant erosion of their hunting grounds frustrated the attempts of village headmen to control the restless, young Cherokee warriors. In addition, a growing influx of unscrupulous and dishonest traders robbed the Cherokee of their valued deerskins.

Further eroding relationships were English efforts to pressure the Cherokee into open support of their conflict with France, which increased following Gen. Edward Braddock's egregious defeat in the Pennsylvania wilderness on July 9, 1755. When Brig. Gen. John Forbes marched north in 1758 to avenge his predecessor's rout, as many as three hundred volunteer Cherokee warriors accompanied his column, having been promised loot and cattle. But quickly offended by British army justice, a number of these warriors started home in May 1758.

Meanwhile, Capt. Raymond Demere, the commander at Fort Loudon, became extremely unpopular among the Cherokee when he indiscreetly involved them in a skirmish with French and Shawnee aggressors that caused heavy losses. A deputation of Over-the-Hill Cherokee leaders traveled to Fort Toulouse near Mobile to sign a document of alliance with the French. When a copy of this document fell into the hands of William Lyttleton, the new South Carolina royal governor, he rashly instituted an immediate embargo on guns, shot, and powder, hunting tools upon which the Cherokee now completely dependant. A delegation of Cherokee chiefs undertook a journey to Charles Town to seek conciliation but more severe repercussions followed.

While negotiations were in progress, a serious raid of some gruesome consequence goaded Lyttleton into imprisoning the entire peace delegation. The hostages were marched westward to Fort Prince George and imprisoned, thirty-one proud Cherokee confined to a cell intended for six. Lyttleton raised a provincial army of almost twelve hundred men, who assembled on the banks of the Keowee but declined to cross into Cherokee territory. Smallpox broke out and in late December his army broke apart and returned to Charles Town, leaving the hostages in the care of the garrison at Fort Prince George. When several red-coats, including an officer, were killed just outside the walls of Fort Prince George by lurking hostiles, Lyttleton ordered the remaining prisoners placed in chains. A detail of soldiers arrived to carry out the order but swiftly encountered resistance, and in the confusing melee that followed all the hostages were slain. Accordingly, the frontier exploded with Indian raids. More than one hundred white settlers were slain or taken captive within weeks and the frontier rolled back a hundred miles.

Lyttleton appealed to the British military for protection, and Col. Archibald Montgomery was dispatched southward with the First and Seventy-seventh Regiments of Foot to put down the uprising. Marching west into the mountains his redcoats burned Keowee, Estatoe, Toxaway, Qualatchee, and most of the Lower Cherokee towns. Proceeding onward on a steep mountain trail Montgomery's troops were ambushed by about six hundred Cherokees in a narrow defile between river and mountain called Crows Creek. After several hours of heated exchange, the Cherokee withdrew, leaving Montgomery with twenty dead, including Capt. Manly Williams of the Royal Scots, and about seventy-six wounded. Not eager to continue, Montgomery placed his wounded on the remaining pack-horses, burned Etchoe, and conducted a strategic retreat to Fort Prince George. While Montgomery loudly proclaimed a victory his foes and his colonial allies recognized a defeat when one occurred. He refurbished his column, marched back to Charles Town, and embarked for New York. Despite the loss of numerous Lower villages the Cherokee still controlled their mountain empire and now danced wildly about the surrounded and besieged Fort Loudon.

When the garrison of Fort Loudon learned of Montgomery's repulse and realized their hopeless position, Capt. John Stuart was dispatched under a flag of truce to Chote, the Cherokee capital, to attempt to negotiate a surrender of Fort Loudon. He reached agreement that the garrison and all dependants could march under arms to Fort Prince George while Fort Loudon with its great guns, powder, balls, and spare weapons would be abandoned for the Cherokee. But the retreat turned into a massacre with thirty soldiers slain and more than two hundred men and dependants stripped, enslaved, and distributed among the Cherokee villages. Captain Stuart, through the efforts of Chief Attakullakulla the lone officer to survive, eventually fled north to reach the encampment of Col. William Byrd's Virginia militia.

Lyttleton, whose tactless diplomacy had precipitated the Cherokee War, was transferred to Jamaica and replaced by William Bull, Jr., who attempted to bargain with the Cherokee. But news of the massacre following the surrender of Fort Loudon precluded any peaceful solution. Bull appealed again for British military assistance to Gen. Jeffrey Amherst, who for once had troops to spare, and he dispatched Lt. Col. James Grant with portions of the First, Twenty-second, and Seventy-seventh Regiments to Charles Town. On May 27, 1761, Grant assembled his redcoats and accompanied by a colonial regiment under Col. William Middleton and Maj. Andrew Pickens, moved upcountry and crossed the Keowee River in a column two miles long.

Grant was a capable but unpopular officer. Demanding, persistent, and well organized, he was also ill tempered and arrogant, particularly in his dealings with colonials. Grant proceeded through the deserted and previously burned Lower towns and turned into the steep mountain path utilized by Montgomery. As he neared the defile where his predecessor had been ambushed, he sent forward a provincial force of thirty men under Capt. Quinton Kennedy and 1st Lt. Francis Marion. Dressed in Indian garb and accompanied by Catawba scouts, these provincials charged boldly into the gap yelling and firing. As war whoops sounded and Indian rifle fire exploded from the crest, Grant poured his regulars into the pass, blandly dismissing casualties. Meanwhile, Marion pressed on, despite twenty-one casualties in his column, distracting the Cherokee. Grant's main force pushed up the Little Tennessee toward a large Indian town called Echoe, then encamped. The following morning he burned Echoe as well as its great council house and moved on to Nikwasi, where he appropriated the council house to serve as a hospital. For thirty days Grant scoured the Middle Cherokee towns, rampaging into the mountain valleys, burning villages and acres of corn. The economic distress inflicted upon the Middle villages was devastating. Coupled with the previous carnage created by Montgomery, almost half the Cherokee nation lay in smoking ruins. Unbeaten in battle but economically destitute the Cherokee were forced to seek a peaceful settlement. An Indian delegation led by Chief Attakullakulla soon appeared at Fort Prince George to negotiate and smoke the pipe of peace, signing a formal treaty on December 16, 1761.

Cherokee-colonial relationships recovered slowly from these punitive expeditions, but as French influence disintegrated the British Indian Department moved expeditiously to fill the resulting power vacuum, adopting a dual policy of limiting colonial expansion into Indian lands and manipulating Cherokee trade policies. British Indian agents were appointed and accorded broad, wide-ranging powers. John Stuart, the red-headed young officer who negotiated the surrender at Fort Loudon, was appointed British superintendent for Southeastern Indian Affairs, a wise and fortuitous assignment. Stuart was a unique, resourceful, and opportunistic individual whose impact on Cherokee and American history was truly astounding. Born in 1718 at Inverness, he was the son of John Steuart and his second wife, Christine MacLeod of the Isle of Skye. Mastering Spanish as a child, he accompanied an expedition in 1740 designed to harass Spanish shipping in the Caribbean. Having dropped the "e" from his last name, in the spring of 1748 he established residence in Charles Town, South Carolina, married, and soon enjoyed a family, three daughters and a son. John Joseph, his only male progeny, would eventually achieve the rank of lieutenant general in the British army, receiving a knighthood after Napoleon's defeat at Calabria.

When appointed Indian agent, Stuart rapidly gained popularity among the Cherokee, who respectfully bestowed on him the title of "Beloved Father." He lived among the Cherokee for several months each year, being called "Bushyhead" to denote his characteristic shock of curly, red-gold hair. He took an Indian wife, Sarah Henry, and sired a son, also called Bushyhead, a tribal surname that was passed on for generations among the mountain residents. As relations between colonies and king became strained, Stuart's continued residence in Charles Town became tenuous. Intercepted by the colonials was a letter addressed to him from Gen. Thomas Gage that stated in case of war, "have them [the Cherokee] take up arms against his majesties [sic] enemies and distress them with all their power." This threat compelled Stuart to flee, first to Savannah, then on to Florida, his English wife and a daughter, Mary Fenwick, being virtually held hostage in Charles Town. Establishing a base of operations in St. Augustine, Stuart continued to advise the activities of the Cherokee tribes through two agents, Andrew Cameron and his brother, Henry Stuart. In 1775-76 when British plans to capture Charles Town were formulated and Stuart was ordered to trigger a concurrent Indian uprising, he refused, fearful that the Cherokee, if once turned loose, would assail Loyalists and rebels alike while acting outside his control. Stuart also correctly and sadly forecast the severity of colonial retribution upon his charges should the English efforts fail.

In June 1776 more than fifty British sailing vessels, warships, and transport vessels appeared off the entrance to Charles Town harbor. Lt. Gen. Sir Henry Clinton, accompanied by Adm. Sir Peter Parker, led a combined force with which they planned to capture Sullivan's Island and seal access to the busy seaport, assuring its eventual surrender. Clinton debarked his infantry on nearby Long Island, planning to deploy and storm across the narrow Breach Inlet onto Sullivan's Island. Colonial defenses on the island consisted only of a low fort constructed of palmetto logs arrayed in double rows about sixteen feet apart, the intervals filled with sand. The fort contained twenty-one artillery pieces: five 18-pounders, nine 12-pounders, and seven 9-pounders. Col. William Moultrie and four hundred members of the Second South Carolina garrisoned the works, assisted by twenty to thirty gunners of the Fourth South Carolina Artillery.

Clinton disembarked twenty-two hundred redcoats and marines on Long Island and prepared to wade across the seventy-five-yard inlet at slack tide. At low tide the water depth was discovered to be seven or eight feet in the wash, with strong rip currents. The land assault thus foiled, on June 20, Admiral Parker carefully brought eleven warships over the tricky Charles Town bar and prepared to bombard Fort Sullivan into submission. However, the spongy palmetto walls absorbed the balls of his 270 guns with minimal damage. Conversely the wooden hulls of the English warships took a pounding from surprisingly accurate Colonial gunners who skipped their cannonballs into the targets. Several ships ran aground and one frigate, the HMS *Actaeon,* was struck so often that she was burned to prevent capture. British naval casualties exceeded two hundred, including several prominent senior officers. Clinton's infantry organized a final bold attempt, utilizing the longboats of Parker's warships to row cross the inlet. But a well-placed 18-pounder and the muskets of Col. William Thompson's militia foiled this final effort. Clinton withdrew his infantry and the fleet sailed back to New York, their exit the cause for celebrations and bonfires on the beach.

As English sails disappeared from view at Breach Inlet, a tragic sidebar in Revolutionary War history ensued. The Cherokee frontier, both east and north, exploded with war whoops and gunfire as raids and incursions were rashly launched on farm and settlement in conjunction with the British assault on Charles Town. While a few Cherokee towns, exercising their city-state like independence, did not participate, most complied with the British-inspired onslaught, though against the advice of their southern Indian commissioner, John Stuart. The attackers found easy victims on isolated farms, but their triumphs initiated a terrible response, much as Stuart had forecast. The Cherokee would pay the price for their alliance with the redcoats.

When the Cherokee took the warpath in 1776, leadership within their towns and villages was shifting from a cadre of older, peace-seeking chiefs to younger, more militant warriors. Emerging rapidly among the Over-the-Hill villagers was the forty-four-year-old chief of Great Island Town, Dragging Canoe. Attributed with great physical prowess as well as oratorical skills second to none, he soared to a highly respected position among his peers. The young chief had attained his unusual name while a youngster. When his father, Chief Attakullakulla, prepared a war party to attack the Shawnee, the ten year old begged to attend, a request adamantly refused. Stealing away, the youngster secreted himself in a dugout canoe. Several warriors discovered the stowaway at the first portage, invoking an angry response from Attakullakulla, who demanded that his son return home unless he could carry a canoe over the one-mile portage. The aspiring little warrior, unable to lift the heavy vessel, began dragging the canoe across the wet sand. As he finally completed the portage the observing warriors, cheering and encouraging his efforts, began calling the young lad by a newly coined name, Dragging Canoe.

The initial Cherokee strikes were northward into the vulnerable Holston, Watauga, and Carter's Valley settlements of Virginia, involving more than seven hundred warriors. Dragging Canoe led several hundred into the Long Island (Kingsport, Tennessee) settlements on the Holston River. Old Abram, a longtime war chief, took a contingent into the Watauga Valley, while the Raven, war chief of the Chota, led warriors up into Carter's Valley to destroy those settlements. All three bands met with less than satisfactory results. Old Abram penetrated to the Watauga stockade but was repelled in a tough fight with John Sevier's militia. The Raven found Carter's Valley empty, all the settlers having fled, and he continued north as far as Abingdon, Virginia. Dragging Canoe became involved in a serious fight at Long Island Flats where the timely maneuvers of Capt. Evan Shelby's militia company checked the Indian leader's promising enveloping movement. Losses were minimal in both combats, but the most serious was the wounding of Dragging Canoe. The charismatic war leader took a rifle ball in the thigh, causing his incapacitation at a crucial moment in Cherokee history.

Subsequently, based on this endeavor, Dragging Canoe altered his style of combat. Defeated when attempting to fight the Colonials in their linear style, he reverted again to Indian fighting methods: using stealth, surprise, unmerciful attacks, and sudden retreat. When the Colonial armies invaded the Cherokee villages he refused to make peace with the attackers; he and his followers left the Cherokee country by canoe and dugout. A hero to Cherokee nationalists, Dragging Canoe symbolized the ultimate, unconquerable Cherokee.

Simultaneously, raids were conducted by war parties of young Cherokee in the frontier areas of North Carolina, South Carolina, and Georgia. When a company of Georgia militia was ambushed, all its members were slain or tortured. The body of Lieutenant Grant, the commander, was dismembered and nailed to a tree. All hope for reconciliation between Cherokee and Colonials disappeared as the voices of numerous Colonial leaders called for a final destruction of the Cherokee nation. The absence of any ongoing revolutionary conflict with British forces following the aborted British attempt to take Charles Town allowed these newly independent states to concentrate their militia power on eradicating the Cherokee threat. Thus the Cherokee raids did more to unite frontier settlers against British policies than any threat of redcoat attack could possibly have achieved. As the Cherokee were proclaimed allies of the British, any deeds they committed were considered British-inspired actions. These sudden attacks provided back country settlers with a common cause, a unifying purpose. Surprisingly the governing officials of four states established frontier defense as a priority and achieved a fair level of cooperative effort. Three separate militia armies were quickly raised to engage the Cherokee: a force from Virginia, a North Carolina army, and a combined South Carolina-Georgia contingent. The South Carolina force would invade the Lower Cherokee towns and then move on to unite with a North Carolina army already active in the Middle towns. Together the two forces would raze the Valley towns. Concurrently, a Virginia army would invade the inner citadel of the Cherokee nation, the secluded Over-the-Hill villages.

As orders to muster circulated in upcountry South Carolina, small local militia units began moving westward in stages, gradually combining with other units in a steady, growing stream. As they neared the frontier the volunteers observed the readily viewable results of Cherokee raids—scalped victims and smoking homesteads. At Prince's Fort on the Tyger River, the militia companies staged and encamped, awaiting direction. Col. Samuel Jack led in a Georgia company that had already destroyed several Cherokee towns on the Tugaloo River while moving north to a rendezvous with Col. Andrew Williamson's South Carolinians.

On August 31, Williamson decided to march, ordering Col. Leroy Hammond with about 350 mounted soldiers to sortie toward Seneca in search of a Cherokee war party that was reportedly led by British agent Alexander Cameron. Moving at night across the Keowee River, Hammond was unexpectedly ambushed by waiting Cherokee. Initially the Colonial soldiers fled, but they were rallied as Hammond profanely tongue-lashed the shirkers. Cameron's small band of warriors soon faded into the mountains. Hammond lost five killed and fourteen wounded, a light casualty list for his inept blunder into a tactical trap. Darkness and the fact that Hammond's men were mounted while the enemy was afoot probably prevented more serious loss of life.

At daybreak, Williamson advanced his entire thirteen-hundred-man force across the river and deliberately deployed. The army then moved forward in three columns: Col. John Thomas's regiment on the right, the light horse on the left, and Col. Thomas Neel's regiment in the center astride an old Indian path. The rear guard followed with supply trains and an extensive cattle herd. Carefully the column approached Estatoe, penetrating into the streets of the large village only to discover the town completely deserted. After the force camped overnight, Estatoe was burned and the men followed Indian trails to Qualatchee, Toxaway, and Tugaloo, villages of considerable size that they also reduced to ashes. Crops and storehouses were burned, while cornfields and orchards were chopped apart with swords and axes. The militia force then turned down the Tugaloo River to a junction with the Keowee. Following that stream the army arrived at the ruined village of

Keowee, across from the remains of old Fort Prince George. The Cherokee Lower towns now lay in abject ruins, once again devastated by hostile force.

Williamson then permitted his militiamen to return home for provisions, preparing for a longer expedition. A 300-man unit remained to erect a fort at Seneca, which was named Fort Rutledge in honor of the newly appointed president of South Carolina. On September 12, Col. Thomas Sumter arrived at Seneca with 270 soldiers and a large supply of gunpowder, having marched from Charles Town to reinforce Williamson's army following the British departure. On the next morning the army departed its camps to the lively beat of drummers, approaching the Ocoee Mountains and Rauban Gap, the gateway to the Middle towns. The unusually rugged nature of the surrounding mountains awed the long line of marchers. Despite the topography, Williamson continued to employ his favorite tactic of advancing three units in a column abreast. Anticipating contact with the enemy by his center column, he planned to envelope the opposition with his wings. While this was a viable practice in open country warfare, the tactic adapted poorly to mountainous terrain. Slow and ungainly movements resulted, with flanking columns often forced to cut their way up and down trackless mountainsides. Such a strategy usually failed to make contact with a mobile enemy, who could easily avoid the advance, remain concealed, and emerge to fight only when opportunity for easy success was presented. On the seventeenth they reached the narrows, a path with steep mountain crags on one hand and an abrupt drop into a river on the other. This was the very spot of previous ambushes of redcoat columns, but surprisingly no opposition materialized and the column proceeded to find the smoldering ruins of Cowee. General Rutherford's North Carolinians had arrived first.

A second Colonial army had been fitted out in back country North Carolina. Assembled in late August from militia regiments, this twenty-four-hundred-man force was commanded by crusty old Gen. Griffith Rutherford. Dressed in dingy hunting shirts with the motto "Liberty or Death" emblazoned across their chests, these backwoods farmers hardly looked the part of a military force, but Rutherford was a warrior, the veteran of many a backwoods fight. Born in Northern Ireland in 1721 and orphaned at an early age, he grew up tough and was not a man to tolerate disobedience. His troops staged at Old Fort, North Carolina. Arrayed before them were high mountain forests containing an enemy whose cunning, skill, and merciless nature were known by each participant. The fires of vengeance that burned brightly in each man were tempered by trepidation over the coming campaign in such a rugged land.

Rutherford's line of march began with the ascension and crossing of the mountains at Swannanoa Gap, where a clear mountain stream was followed to a juncture with the beautiful French Broad River. Crossing at War Ford, the column followed tributaries until they passed over the Cowee Mountains, where Indians fired on the van. Climbing a ridge, the North Carolina militia pursued a trail to the Tuckasegee River and crossed to the west bank, discovering an Indian trail leading to the deserted village of Sticoy. Rutherford destroyed Sticoy and sent detachments to burn all the villages on the Tuskasegee. He then advanced to the Little Tennessee River, camping for several days opposite Nikwasi to await the South Carolinians. Rutherford's men enjoyed the respite amid the early fall beauty of the region, finding adequate provisions among the Indian storehouses, gardens, and limitless population of swine. Then, the large Cherokee Middle towns of Nikwasi, Etchoe, Cowee, Cullasaja, and Watoga were methodically torn apart and burned. The only resistance came when Maj. Daniel Bryson led a troop to burn Sugartown, or Callasatchee, and was briefly ambushed. Entering an empty town and seeking loot the reckless invaders were suddenly fired on as the Cherokee war whoop echoed down the valley. Forced to seek shelter in the Indian huts, the soldiers were pressed for a time until a relief contingent arrived.

Meanwhile, uncertain of Rutherford's exact location and growing impatient, Williamson directed forays into the nearby valleys. Leaving the village of Nikwasi, on the banks of the Little Tennessee, he advanced into a long, horseshoe-shaped valley surrounded by brooding mountains. Forcing a passage he deployed Hammond with a column left and Sumter right, ordering Neel's militia to advance across the valley floor. Capt. William Hampton spied Indians ahead hiding in the fields and realized that Neel was about to be ambushed. He charged forward with his riders directly into the Indians and then deployed his men with Neel's men in a defensive circle. For almost two hours a hot fight ensued. Neel's regiment lost thirteen killed and eighteen wounded and Hampton several more. The inspired Hampton led brief charges from the protective ring, falling back into safety when pressed. Observing Sumter's advancing column drawing near, the Cherokee gave up their surrounding position and retreated into the mountains. The soldiers burned or razed every hut and field in the forbidding "Black Hole" as Cherokee women and children watched, weeping, from the mountaintops.

Colonel Sumter sortied several days later, leading three hundred riders into the Nacoochee Valley. Crossing the continental divide on a path so perilous and narrow that they were forced to dismount and lead their horses, his riders emerged into a lush valley of apple orchards and fertile fields near Frog Town. Sumter's horsemen swept down the valley, killing livestock, cutting trees, and burning cornfields. The beautiful little oasis was turned into a wasteland. After nightfall the column set out by the same dangerous path to Nikwasi.

Having completed the destruction of the Middle towns, Rutherford in turn grew restless waiting for Colonel Williamson and decided to move on the Valley towns without support. Moving westward from his camp at Nikwasi he led his force into the Nantahala Mountains, planning a crossing at Wayah Gap. At an angle formed by two ridges, a Cherokee party opened a scalding fire on the Carolina troops. Pinned down without sight of an enemy the column began taking casualties, suffering forty wounded in two hours, until without warning the Cherokee disappeared. Once again, the Cherokee warriors had gained some advantage but run short of ammunition and were forced to disengage.

Rutherford's column moved on to the Hiwassee River and into the Valley towns where a juncture was affected with Andrew Pickens' South Carolina horsemen on September 26. When Williamson's infantry arrived the two columns united to raze the valley of the Hiwassee River and its tributaries. Large, prosperous Cherokee towns such as Hiwassee, Tellico, Tommotley, Chatoga, and Ustally simply ceased to exist. This combined army, numbering more than four thousand men, encountering slight Cherokee opposition, destroyed more than thirty-six Cherokee towns.

Both armies returned to their individual mustering points by following their earlier respective routes of advance. Williamson's army suffered a total of ninety-nine casualties while Rutherford's losses were probably less. Little fighting occurred during the campaign; however, the Cherokee Lower, Middle, and Valley settlements—three-fourths of their nation—were utterly devastated. Thousands of homeless Cherokee were forced into the forest to starve or live as best they could, even as the chills of winter approached. Many fled across the mountains to find safety in the Over-the-Hill settlements while still others moved west, seeking succor with Dragging Canoe's Chickamauga villages or even south to beg from their ancestral enemies, the Creek.

The Virginia Army

The Carolina campaigns were almost concluded when a Virginia army launched its own retaliatory attack. Virginia governor Patrick Henry appointed his brother-in-law, Col. William Christian, to assemble an army, which he ordered to invade the Over-the-Hill villages. Lt. Col. William Russell had earlier constructed a new fort at Long Island, christened Fort Patrick Henry, and this site was designated as a rendezvous for the Virginia army.

Christian, a veteran of Dunmore's War, was an experienced and intelligent leader. Well acquainted with Indian warfare, he would prove a capable if somewhat methodical soldier, moving slowly and carefully forward in well-planned stages. While Rutherford and Williamson campaigned along Indian trade routes, Christian would endeavor to cross the mountains through near impassable paths to fall on the flank of the Indian villages alongside the upper Little Tennessee, or Cherokee River. Few white men had ever seen this bastion of Cherokee power.

On October 6, his men advanced to the Nolichucky River. Camping at a ford, Christian, who suspected an ambush, marched at night, leaving campfires burning to delude the enemy. Moving down an old warrior path he soon reached the French Broad River crossing at Buckingham Island Ford. There Capt. John Sevier joined the column with a mounted company that proved invaluable for scout duty. Christian wrote to Gov. Patrick Henry: "I am crossing the French Broad, I will be attacked or meet proposals of peace. . . . Cameron remains among the Cherokee and daily encourages them to defend their country. . . . I heartily wish they will attack me."

Soon a peace embassy, a white trader named Ellis Harden, appeared to inquire if Christian would talk peace with Chief Raven. He also warned of a possible ambush should Christian refuse, but the Virginian replied that he and his men would advance to the Cherokee towns and distinguish between those Cherokee who behaved well and those who did not. Those involved in the conflict would be punished. This bellicose message caused a vicious debate in the great council house at Chote. Dragging Canoe and Alexander Cameron exhausted their appeals for war and left the village, moving southward down the Tennessee.

Christian's army, led by John Sevier's scouts, crossed the river near Toqua. The column then moved upstream to Tommotley. On the following day the column marched past Tuskasegee and the blackened ruins of Old Fort Loudon before pitching camp at the Great Island Town of Mialaquo. Most of the Cherokee had fled, uncertain of Christian's intentions, so the soldiers moved into the deserted Indian homes and council house at Island Town.

From this encampment, Christian sent messages to the Cherokee chiefs requesting that they attend a parley at his camp. Christian wrote to Patrick Henry, "Tomorrow I expect The Raven, Oconostota, and Little Carpenter along with other officials to open talks. . . . I know I can kill and take hundreds of them . . . but it would be mostly women and children for the men retreat faster than I can follow."

These aging chiefs came to face Christian and listen to his ultimatum—"cooperate or be destroyed"—and each was convinced of his sincerity. Christian further requested that all white prisoners be released and that Dragging Canoe and Cameron be delivered to him as prisoners. While the chiefs accepted his demands for prisoner release, they explained that the two men he desired to incarcerate had fled to Florida, finding refuge in British domains. Apparently content with the outcome of the talks, Christian refrained from the wholesale destruction that had occurred in the Lower, Middle, and Valley settlements, for so destitute was the plight of the Cherokee that he felt further burning unnecessary. Only two particular villages, Tuskasegee and Toqua, where atrocities had been committed upon whites, were torched.

Christian completed plans for a June treaty meeting with the Cherokee at Long Island and marched his army north, arriving at Bristol, Virginia, on November 12, 1776. While Col. Joseph Williams and others criticized Christian for extending leniency to the Cherokee survivors, his campaign was concluded successfully with the previously impregnable Cherokee citadel breached and broken while he absorbed only scattered casualties.

The departure of Christian's Virginia army from the Over-the-Hill settlements signaled the end of the large-scale expeditions to subjugate the Cherokee. Scarcely two and a half months had elapsed since the initiation of warfare by Williamson and Rutherford to the conclusion of Christian's campaign. In this brief span the Cherokee nation was almost completely destroyed. Only a determined few warriors continued to resist, sallying forth from their lower Tennessee River bases to harass settlers on the Holston and Clinch Rivers. Possibly, only the charismatic leadership of their resolute war chief, Dragging Canoe, sustained and inspired these unconquered warriors.

Two separate treaties were negotiated. The first, drawn up on May 20, 1777, at Dewitt's Corner, South Carolina, was initiated by the governments of Georgia and South Carolina and demanded extensive concessions of land located along the Tugaloo, Saluda, and Keowee Rivers. While much larger concessions were agreed upon at Dewitt's Corner, a second treaty at Long Island in Virginia resounded with axioms of critical importance to both Cherokee and settlers. These negotiations began on June 28, 1777, with aging chiefs Oconostota and Attakullakulla representing the Cherokee, while Colonels Christian, Preston, Shelby, Winston, and Lanier embodied the interests of Virginia and North Carolina. The Cherokee deftly deflected inquiries by the Virginians about Dragging Canoe and Alexander Cameron. Old Tassel, a well-respected chief, best reflected the Cherokee position when he stated, "The Great Spirit has placed us [Indian and white] in different situations. . . . he has not created us to be your slave. *We are a separate people.*" With these words the seeds of a new form of Cherokee independence were sown among the tribe. By recognizing that Cherokee settlement and culture differed from white and refusing assimilation, they showed faith that their future as a nation could be ensured. Those Cherokee who joined the followers of

Dragging Canoe, floating down the Tennessee to the Chickamauga towns, derisively taunted those Cherokee who remained in the villages as "Virginians."

The commissioners, moved by the eloquent pleas of Cherokee speakers, limited the land requests from the nation, insisting only on those areas already settled by white farmers, although much of those holdings were nefariously attained. A shaky agreement was attained as Colonials promised to furnish aid and supplies, goods previously provided by the British. Regretabably, they could not or did not deliver, reigniting tensions on both sides.

Angered by the escape of Dragging Canoe and his adherents and fueled by new rumors of arms shipments to the Chickamauga villages by Crown officials, an expedition was authorized by Gov. Patrick Henry to preempt the raiding ability of the Cherokee. Col. Evan Shelby, assisted by his son, Isaac, enlisted a six-hundred-man assault force and mounted a downriver raid. Utilizing canoes and pirogues the little force cast off from Big Creek on the Holston River on April 10, 1779. With the Tennessee River running full flood, Shelby's men reached Chickamauga Creek in five days, catching the Indians unaware. But as the Colonials stormed ashore, the Cherokee scattered into the woods and fields, abandoning their homes while Shelby's men remained in the area almost two weeks, burning eleven villages. Crops were not yet planted so little long-term damage was possible. The militiamen then destroyed their vessels and marched afoot up the Tennessee River while a contingent of the Virginia regulars under Col. John Montgomery journeyed overland to join George Rogers Clark in Kentucky.

Sporadic retaliatory raids by Cherokee groups continued throughout the winter of 1779-80 when British columns marched out from Charles Town and Savannah. Those Cherokee who remained loyal to George III were now able to obtain supplies, guns, and powder at a depot located on the Savannah River at Augusta, Georgia. In October, when the settlers of Tennessee and Virginia crossed the mountain range in pursuit of Maj. Patrick Ferguson, his scouts informed Dragging Canoe. Recognizing an opportunity to strike the homes of frontiersmen, the Cherokee chief rallied his warriors and started north. But Sevier, Shelby, and Campbell met at Sycamore Shoals, crossed the divide, chased and trapped Ferguson on Kings Mountain, and returned home so quickly they averted the Cherokee attack and moved south to fight them at Boyd's Creek.

Approaching the Indian encampment, Sevier discovered the Cherokee were advancing and moved forward to meet them. The Indian attack party was concealed in tall grass, seeking to ambush Sevier's horsemen. The ambush discovered, Sevier dismounted his forward riders to form a skirmish line and ordered his following riders to gallop to each flank, enveloping the warriors. When the Cherokee began to retreat, the Colonials charged all along their line, riding hard to surround the Indians, but the pursuit led into a nearby swamp and most of the Cherokees escaped. Camping on the field, Sevier awaited the reinforcing column of Col. Arthur Campbell that arrived on December 22. Campbell, the cousin of Gen. William Campbell, joined with Sevier and they led their combined force into the Over-the-Hill settlements, arriving at Chote on Christmas Eve. Despite the peaceful intentions of the inhabitants, they burned the villages of Chote, Chilhowee, Toqua, Kaiatee, Tellico, and Hiwassee, a total of more than one thousand Indian cabins. Save for the few Chickamauga towns, the Cherokee villages lay in ruins.

From his bastion near Chattanooga, Dragging Canoe continued his resistance, leading a brilliant raid on Nashborough, Tennessee, that almost destroyed a recently established settlement at French Lick. Unrepentant and uncompromising, the war chief continued his own personal war until his untimely death following an all-night marathon dance on March 1, 1792. The demise of the sixty-year-old chief removed the heart and spirit of Cherokee resistance.

The merciless campaign against the Cherokee nation in 1776, although of brief duration, so disassembled the Indian tribe that in 1780, when another British military campaign was introduced into the south, minimal Indian support was forthcoming. From the war's inception the Cherokee were at a marked disadvantage. Betrayed by a British alliance that left them to face the punitive columns of revenge-seeking Colonial militia, the tribes suffered tremendous economic destruction and for all practical purposes were removed from the war in one massive strike.

The developed culture of the Cherokee actually proved disadvantageous. Having adopted fairly sophisticated dwelling patterns, leaving the nomadic lifestyle of earlier times for agricultural pursuits, the Cherokee became markedly more vulnerable. Depending on the brooding mountain fastness of their villages for safety, they were shocked to observe the overwhelming number of enemies traversing their valleys. Further, the Cherokee did not fathom the effects of the recent migratory waves into the southern back country. Thousands of land seekers had journeyed south, many locating adjacent to Cherokee land. A multitude of riflemen could thus be assembled to march on the Cherokee within brief weeks. Well-armed, provided with unlimited ammunition, and driving herds of provisions on the hoof, long lines of riflemen filed through the mountain valleys, watched with awe by Cherokees from hidden lairs. Little direct resistance occurred during the invasion as the outnumbered Cherokee abandoned their beloved villages and fled into the mountains to watch the violent destruction of their world. This scorched-earth philosophy depicted a total Colonial disregard for Cherokee culture but was a tactic deployed some hundred years later, when Sherman's bummers cut wide swaths through the lands of these same settlers.

Despite the one-sided aspects of the Cherokee War, its effects were overwhelmingly beneficial for rebel purposes. The Cherokee expeditions, whatever their outcomes, were Colonial operations from inception to conclusion. Similar to the Virginian march to Point Pleasant in 1774, all the participants were back country militia, organized in battalion-size units for the first time. Now their actions were authorized by newly appointed state administrators, not royal governors and their cumbersome array of operations; organization, communication, supply, and armament were distinctly Colonial ventures. Poorly or well done, these initiatives laid the foundations of a new Colonial identity.

Several byproducts of the Cherokee War were imperative for the future operation of Colonial armies in the south, particularly in the back country. The British decision to abandon the Charles Town attack in 1776 provided several years of relief from military activity for patriot forces in the south, and all militia efforts could be concentrated on Indian defeat. Such punitive treatment would discourage the Indian nation from active participation when the British later invaded the back country, in 1780. Additionally, Tories in the area were placed at a disadvantage since public knowledge linked British armies with

Indian tactics, discrediting all those who professed loyalty to King George. Opposition to Indian warfare generated a spirit of unification, however feeble, amongst back country rebels, neutrals, and even some of Loyalist leaning. Rebellion was not always universally popular in the back country, but defense of one's hearth and family were unfaltering.

Another important benefit to the Colonials was the discriminating process that evolved within militia leadership ranks. Just as the Point Pleasant campaign culled many incompetents from those who would be military leaders in Virginia, the Indian campaign in the Carolinas affirmed the abilities of some and proved the demise of others. The expeditions served as "schools of the army" for the actions to come against British foes. Men learned how to provision and supply a military force, what forms of shelter and camp accommodations were necessary, and what training activities might turn diverse individuals into an active, disciplined military body.

The three great partisan leaders of South Carolina all found their military "legs" in the campaigns against the Cherokee. Francis Marion, the "Swamp Fox" of the Low Country, learned to use the hit-and-run tactics of the Cherokee while marching with Grant's redcoats. Likewise, the irascible Thomas Sumter, who effectively led a regiment with Williamson's column, developed strategies to confuse and bedazzle British units in scores of upcountry fights. Finally, the dour Presbyterian Andrew Pickens, who rode alongside Williamson, led partisan raids of effect on numerous occasions and commanded Daniel Morgan's second line in the critical stand-up fight at Cowpens.

Also from Williamson's column a contingent of valuable militia officers emerged, men who could lead regiments and brigades. James Williams, lieutenant colonel of militia, later served with Sumter, filling important roles in that officer's partisan corps although the two argued vociferously. Irritatingly ambitious, Williams' ardent patriotism led to his death on the slopes of Kings Mountain. Bold and incautious, Lt. Col. Joseph Hayes was a veteran officer whose leadership on the second American line at Cowpens was critical. Captured in November 1781 at Hayes Station, he was unjustifiably hung by Bill Cunningham, a Tory leader of note. Samuel Hammond, a veteran of many a clash in the south, was also at Cowpens. He led the left wing of the Colonial skirmish line and rallied his riflemen after their retreat through the second line to emerge on the right flank and assist in the surrounding and capture of a battalion of the Seventy-first Highlanders.

Christian's column, too, included frontiersmen destined for positions of repute. Maj. William Edmondson served as a captain on the Cherokee expedition as well as during Shelby's Chickamauga raid. He then joined William Campbell's force on the march to Kings Mountain. Eight members of his family followed him, three to die on the mountain. Isaac Shelby fought in his father's company on Christian's raid to Point Pleasant and in almost any fight in which long riflemen were involved. He led a force at Kings Mountain that stormed the north ridge, his inspirational leadership contributing much to the victory. Shelby was elected the first governor of Kentucky after statehood was achieved. John Sevier must also be recognized. His service as chief scout and cavalry leader on Christian's assault proved invaluable. A hero at Kings Mountain, he commanded the frontiersmen at Boyd's Creek and was eventually selected as the first governor of the State of Tennessee.

These and many others fashioned the militia forces that

later dared to face red-coated professionals on fields of battle. From Dunmore's War and the Cherokee War came the experience that produced worthy foes for the British southern campaign of 1780. Undisciplined, uneducated, but determined, rebels emerged who served well in command during the three great decisive battles of the southern campaign: Kings Mountain, Cowpens, and Guilford Court House.

CHAPTER 3

Thunder on Spring Hill

"D'Estaing, a true Grenadier in this affair but a poor General . . . It was not the fault of the troops that Savannah did not fall, but rather of him who commanded us."
French staff officer at Savannah

At daybreak on October 9, 1779, nervous, anxious files of French and American soldiers had arrayed in the swamps near the Augusta turnpike to await the orders of their French commanding officer, the pompous Comte d'Estaing, who was prepared to launch an attack upon British redoubts located on Spring Hill, southwest of Savannah. The sophisticated French commander had prepared his surprise, early-morning frontal assault in a final, almost desperate, attempt to bring a successful conclusion to a frustrating month-long siege of Savannah. The brutal repulse that ensued, aggravated by ghastly, exorbitant casualty lists, brought a savage ending to the allied French and American expedition into Georgia. As American soldiers moved north in retreat across the Savannah River toward Charles Town following the repulse, d'Estaing's Frenchmen prepared to again board their ships. The one-sided British victory at Spring Hill provided support for and rekindled interest in George III's and Lord Germain's plans to capture the southern provinces as a two-year campaign for domination of the Carolinas and Georgia began, a movement characterized by moments of tactical brilliance, uncommon valor by redcoat and rebel alike, and the unveiling of an unprecedented scale of violence between Whig and Tory. Revolutionary warfare in the south was truly initiated.

As the war came to Georgia, the populace began to divide in allegiance. Most government officials, business leaders, merchants, and Anglican Church members allied themselves with the king and his policies. These Tories, or Loyalists, maintained control of Savannah and launched sporadic expeditions into the back country, attempting to establish outposts. Augusta, on the Savannah, was captured and recaptured three times. The Georgia back country was more divided, with Whigs and Tories contending for supremacy in given areas. Soon enclaves of either party existed and raided the opposition as violence escalated and a real civil war emerged from the fluid chaos, with atrocities a common occurrence. Cherokee and men of color, free or slave, supported the Tories, but as immigrants moved south, the back country, Presbyterian in faith, became patriot territory. Neutrality was impossible. An individual must declare for one side or the other and be willing to take up arms in support of that cause.

More than a year before Georgia became the focus of the British campaign and the colony's citizens were forced to align themselves with either their new country or the motherland, Col. Archibald Campbell, an English officer of exceptional talent, was ordered south from Sandy Hook, New Jersey, with almost thirty-five hundred soldiers, including two of three battalions of the Seventy-first

Highlanders, two Hessian regiments, four Loyalist battalions, and a small detachment of Royal Artillery. His objective was the capture of the valuable Georgia seaport, considered second only to Charles Town in economic importance or political prominence. Possession of Savannah would additionally provide a buffer between worrisome British fortification in Florida and the rebel brigades of the south.

British white ensigns appeared off Tybee Island on December 23, 1778, and soon small vessels maneuvered upstream toward Girardeau's Plantation, where a vanguard of redcoats was disembarked and entrenched. Lt. Col. John Maitland, a crusty old Royal Marine veteran who was transferred to command the Seventy-first Highland Regiment, led the advance, his skirmish line mounting the plantation wharf and scaling a steep twenty-foot bluff to establish the beachhead. The American army commander, Maj. Gen. Robert Howe, was compelled to attempt a defense of Savannah with about 700 militiamen weakly entrenched in hastily constructed revetments. Quamino Dolly, a runaway slave, voluntarily guided Sir James Baird's British light infantry through nearby swamps, traversing a hidden pathway that emerged on an unprepared American flank. In the ensuing rout rebel units fled wildly, suffering nearly 100 casualties and leaving more than 450 men to be incarcerated on prison hulks. British losses totaled less than 50. This relatively easy victory firmly reestablished British presence in the south, effectively recapturing most of the Georgia colony and creating a base for future operations.

The popular Campbell was transferred elsewhere, and Swiss-born Maj. Gen. Augustine Prevost of French Huguenot lineage moved north from Florida to unite with royal governor James Wright and reestablish British government in Georgia. From a comfortable house on Broughton Street, between Bull and Drayton, Prevost seemed content to peaceably administer his newly acquired dominion. But when Gen. Benjamin Lincoln, who replaced the defeated Howe, moved west toward Augusta with rebel militia, Prevost suddenly exploded into action. Crossing the Savannah River near Purysburg with two thousand regulars and an intimidating force of Creek and Cherokee warriors, he brushed aside William Moultrie's blocking force and marched directly toward Charles Town. The hesitant British commander delayed his advance for several days while considering his various options, however, tossing away his early advantage. Local rebel militiamen labored frantically to erect defensive works and batteries about Charles Town as Lincoln countermarched to rescue the threatened port city. Suddenly outmaneuvered and outnumbered, Prevost abandoned the main road and decided to retreat across James Island, temporarily entrenching at Stono Ferry, where a boat bridge was erected that connected to nearby Johns Island. He left Colonel Maitland with five hundred to seven hundred members from the Seventy-first and the Trumbach Hessian regiments and continued to fall back from island to island, surrounded by and encumbered by hundreds of freedom-seeking slaves, refugees from the sea islands. The Hessian regiment at Stono Ferry recruited a group of slave boys from the Simmons Plantation for service as regimental drummers, a practice soon to be widely copied in most German and Loyalist battalions.

Colonel Maitland arrayed this small force at Stono Ferry in three stout earthen redoubts, batteries deployed between each earthwork. Capt. Colin Cameron, with four officers and fifty-six Highlanders, was dispatched forward, advancing beyond a grove of screening pine trees to serve as skirmishers. Lincoln, learning of Maitland's small force in such an exposed position, promptly advanced with almost twelve hundred Colonials. Initially Lincoln encountered a vicious firefight with Campbell's skirmishers, who resolutely refused to retreat. After finally breaking their resistance he continued forward toward the redoubts. Concentrating his attack on the British left redoubt, where the Trumbach troops were posted, Lincoln achieved some early success but Maitland adroitly shifted units to counter the attack. Following a lengthy exchange of musket fire, the rebel force began a deliberate withdrawal that gradually became somewhat disordered. The aggressive Maitland advanced his men in line of battle until Lincoln ordered a countering cavalry charge. Maitland closed ranks into an abbreviated square; the rear rank fired by platoons and the front rank kneeled with fixed bayonets. This maneuver broke up the cavalry assault but also concluded further British pursuit. Casualties were unusually heavy in both small forces. Maitland suffered 26 killed and 126 wounded of his 500 men, most of these among the Highland skirmishers and exposed gunners. American losses totaled 150 with another 150 missing, militiamen who would reappear later.

Without continued opposition, Maitland withdrew by stages to Edisto Island and then to Port Royal Island, where his soldiers moved into the tabby and frame houses of the sleepy village of Beaufort. He established a personal residence amid palmettos and live oaks in a comfortable estate on the corner of Carteret and Port Republic Streets. The First and Second Battalions of the Seventy-first and an attached company of New York Volunteers were garrisoned in Beaufort, while the Hessians and their attached artillery unit constructed revetments and comfortable camps at Miles End, a narrow neck commanding access to the village. Since the British navy controlled the coastal waters, the lodgments at both Savannah and Beaufort were seemingly easily defended. The torrid heat of a Low-Country summer prevented continued campaigning, as did accompanying episodes of bilious fever. Lincoln emplaced a comparable force at the village of Sheldon to shadow Maitland, whose little outpost had now grown to almost thirteen hundred by the addition of numerous noncombatants and runaway slaves. While comfortable and secure in Beaufort, the escalating illness rate forced Maitland to convert the jail and courthouse into hospitals.

Invasion

Similar to the destructive hurricanes that fitfully savaged the Carolina coastline without warning, so too did an unexpected armada of French warships sweep north from the West Indies to threaten the City on a Bluff. In September more than twenty-five men of war, vessels ranging in size up to seventy-four guns and accompanied by transports conveying more than four thousand soldiers, materialized out of the mists at the mouth of the Savannah River. It was commanded by the courtly and ambitious Charles-Henri, Comte d'Estaing, whose career had somewhat recovered from earlier 1778 setbacks off New York and Rhode Island by his capture of Grenada and the defeat of British admiral Byron's fleet. Basking in the accolades of these recent victories, d'Estaing was convinced by an aide, Colonel Bretigny, and Gov. John Rutledge of South Carolina that he could expect another quick victory at Savannah.

The French fleet, anchored warily in the open ocean

and spread from Beaufort to Tybee Island, was led by an elaborately titled, well-qualified, although somewhat contentious officer corps jealous of favor and position. D'Estaing began disembarking his soldiers after several aborted attempts. The troops were crammed into ungainly, uncomfortable longboats, rowing up the Vernon River to come ashore at Beaulieu Plantation. About twelve hundred men landed without opposition, although their task was endangered by inexperienced river pilots, high winds, rolling surf, and a constant, driving rain.

By the sixteenth of September, twenty-four hundred soldiers had advanced to within three miles of the city and united with Lincoln's Americans. The brightly attired French troops were drawn from fourteen regiments, ten of which were line battalions such as the Armagac, Dillon, Foix, and Gastinas, all possessing impressive colorful flags adorned with fleurs-de-lis and numerous battle streamers. Several additional units had long been on garrison duty in the Indies and were sorely depleted by disease and had grown soft by lengthy inaction. The largest contingent of French regular troops was the Dillon Regiment, a unit based of Irish volunteers but now including soldiers of Dutch, German, Swiss, and French origin. This unit contained 434 officers and men. Count Arthur Dillon, the commander, was born in Ireland in 1758 but like most of his family had spent his adult life in French service. A regiment of free blacks, the Chasseurs Volontaires de St. Dominique, ten companies of 545 volunteers, dressed in blue and green, under Col. Laurent de Rouvary, also accompanied d'Estaing, and a small detachment of the Royal Metz Artillery completed his force. Marching with the Haitian unit was Henry Christophe, a young mulatto soldier destined to become renowned as the "King of Haiti."

Meanwhile Lincoln's small American army was encountering difficulties in their efforts to unite with d'Estaing. They were frustrated in crossing the Savannah River at Zubly's Ferry, the logical crossing point, where Loyalists had burned both bridges and all available boats. A shuttle of skiffs and canoes finally proved sufficient, and Lincoln was able to convey into Georgia six understrength South Carolina Continental regiments totaling less than one thousand men, accompanied by militia units from South Carolina, Georgia, and Virginia. His officers included an array of American talent, men who would be well known in various endeavors in future days, such as John Laurens, Francis Marion, Charles Pinckney, Thomas Pinckney, Casimir Pulaski, and Isaac Huger. Marching in the militia ranks was a soldier named Sam Davis, whose son would become the famed Jefferson Davis, president of the Confederacy. Garbed in unusual combinations of militia uniform and civil dress, Lincoln's men were the source of great derision among their well-uniformed allies, but the Colonial soldiers continued exuberantly, expecting victory in this first joint venture with their French ground troops.

As French and American soldiers surrounded Savannah, Cherokee warriors joined the British defenders, slipping through the allied lines after nightfall. Having reestablished supply links with Crown authorities after Campbell's swift coup, the Cherokee became active in support of local Tories. A contingent of the warriors served General Prevost as scouts, delaying the American effort to cross the Savannah and join their French allies. As the siege of the city progressed, d'Estaing employed his fifty-three heavy guns to pound the city until most civilians were hiding in the cellars. Prevost decided to send all the women and children across the river to Hutcherson's

Island, where he erected a tent city. This island was low and opposite the tall bluffs that marked the city's business district; therefore, the siege guns could not fire on the island. Prevost selected the Cherokee to accompany the refugees, scattering the warriors about the island perimeter and posting guard details downstream. On October 1, a French frigate, the *Ramain,* sailed as far as possible upstream and opened fire on the encampment. Quickly the Cherokee sprinted to the river bank and opened fire, forcing the vessel to withdraw.

While Prevost collected defenders and strengthened his entrenchments, he obtained the services of Capt. James Moncrief of the Eighty-first Foot, a gifted military engineer. With the assistance of more than five hundred slaves, Moncrief transformed the crumbling old defense line into a strong series of at least thirteen redoubts with interconnected entrenchments and gun batteries. While not contiguous, the works took advantage of terrain features, provided supportive fields of fire, and were totally encompassed by a strong abatis of cedar and pine branches. On September 14, seamen from British ships in the harbor began hoisting and landing naval guns, 18- and 9-pounders on wooden sea-carriages, to be rolled through the sand streets for relocation in prepared emplacements. Soon more than eighty naval guns frowned from mounts in earthen batteries. Marines from the warships also filed ashore and were organized into units to be attached to the Sixtieth Regiment of Foot. Additionally, Prevost could count on Delancey's New York Volunteers, the Hessian Wissenbach Regiment, and Loyalist units from North Carolina, South Carolina, and Georgia. But the troops with Colonel Maitland at Beaufort, the Seventy-first Highlanders and Trumbach Hessians, were considered the most experienced soldiers in the British southern army, and Maitland was in danger of being cut off, by land and sea.

The arrival of the French fleet at Savannah was noted in Beaufort by the appearance off Port Royal Sound of a fifty-gun French warship, the swift-sailing *Sagittaire*. Commanded by d'Albert de Rions, she was dispatched by d'Estaing to blockade Beaufort and prevent Maitland's exiting his island encampment. Accompanied by American pilots, who first hesitated then refused to cross the tricky bar at the river's mouth, de Rions was forced to content himself with sealing Maitland off from any access to the Atlantic. Already denied a land route to Savannah, Maitland would have been neatly corked, as if in a bottle, should de Rions have warped his warship a mile or two upstream and anchored, an action that was readily accomplishable and would have virtually ensured the surrender of Savannah. The *Sagittaire* did manage to capture the British vessel *Experiment* off Port Royal. On board were Maj. Gen. George Garth, detailed as a replacement for Prevost; Garth's wife; the daughter of Governor Wright; 660,000 silver lires; and large amounts of foodstuffs onboard, although Savannah was well provisioned.

Upon receipt of a summons from Prevost, Maitland loaded his garrison into a small fleet of vessels, including a schooner, the *Vigilant*; two galleys, *Scourge* and *Vindictive*; and an unusual assortment of smaller craft, even canoes. Carefully proceeding across unguarded Port Royal Sound, the little flotilla turned down Skull Creek, between Pinckney and Trench (Hilton Head) Island. Discovering an easily defendable position near Buck Island, Maitland unloaded the invalids, noncombatants, and Hessian artillery, placing naval captain Christian in command with two companies of the Seventy-first as garrison. Christian anchored his vessels in an arc, establishing a complementary shore battery on Buck

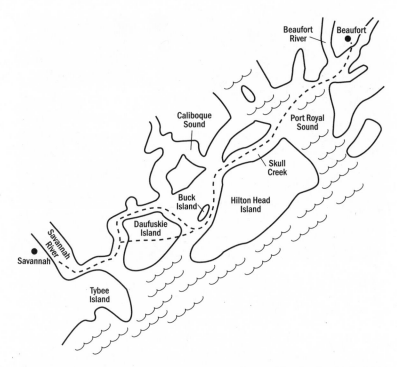

Maitland's route to Savannah. Lt. Col. John Maitland adeptly led his relief column through the swamps from Beaufort to Savannah. Avoiding French and American forces, he arrived in Savannah to reinforce the besieged city.

Island, thereby creating a formidable base. With the assistance of two Gullah fishermen, Maitland then led his eight hundred to nine hundred effective infantrymen through Wall's Cut and additional interconnected tidal creeks behind Daufuskie Island to emerge into the Savannah River some ten miles below the city. Rowing upstream through a dense fog, his regulars completed their remarkable journey by scaling the bluffs to Savannah amid cheers from its defenders. This bold march added troops of proven ability to the defenses as well as an officer of great skill and zeal. Even the French

Skull Creek. John Maitland withdrew his garrison from Beaufort and sailed through Skull Creek and Caliboque Sound to Savannah, rescuing the besieged city. (*Photo by Penny Swisher*)

besiegers later admitted that the arrival of Maitland's column altered the circumstances of their campaign.

Prior to Maitland's arrival, capture of the city seemed sure. Early on the fifteenth d'Estaing issued an imperious summons demanding that Prevost surrender Savannah to the "Arms of the King of France." The British commander's coy response requested a twelve-hour truce to consider terms, followed by a request for an extension until the seventeenth. Maitland arrived in the interim, and Prevost promptly rejected the French officer's terms, stating that hostilities should recommence. D'Estaing's attempts to negotiate a victory having failed, the time afforded by the delay was well utilized by the defenders. D'Estaing's officers complained bitterly and even the mild-mannered Col. Francis Marion openly expressed his disdain at a commander who would allow the enemy to

Daufuskie Island. Maitland proceeded with the Seventy-first Highlanders and von Bose Hessian regiment behind Daufuskie Island, up Wright's Creek, and into the Savannah River. (*Photo by Penny Swisher*)

complete his preparations and receive reinforcements under a flag of truce. He deemed d'Estaing's actions "unthinkable."

During this period of truce, the inexhaustible Moncrief continued his labors, completing the thirteenth of the Savannah redoubts. These little forts were almost square, formed of sod walls mounded with dirt and sand six to six and half feet in height. Interior firing steps were installed and a five- to six-foot ditch surrounded each redoubt. A single sally port faced rearward. Horseshoe-shaped batteries were located between the redoubts whereby the guns enfiladed the redoubt walls to repulse attacking troops. An abatis of sharpened tree limbs completed the obstacles. Not an impressive appearing series of works, but defenses that would prove most effective against the French and American storming attack.

Initially d'Estaing began preparing for siege operations, digging parallels and saps within which he emplaced his heavy guns. Maj. Colin Graham led a British light infantry assault of four Highland companies on September 24 in an attempt to disrupt the battery construction. When repulsed, he and his men retreated rapidly, but an overzealous French officer, Lt. Col. Thadee-Humphrey O'Dunne of Walsh's regiment, permitted his pursuing troops, including the Haitian Chasseurs, to be caught in the open by British batteries and suffer more than one hundred casualties, a harbinger of the effectiveness of British gunners. On the twenty-seventh Maj. Archibald McArthur led a second sortie, again without much success, although allied units fired into one another in the darkness. Undeterred, d'Estaing continued to emplace his siege artillery preparatory to opening the bombardment.

On October 3 his guns opened, and within a five-day period, fifty-three heavy guns and fourteen mortars deposited more than one thousand shells into Savannah, many of them carcasses or combustible shells. A number of civilians were dispatched across the river to Hutchinson's Island, out of artillery range, where they were afforded protection by Cherokees and armed slaves. Governor Wright and Lieutenant Governor Graham moved into tents alongside Maitland's camp near the twelfth redoubt. Some houses were set afire and almost forty civilians slain, but as time passed and the defenders learned to utilize earthworks and gun-proof shelters, terror of the bombardment abated. Defenders demolished the grand new barracks, using its timbers in redoubt construction and mounding the brick walls with dirt to parapet height for 9-pound guns installed to fire *en barbette*.

As days passed with no sign of British weakening, d'Estaing grew impatient. His supplies were growing scarce, bread could not be found, and the French soldiers detested the readily available rice. He also feared that a storm might wreck his vulnerable fleet. So the French commander made a rash and fateful decision. He would storm by coup de main, or direct assault, a portion of the defensive line, breaking through and permitting his attackers to drive into the city. He elected to attack the northwest corner of the defensive arc where marshy ground and underbrush would permit his assault columns to mass close to the works. British deserters had informed d'Estaing that the enemy redoubts in the Spring Hill area were manned by militia units and would prove easy to penetrate. While somewhat accurate the report did not mention that Maitland and a corps of professional officers commanded those redoubts as well as units such as the Sixtieth Foot and attached marines and that a battalion of the Seventy-first was posted in close support. D'Estaing determined to launch his surprise dawn attack in French fashion—troops advancing in massed vertical columns—and hoped the attackers would penetrate the defenses along the Augusta Road, a throughway that would further facilitate their reaching the city's core. Impatience, inexperience, and a gross underestimation of the effectiveness of the sand-filled defenses of Moncrief combined to convince the arrogant French commander to order an assault destined to cost more blood through losses on one side than any other action in the revolution, save Bunker Hill. Early on the morning of the eighth, Capt. Pierre l'Enfant, the future architect of Washington, D.C., assisted by a squad of brave soldiers, attempted to ignite the abatis in front of the British lines. The effort failed due to dampness and the greenness of the wood.

Attack on Spring Hill

Shortly after 1 A.M. on October 9, colorfully attired grenadiers and soldiers of the French king quietly assembled in their camps and began moving north in the cool darkness, seeking their jumping-off points. Concurrently, American columns filed south and north to designated locations, often crossing the route of their allies. D'Estaing understood well the desperate nature of this onslaught, but he dismissed these reservations amid evidence of a prideful desire to demonstrate to the Colonials the ability of French soldiers and a corresponding flagrant disrespect for Savannah's defenders.

Upon arrival among the marshes and scrub pine some two hundred yards from the British works on Spring Hill, the assault troops lay in wait as a heavy mist rolled in off the Atlantic. Nervous grenadiers were startled to hear the mournful wail of a solitary bagpiper as he paced the walls of the British revetments, his melancholy song seemingly an ominous warning. Despite repeated disparaging pleas by subordinates, d'Estaing resolutely massed almost thirty-five hundred French and American soldiers in the underbrush, determined to gamble on this single attempt to capture two redoubts and an adjacent battery composing a corner of the northwest arc of British defenses. The little sand fort on Spring Hill, called the Carolina Redoubt Hill (or Spring Hill Redoubt), the adjoining redoubt to the north (near Maitland's headquarters), and the gun battery between Ebenezer Battery covered Yamacraw Creek and the road to both Augusta and Ebenezer and were the focus of d'Estaing's assault.

The redoubts were small, square, earthen forts, hardly larger than outposts. Few more than four hundred soldiers

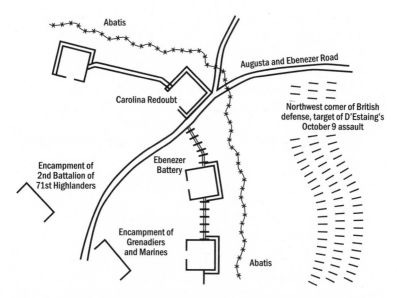

The southwest corner, Savannah defenses. On this position, centered about the Carolina, or Spring Hill Redoubt, d'Estaing launched his desperate and ill-fated assault on October 9, 1779.

manned the targeted positions, although ample reserves were posted nearby. The Carolina Redoubt was held by twenty-eight dismounted dragoons of the Seventy-first led by Bvt. Capt. Thomas Tawse, twenty-eight stalwarts of the Sixtieth Foot under a Lieutenant Wickham, and fifty-four of Lt. Col. Thomas Browne's South Carolina Loyalist battalion. Ninety members of Col. John Hamilton's North Carolina Loyalists and seventy-five militiamen manned the redoubt to the north, while thirty-one tars under Captain Manley and Lieutenant Stiel served the 18- and 9-pound guns of the Ebenezer Battery. The battery was horseshoe shaped with traverses. Two 18-pounders on field carriages were the key to the Ebenezer Battery, one of which, charged with canister, was positioned at the head of the Ebenezer Road. Upon this small force of soldiers, sailors, and Loyalists, critically arrayed in low earthen revetments, the fury of d'Estaing's massive assault would fall.

The French commander's attack scheme was elaborate and complicated but not without merit if properly executed. He scheduled two spoiling attacks on the British left and center for 5 A.M. American militia under Generals Andrew Williamson and Huger would attack on the far British left while volunteers from the West Indies, assisted by French marines under M. de Sablieses, would feint into the center. A third demonstration launched from the river would hopefully further confuse the English.

D'Estaing prepared five columns to actually deliver the assault. A vanguard of French grenadiers, between 250 and 275 strong, veterans in white coats with black gaiters, would dash forward to capture the Carolina Redoubt, overwhelming the defenders with speed and surprise. Two following columns of picked French soldiers, each of one thousand to twelve hundred men, would attack left of and in concert with the vanguard, striking the entrenchments on either side of the Augusta Road. Selecting soldiers from the various regiments with little thought to cohesion, he assembled the columns. Two American units, each of about six hundred men, would support the French columns. Count Casimir Pulaski, a Polish officer leading American cavalry, would walk his cavalry forward in concert with the first American column, ready to exploit the expected breakthrough by releasing his cavalrymen into the city. If, as rumored later, deserters or spies had passed warning of the attack to the British, little special preparation was apparent; however, the sleepy defenders, crouching in the sand redoubts, must surely have noted the movements of large columns of men.

Sometime after dawn, about 5:30 A.M., the sound of firing could be heard from the fake attacks to the south, and despite the fact that not all his units were in position, d'Estaing ordered his vanguard to advance at the "double quick." Charging out of the fog to the strident pulse of drummers and shouting, "Viva de Roi!" the grenadiers dashed forward to collide suddenly with an abatis that blunted their impetus. Col. Baron Bethiny, in command of this select unit, sprinted forward, screaming to his grenadiers to press on, and many did, crawling over or through the maze of tree limbs, using the few axes they possessed to hack away protruding branches, and entering the ditch before the Carolina Redoubt. There they found themselves unable to scale the twelve-foot sand wall while subjected to the enfilade fire of guns from batteries on either side of the redoubt. Suffering from the cannon fire and confronted by the musketry of the defenders, the grenadiers slowly began to fall back, carrying their wounded, including Colonel de Bethiny. Bearing slightly left toward the Augusta Road, which seemed a likely avenue of escape, the grenadiers actually became entrapped. They collided with the late arriving main column of Count Arthur Dillon while the 18-pound naval guns began to flay the roadway with iron, smashing the head of the massed French column as well as the defeated grenadiers.

Both d'Estaing and Dillon arrived as the bloodied grenadiers retreated. Their column had become disorganized in the spongy marsh, losing its compactness, but the bold Dillon led eighty men in a charge on the north wall of the Carolina Redoubt, planting a flag on the parapet. Tawse and Wickham issued forth with their defenders, initiating a fierce hand-to-hand melee on the walls during which Tawse was slain after dispatching three antagonists.

Unsupported, Dillon's attackers fell back into the causeway, into the still-thundering British guns. D'Estaing, wounded in the arm, refused to concede, rallying the mass of men in the roadway on three occasions to advance, but his efforts were in vain. D'Estaing went down a second time, this time a bullet in his thigh, and the spirit of the French column dissolved.

The second French column, led by Baron Curt von Stedingk, a dashing Swede, approached the cauldron of gunfire. Like the initial column, this unit lost cohesion in the morass but swung right, crossing the Augusta Road, and continued farther north. Stedingk was wounded on the causeway but gathered nine hundred men to charge the entrenchments near Maitland's headquarters. Surging forward, they captured a portion of the revetments and Stedingk, convinced that the day was his, cried out, "Victory at last!" However, Maitland, observing the breakthrough, coolly ordered Maj. Beamsley Glasier of the Sixtieth to advance with his grenadiers and Royal Marines. Glasier's 111 stalwarts closed on the breakthrough with measured tread and gleaming bayonets, a sign of British veteran infantry. Within minutes, Stedingk's survivors dispersed, joining the milling mass on the causeway still absorbing grapeshot and langrel. Many fled into the swamps to avoid thundering death.

As the French columns hesitated an American unit composed of the Second South Carolina Continentals and the First Battalion of Charles Town militia sprinted past to jump into the ditch before the Carolina Redoubt. Col. John Laurens led this unit, determined to rectify the French repulse and to demonstrate the ability of Colonial troops. However, attaining the ditch was only the first part of their struggle. The colors of the Second South Carolina were planted on the berm, the midpoint where the ditch and wall met, but the valiant Carolinians, like the grenadiers before them, found the sand walls unassailable under heavy musketry and cannon fire. Count Casimir Pulaski, who accompanied Laurens' column, proceeded forward to the abatises, where he sat on his horse awaiting a break-through. Suddenly cannon fire from a British vessel anchored in the Savannah struck him in the groin, an instantly recognizable fatal wound. As Pulaski was borne rearward, a disgusted Laurens threw down his sword and permitted his men to retreat.

Into the midst of the chaos on the causeway a second American column arrived. Gen. Lachlan McIntosh led the First and Fifth South Carolina Continentals and attached Virginia Militia into the fray, proceeding over the dead and maimed. Unable to advance through the milling, retreating troops, McIntosh sent Col. Thomas Pinckney forward to

The Attack on Savannah. (*National Archives*)

reconnoiter the redoubt, vainly hoping to discover a new means of assault, but Pinckney reported the area now covered with dead and wounded men. Their efforts became useless when it was evident the attack had failed and all other allied units were retiring. The two officers were appalled at the ditch full of moaning wounded, both French grenadiers and rebels. Maj. T. W. Moore of Prevost's staff commented that "the ditch before the Carolina redoubt was filled with dead for fifty yards . . . many dead and wounded hung on the abates . . . the plain inside the abatis being strewn with mangled bodies, most caused by the grapeshot or langrel."

Seeing the confusion and terror among the defeated enemy, Maitland, eager to punish the attackers, organized an advance, but Viscount Louis Marie de Noailles, his battle line stationed near the old Jewish Cemetery, countered this action. He advanced his reserve force of Haitians, American militia, and French troops forward in tight order, artillery on the flanks, discouraging any British advance and providing shelter for retreating survivors. Until almost noon groups of French and American soldiers emerged from the swamps into which they had fled. A French officer stated, "The disorder was so complete . . . that not ten soldiers out of the same company returned to camp together." Noailles's column took casualties from the English guns but his actions probably saved many wounded and discouraged soldiers. Casualties among the attacking troops were horrific. Estimates vary among observers, French, American, and British, but most consistent sources count 821 French casualties and 312 American for a total loss of 1,133 men. More than 270 dead were found in the ditch before the redoubt on Spring Hill. The units suffering heaviest were the Dillon Irish regiment, which lost 42 killed and 105 wounded, the French grenadiers, the Second South Carolina Continentals, and the Virginia militia. A truce was requested to evacuate the wounded, scheduled to last from 10 A.M. to 3 P.M., but extended until dark. The wounded received little care. While the British provided two carriages to transport the injured, a lack of bandages and physicians condemned any hope of recovery for the seriously wounded.

The decisive nature of the repulse shocked the allied army, destroying its morale and eliminating any hope of future operations, save a rapid evacuation of Georgia. Credit for the decisive outcome is often attributed to Lt. Col. John Maitland, Capt. James Moncrief, Capt. Thomas Tawse, Maj. Beamsley Glasier, and Col. Frederich von Porbeck, men whose professional leadership and abilities largely dictated the repulse. D'Estaing is credited with much of the blame for his poor leadership and staff work although his personal bravery seemed worthy of a grenadier. In truth, several salient factors influenced the battle's outcome, some outside the purview of the French commander. Firstly, the presence of the huge naval guns in the Ebenezer Battery and the expert handling of these weapons by their sailor crews actually dominated the battlefield. Well situated to enfilade attackers on both redoubts and perfectly positioned to sweep the causeway that collected the retreating soldiers, these remarkable weapons, not commonly used on a military field, caused a high percentage of allied losses, completely pulverizing the French massed columns.

Secondly, the redoubts themselves, small square forts well designed by Moncrief, influenced the outcome. Defended by few troops, the six-foot sand walls with six-foot ditches attached presented a formidable, perhaps unassailable obstacle to attackers attempting to scale their sides much as the difficulty encountered in attempting to ascend sand dunes carrying heavy equipment. Even without palisades or fraises these ugly dirt redoubts proved formidable.

The tactical attack plan employed by d'Estaing and his officers, deploying troops in shoulder-to-shoulder massed fashion, designed to penetrate a position despite losses at the column's head, was rendered ineffective, the columns being pummeled as they marched into the British 18-pound guns. The extremely poor coordination of the attacking columns complicated this strategy, as each formation struck the entrenchments of the enemy independently and in succeeding order. Thus the gunners could concentrate on each attack, defeating them one by one. All five columns should have struck as one, denying the gunners the ability to concentrate on each. About 3,500 men were severely repulsed, suffering about 1,100 casualties by an opposing force of 417 soldiers.

While d'Estaing was being treated for wounds he expressed a desire to continue the siege, but in reality he had conceded the campaign. Informing his allies of his intentions, he began moving his wounded downriver for embarkation. Lincoln's troops crossed the Savannah and marched north as the French regiments filed quickly down to Causton's Bluff and boarded ships. Vessels sailed as they were loaded, with wounded being conveyed north to Charles Town or Virginia, while other ships found refuge in the Leeward Islands. D'Estaing returned to France surprised to be accorded a hero's welcome. Years later in 1794, caught up in political changes, he was scheduled to meet the guillotine. As he mounted the platform, he exclaimed: "You should send my head to the English, they will pay well for it."

The allied withdrawal proved a signal occurrence in the course of the revolution. As an initial measure of compatibility between French and Colonial forces, the campaign produced only mutual recriminations. American criticism of French organization, implementation, and arrogance was widespread. Despite his bravery, d'Estaing was judged an ineffective and uninspiring leader. Conversely, the undisciplined appearance of Lincoln's troops and his laissez-faire leadership, characterized by frequent unscheduled naps, generated widespread French derision. In each instance, the alliance suffered.

The clear-cut defeat elevated the aspirations and spirit of Tories throughout the southern colonies, increasing recruitment and intensifying the animosity and scope of conflict, which widened from resistance to British invasion to full-blown civil war of unprecedented brutality. The defeat further provided Sir Henry Clinton with a springboard that he could utilize to initiate a southern campaign. Without a successful British defense of Savannah it is certainly doubtful that Clinton would have so rapidly invested Charles Town, nor could he and General Charles Cornwallis have subjugated South Carolina so quickly in the winter campaign of 1780-81, with its demanding marches and brutal clashes. At length, through a combination of British military inertia, French naval fortune, and Washington's audacious march south from West Point, the alliance of French and American soldiers reconvened at a small village on the York River in 1781, this time with decisive results.

CHAPTER 4

The Redcoats Return to Charles Town

"It was the greatest British victory of the war, and it belonged to Sir Henry Clinton who was at the peak of his career."

William B. Willcox, *Portrait of a General*

Charles Town, South Carolina, the Queen City of the southern British colonies, lay peacefully secure behind harbor forts, sea islands, and sand bars, its populace largely undisturbed by the formidable British military presence in Savannah, Georgia, only ninety miles south. This city of ten thousand persons, a humid, semitropical seaport, was ideally located on the eastern tip of a narrow peninsula between two tidal rivers, the Ashley and the Cooper. The twin streams merged in front of the city to create an expansive but shallow anchorage tricky to navigate due to shifting sand bars and treacherous currents. The defeat of a British incursion in 1776 and the repulse of Gen. Augustine Prevost's precipitous foray in 1779 afforded an unmerited sense of security to the South Carolina rice planters who now assumed control of local government following the sudden exodus of Crown officials.

The peace of the Queen City was soon to be shattered

by forces of the diminutive Sir Henry Clinton, the British commander in North America, who having once failed to capture Charles Town was meticulously preparing for a return in the winter of 1779-80. Encouraged by Crown officials, he determined to gain possession of this fourth most populous city in North America and center of the southern rice and indigo trade, remarking, "I had long determined on an expedition against Charlestown." Clinton's expectations were increased by the recent capture of Savannah by Col. Archibald Campbell and the subsequent rout of a recapture attempt by the allied French and American army under Comte d'Estaing and Gen. Benjamin Lincoln.

Clinton was a somewhat stuffy product of the British elite. Born in 1730, he accompanied his father, Adm. George Clinton, to North America and was reared in the Colonies as his father filled an array of important civil posts. He purchased a commission as a lieutenant colonel in the prestigious Grenadier Guards, and his military career seemed destined for great success, but the tragic death of a young wife plunged the ambitious officer into a severe depression and lengthy leave of absence. Upon return to active duty Clinton was assigned service in North America, where he immediately demonstrated organizational abilities fundamental to the conduct of a comprehensive military campaign. Unfortunately these administrative attributes were offset by his distinctly flawed and cantankerous personality. Promoted to army commander in North America, his tactical planning skills rapidly emerged as superior to most of his contemporaries, and his preference for flanking movements rather than direct assaults was greatly appreciated by his officers and men. Nevertheless, Clinton's plans usually deteriorated in application, as his caution and lack of tact precipitated what were often rancorous encounters with superiors, peers, and subordinates. Reluctant to commit his forces to battle, Clinton seemed to fear failure and when under stress he searched for others to blame. He, like George McClellan of Union Civil War command, had few peers in the preparation of an army for a campaign but then seemed actually afraid to endanger this force by engaging it in combat.

In the fall of 1779, Clinton, realizing he was unable to bring George Washington to a decisive land battle, collected a force of almost eighty-five hundred soldiers, which he packed into more than ninety transports, and prepared to debark from New York. Uneasily, he delegated operational command in New York to Hessian lieutenant general Wilhelm von Knyhausen. Clinton felt that he could capture the Holy City of South Carolina by spring and return to New York before the American army reassembled.

Clinton's naval counterpart was the indecisive, sixty-seven-year-old admiral Marriott Arbuthnot. The two men clashed over almost every detail of naval operations, and only the intervention of capable subordinate naval officers such as Capt. George Elphinstone provided enough cooperative liaison for the supporting naval flotilla and army to coexist. Maj. Gen. Charles Cornwallis, an able tactician, absolutely fearless, and revered by his men, was also detailed south, to serve as Clinton's second in command. However, earlier disagreements between the two, combined with Cornwallis's aggressive nature, soon brought him into conflict with his neurotic commander. Two additional young officers of talent and reputation, Banastre Tarleton and Patrick Ferguson, both favorites of Clinton, accompanied the expedition. Despite constant personal conflicts and assorted disagreements, Clinton prepared to embark on an expedition that would unfold as a classic example of the investiture of a defended seaport by a combined naval-military arms force. Clinton's careful, methodical approach actually increased the scale of his eventual success, for his snail-like pace permitted additional American defenders, particularly the highly valued Continental regiments, to reach and enter the city defenses only to be enveloped by British siege lines.

Clinton's handpicked army was formidable, diverse, and experienced. British units included the Seventh, Twenty-third, Thirty-third, Sixty-third, and Sixty-Fourth Foot Regiments, joined by a portion of the Seventy-first Highland Regiment. Two battalions of British light infantry and two battalions of grenadiers were also aboard the ships. Light infantry companies were transferred from four or more regular infantry regiments and combined into battalions that could be utilized as a quick, mobile striking forces. Likewise, combining grenadier companies from various regiments, grenadier battalions were to serve as shock units. Occasionally effective these ad hoc units were considered parasitical by military purists, robbing the strength from the parent regiments.

Numerous Hessian troops accompanied Clinton. They consisted of the von Huyn Regiment and the four Hessian grenadier battalions: von Graft, von Langerke, von Lindsing, and von Minnegerode. Hessian units were named for their commanding officer and alterations due to illness, death, or transfer frequently changed their designated names, confusing their battle histories. About 250 Hessian jaegers in three companies were detailed to attend the force. They were superb light infantry and possibly in this instance the most valuable units in the army. Unlike

British light infantry companies, these jaeger units were recruited as chasseurs of light infantrymen from among German foresters or hunters and had long developed a history of successful independent operation. A Royal Artillery unit, attired in dark blue coats, was also included, as were the Loyalist American Regiment and the New York Volunteers.

Reinforcements from New York and Savannah would increase Clinton's force to over ten thousand men, including the Hessian von Dittfurth Regiment, the remainder of the Seventy-first Highlanders, the Forty-second Highlanders, the Prince of Wales Regiment, and additional Loyalist units including the Volunteers of Ireland, which later became known as the 105th Foot.

Maj. Gen. Benjamin Lincoln, assigned command of the Colonial southern army, prepared to defend Charles Town primarily with militia units. He was an amiable gentleman of some ability, but handicapped by narcolepsy, a condition that often caused him to fall into a deep sleep in mid-sentence. Combined with this sleeping affliction, his physical stature of 5' 9", 240 pounds, and a noticeable limp from a severely shattered ankle compromised his leadership persona. A veteran of the French and Indian Wars, Lincoln was active in Massachusetts militia affairs and had risen rapidly in rank upon the outbreak of the revolution. His skills in organizing local militia units were quickly noted and appreciated by General Washington, who had few officers to praise. Washington detailed Lincoln north to recruit and assemble militia in opposition to Maj. Gen. John Burgoyne's advance down the Hudson River. His performance, loyal and capable, was critical in Burgoyne's encirclement. He was credited with cutting the British supply line, but in the fighting about Saratoga his ankle was shattered by a Hessian musket ball. A friendly, gentle man, Lincoln adroitly avoided the political infighting between Gen. Horatio Gates and Gen. Benedict Arnold, emerging from the Saratoga campaign with an honorable reputation. But his future was to be disappointing, and he would receive more than his share of blame for the poor performance of the southern Colonial army.

Having learned of the departure of the British fleet from New York, Lincoln correctly surmised that Charles Town or the Chesapeake was the British target, and he desperately appealed to Congress for assistance. Drafting hundreds of slaves to repair the eroding walls of Fort Moultrie on Sullivan's Island and Fort Johnson on James Island, he also began reconstruction of the works on the "neck" behind the city. Congress assured Lincoln that Continental regiments were en route. A flotilla of four American warships sailed into the harbor, including the frigates *Providence, Boston,* and *Queen of France* and the sloop *Ranger.* Commodore Abraham Whipple led this little fleet, to be reinforced by four South Carolina vessels and a pair of French warships. Soon Continental regiments began to arrive, three each from the colonies of North Carolina (the First, Second, and Third), South Carolina, (First, Second, and Fourth), and Virginia (First, Second, and Third). More than five thousand defenders were eventually scattered along the defensive lines.

The Campaign Moves South

Red-coated British infantrymen, blue-jacketed Hessians, and jaegers attired in green shivered uncomfortably waiting aboard transport vessels in the frozen Hudson River. One ship, the *Pan,* was encased by ice floes and crushed, requiring a hazardous rescue operation to save her cargo of Hessian jaegers. When orders arrived to hoist anchor and move seaward at 8 A.M. on the twenty-sixth of December, the ships tacked smartly out on a northwest wind, clearing the shoals Hook and Middle Ground and turning south. Within days, however, the vessels were buffeted and scattered by a tremendous winter storm, a nor'easter lashing the ships with snow, sleet, high winds, and fifty-foot waves. The tempest finally eased on December 29, to the relief of many seasick soldiers, but as the vessels approached Cape Hatterras, another even stronger storm enveloped the armada. For five long days the struggling ships clawed desperately seaward, circling widely away from the cape and its shoals, all order, discipline, and physical contact disappearing amid watery chaos. On the ninth and tenth of January a third storm drove the fleet south to a position below St. Augustine, Florida. Forty-foot waves battered the ships wildly, felling masts and causing fatal injury to almost the entire contingent of cavalry, artillery, and officers' horses. The tired soldiers labored to toss overboard the carcasses.

On February 1, after more than a month at sea, the flotilla anchored securely in the Savannah River near Tybee Island, Georgia. Surprisingly, only one important vessel was missing, the *Russian Merchant,* a cargo vessel carrying the heavy siege guns and shells. Clinton set ashore a force of fifteen hundred men under Brig. Gen. James Paterson, including the light infantry battalion of Maj. Colin Graham, the Seventy-first Highland Battalion of Maj. Archibald McArthur, Patrick Ferguson's Tories, and Banastre Tarleton and the horseless cavalrymen of Tarleton and Ferguson. Soon this contingent was marching laboriously over rough, sandy roads between the Savannah and the Pon Pon Rivers, searching desperately for horses of any kind, marsh tackies or blooded Arabians. Tarleton conducted a raid into Beaufort in a fruitless search for horses, realizing that Clinton was severely handicapped by the absence of any serviceable cavalry.

Hoisting sea anchors the fleet proceeded northward under reduced sails. After anchoring safely off Hilton Head on the evening of the tenth, the ships drifted northward and, slipping over the narrow, difficult bar into the North Edisto River on the afternoon of the eleventh, found safe haven behind Simmons Island (now Seabrook Island). The tricky passage over Deveroux Bank into the North Edisto required the touch of a master seaman, and Capt. George Elphinstone of the Royal Navy adroitly completed that maneuver without the loss of a ship, his dexterity closely observed and appreciated by Clinton.

Despite the horrific voyage and the ceaseless battering of ships and men, Clinton's assault force was now positioned to debark unopposed only thirty miles from the downtown Charles Town Exchange Building. This sudden appearance of a powerful army and fleet from a totally unexpected direction shocked and surprised the defenders and residents. Peter Timothy, a Charles Town printer, maintained a position in the steeple of St. Michael's Church, his glass searching the sea as well as counting the cooking fires on James Island. He then relayed his knowledge to Lincoln. But between the North Edisto and Charles Town was a warren of tidal creeks, quicksand, mud flats, snakes, and alligators, with few roads or paths save water.

Late on the afternoon of the eleventh, Clinton's vanguard splashed ashore from flatboats amid roaring surf and driving rain to alight in deep sand or within dank woods covered by the all-encompassing Spanish moss. Both

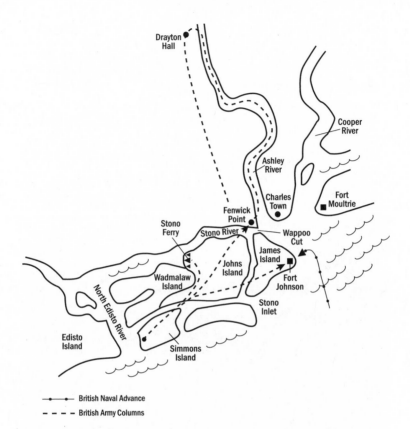

Drayton
Hall

Cooper
River

Ashley
River

Charles
Town

Fort
Moultrie

Fenwick
Point

Stono
Ferry

Stono River

Wappoo
Cut

James
Island

Johns
Island

Wadmalaw
Island

Fort
Johnson

North Edisto River

Stono
Inlet

Edisto
Island

Simmons
Island

——•—— British Naval Advance

– – – – British Army Columns

The sea islands. The British army disembarked in February 1780 on Simmons Island, south of Charles Town, and slowly advanced through the swamps to surround and invest the city.

Clinton and Cornwallis accompanied the initial wave of troops, and when rising surf interrupted the landings the duo was forced to spend the night in the rain, sheltered under the live oak trees. They, like all officers, were without mounts and forced to march alongside their troop columns. The foul weather prevented the landing of artillery save four hand-carried 1-pound amusettes of debatable value.

St. Johns crossing. Capt. Johann Ewald's jaegers lead the advance of Clinton's army, wading from Simmons Island to Johns Island. (*Photo by Penny Swisher*)

Lt. Col. James Webster, as fine a field officer as the Empire ever produced, led ashore his Thirty-third Regiment of Foot, two Hessian and British grenadier battalions, and the light-footed jaegers of the irrepressible, one-eyed Capt. Johann Ewald. Ewald's green-coated foresters initiated a measured advance across Simmons Island and proceeded onto and up the west side of Johns Island, accompanied by an eleven- or twelve-year-old Gullah-speaking slave. Although the language barrier between Hessian skirmishers and runaway slave proved amusing and frustrating, both parties managed to communicate well enough to facilitate the guided advance without major incident. The skirmishers slowly approached Stono Ferry, a principal crossing to the mainland and an anticipated supply base, Ewald noting the ferocious-appearing sixteen-foot alligators in the wide tidal creek called the Upper Stono or Wadammacaw Creek.

Stono River crossing. The tide-swept Stono River was crossed at this site by Ewald's jaegers as they searched for a fortifiable location. (*Photo by author*)

The remains of the Hessian redoubt on Stono River, now on the fourteenth fairway of the Stono River Golf Course. (*Photo by author*)

Ewald collected enough scattered boats and rafts to transport his column across the Stono and there he wisely entrenched, building three redoubts and surrounding them with a stout abatis. Soon Stono Ferry was secure.

Clinton, however, never intended to cross his entire army to the mainland at Stono Ferry. He merely wanted the site as a supply base and so that he could protect his rear from American cavalry. He appointed a captain and one hundred soldiers as garrison and proceeded closer to the city with his army, intent on crossing near the Ashley River after a feint toward Dorchester. Upstream on the Ashley at Bacon's Bridge, General William Moultrie and Colonel Marion had constructed earthworks and were preparing to resist a crossing of the Ashley, but Clinton's plans were of an amphibious nature. His dual objective was to place his army on the neck above Charles Town, cutting off the city, and to force his fleet into the harbor. These two maneuvers should cause capitulation.

Slowly Clinton's grenadiers spread out across James Island, experiencing difficulties from the semitropical environment and a hurricane-like storm of several days' duration. British redcoats approached Matthew's Ferry on the Lower Stono, crossing and establishing a second supply depot. Elphinstone led his supply ships directly into Stono Inlet, and schooners sailed upstream to Matthew's Ferry as the Hessian von Huyn Regiment arrived and prepared a defensive perimeter. Maj. Gen. Heinrich von Kospath led a contingent of Hessians, reinforced by the newly arrived Forty-second Highlanders, on a cross-island march through tropical foliage to attack Fort Johnson, while farther upstream the British army crossed to Johns Island near Fenwick Plantation. The ruins of the bridge over Wappoo Cut still smoldered, torched by American cavalrymen.

The Hessians arrived at Fort Johnson to find the four-bastion quadrangle in ruins. The Germans immediately began construction of a redoubt on the site, emplacing heavy guns. But, harassed by ranging fire from Commodore Whipple's frigates, they were compelled to fall back. When the Colonial warships suddenly withdrew, the redoubt was hastily completed. One Major Mear and 120 soldiers of the von Huyn Regiment were detailed as a garrison with two 24-pound guns and two 12-pound guns that were hauled from the sandy roadway. Possession of this critical position secured the south side of Charles Town Harbor as a haven for the British fleet. Clinton could now abandon his base at Stono Ferry, shifting his supply line to Matthew's and up the Lower Stono River. The bridge at Wappoo Cut was rebuilt and the British army crossed to the mainland almost within sight of the Ashley River.

Captain Elphinstone took charge of supply operations in

the tidal creeks and flats, moving schooners and barges containing the heavy naval guns up the Stono River and ferrying provisions and weapons from the Stono into Wappoo Cut, then directing them to the banks of the Ashley. Strong dual redoubts were erected directly opposite the city at Fenwick Point. The larger of the two was a triangular bastion mounting ten heavy naval guns (four 32-pound, four 24-pound, and two 6-pound guns). Charles Town residents could now see British troops entrenching at close range. Soon the roar of cannon and the exchange of balls confirmed their presence.

Clinton's continual prodding of Admiral Arbuthnot eventually brought about belated naval activity in late March. On the twentieth the admiral undertook the tricky crossing of the bar into Charles Town Harbor. Leaving his heavy ships of the line outside the harbor entrance, Arbuthnot unloaded the heavy guns from the *Renown*, *Roebuck,* and *Romulus,* placing these weapons in cargo vessels. Accompanied by four frigates and the transport vessels carrying the spare guns, he took advantage of a favoring wind and high tide to parade his ships over the formidable bar and safely anchor in a five-fathom hole. Lincoln, who had encouraged Commodore Whipple to anchor his vessels just inside the passageway and dispute the British crossing, was angry and horrified at the lack of opposition, but the American naval commander avowed that Lincoln's request was impractical, stating that water depth, tides, and prevailing winds prevented his stationing his fleet inside the bar. Arbuthnot's action closed the port to further American or French entry, isolating the city from the sea. Whipple, who scattered his fleet near Fort Moultrie, was forced to retreat farther, anchoring in the mouth of the Cooper River. The hesitant, unaggressive

British naval commander, Arbuthnot, had been coerced by General Clinton into confronting and intimidating an even more timid American officer, thereby achieving a major British naval success without battle losses.

In the predawn hours of March 29, amid a heavy fog, Clinton undertook a bold and inspired military action that, coupled with the navy's recent success, sealed the fate of the seaport. At Bacon's Bridge, upstream on the Ashley, the still-waiting American militia was bypassed when British soldiers stormed directly across the river. Clinton neatly circumvented this force by dispatching twenty-two barges, powered by sailors and protected by armed galleys, from the Wappoo Cut up the Ashley. Gliding quietly with muffled oars past rebel outposts on the Charles Town shore, the flatboats proceeded thirteen miles upstream to Drayton Hall, grounding in the moonlight near the impressive manor house.

Crossing of the Ashley. British forces stormed across the Ashley River in a surprise amphibious night attack to gain possession of the "neck" and isolated the city. (Photo by Penny Swisher)

Assembled in the river gardens at Drayton Hall was a large strike force that immediately began to board the barges. Ewald's jaegers, as usual, led the assemblage and were followed by a light infantry battalion, two Hessian and British grenadier battalions, Webster's Thirty-third Foot, and the Seventy-first Highlanders. Silently casting loose and rowing hard, by 8 A.M. Ewald's lead elements were across the river and unloading at the dock on Fuller's Plantation. Deploying into line the grenadiers advanced eastward from the Dorchester plantation, preceded by the jaeger companies in a crescent-shaped formation. By midday artillery units had joined the column. Opposition continued to be slight and by 9 P.M. the advance halted only six miles from the Charles Town defensive lines. A major coup was completed, characterized by an unprecedented outburst of energy from the usually lethargic Clinton. He had suddenly placed the seaport in a vise, a British fist about its "neck."

The second day's advance was not as easily successful. The jaegers advanced more slowly under intermittent fire, closely followed by Clinton, Cornwallis, and a light infantry regiment. As they approached a *fleche* in advance of the Colonial lines garrisoned by Lt. Col. John Laurens and his corps of riflemen, resistance markedly stiffened. At this point the British commander attained his initial view of the elaborate Colonial defenses spanning the neck. These works had been designed and constructed by Lincoln's French engineers, Col. Joseph Laumoy and Col. Jean Cambray-Digny. Clinton was forced to deploy his light infantry in order to drive Laurens and his men back into the American works.

The Colonial revetments, which extended from the Ashley River to the Cooper River, were based behind a water ditch or man-made canal twelve to eighteen feet in

Charles Town defenses. The only remaining portion of the hornwork that anchored the defenses of Charles Town. Located on Marion Square in the center of the present city. (*Photo by Penny Swisher*)

width, six feet in depth, adroitly controlled by a system of dams and sluices located on each riverbank. An imposing hornwork called the Old Royal Work, or The Citadel, was located in the center of the American lines, sited in present Marion Square. Based on earlier gated fortifications and eventually destined to become the home of the Military Academy of South Carolina, the hornwork contained two substantial bastions connected by a curtain wall covering the road to the west and serving as Lincoln's command post. Constructed of brick and faced with several feet of concrete-like tabby, the fortification was almost impervious to destruction by smoothbore artillery balls. Eighteen Colonial guns were mounted on the hornwork, firing *en barberette*. Double palisades edged the water ditch, strengthened by two rows of abatis, one of *cheval de fraises* and a second of sharpened and anchored tree limbs. A second ditch and a series of crescent-shaped redans, extending from river to river, solidified defenses on the neck. Stout forts were erected on either flank to enfilade any advance on the hornwork and to protect the dams controlling the flow of water into the ditch. Trees were cut down and houses razed to clear a field of fire. Further gun batteries were erected behind palmetto and sand walls. Six small forts of four to nine guns were placed alongside the Ashley and seven forts containing three to seven guns were scattered on the Cooper. A strong multi-tiered redoubt of sixteen guns was erected on Battery Point, facing the harbor. About eighty guns were sited across the neck, all carefully placed by the capable Gen. William Moultrie, a future governor of South Carolina.

Clinton realized the cost of storming such formidable works would be severe, and he ordered his engineer, James Moncrief, to begin formal siege operations. This capable officer, who had designed the successful defenses of Savannah, employed the classic European-style siege advocated by the Frenchman Vauban, whose model epitomized the investiture of a city by use of traverse and parallel trenches, all designed to complete capture with a minimum loss of life. Parallels, usually between one and four, were advanced one in front of the other, each progressing closer to the enemy line by utilization of saps or zigzag trenches. Field guns, many weighing up to five thousand pounds, were laboriously dragged forward and emplaced in batteries along the parallels and advanced farther as new parallels were completed. The closer the guns were positioned to their target, the higher the velocity of their projectiles, and correspondingly, the more damage incurred. Any gun placed within one thousand yards was in effective range.

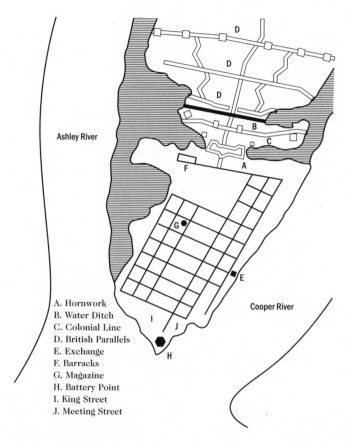

A. Hornwork
B. Water Ditch
C. Colonial Line
D. British Parallels
E. Exchange
F. Barracks
G. Magazine
H. Battery Point
I. King Street
J. Meeting Street

The siege of Charles Town. Crossing to the "neck" west of Charles Town and advancing the fleet over the bar into the harbor, British forces surrounded and besieged Charles Town completely by April 1780.

Charles Town Under Siege

A slow, methodical investiture of the American lines was begun, with most of the digging, completed by sappers and slaves, occurring after midnight. At nightfall on April 2, hundreds of sappers advanced carrying six by sixteen foot mantelets, or wooden shields. Constructed in New York and shipped south, they were assembled at Gibbes's Plantation, just behind the first line. These shields were quickly braced on three legs and dirt frantically heaped upon their frames to afford rapid, but temporary protection. The diggers were guarded from enemy attack by a like number of light infantrymen. Construction was begun on the first of three earthen redoubts located about six hundred yards apart and eight hundred yards from the Colonial works. A ditch was completed connecting these redoubts, and this ditch became the first parallel trench. The trench was twelve to fifteen feet in width to permit passage of the heavy guns and three feet deep, with all excavated dirt encased in gabions and stacked on the enemy side. Two extensive crescent-shaped works were constructed at the extremities, opposite the American riverside forts. While the digging continued, sailors and slaves labored to float and drag the heavy naval guns from the North Edisto anchorage: dirty, sweaty work but sparing of human costs. As the first parallel neared completion, a battery of nine 24 pounders on sea carriages and served by skilled naval gunners was installed between the two center redoubts. American cannon fire rose to a crescendo in a vain attempt to impede British construction. Wing redoubts were added along the riverbanks and connected to the first parallel, thus completing the investiture of the "neck." Zigzag trenches were advanced after nightfall: a dangerous duty for sappers vulnerable to sorties from the defenders. As this labor-intensive process proceeded, additional guns were emplaced ever closer to the enemy. Serious battering of the Colonial works would follow. Clinton resisted the impulse to fire carcasses or fire bombs, for he wished to capture an intact city, not a field of smoking ruins. He remarked that it seemed absurd, impolitic, and even inhuman to burn a town that you mean to occupy.

On April 7, eleven schooners laden with American Continentals sailed smartly down the Cooper River and into the city. Brig. Gen. William Woodford had arrived with seven hundred Virginians of the First, Second, and Third Virginia Continental Regiments, to the joyous celebration of the garrison and the ringing of church bells. A door to the back country along the Cooper was still ajar and must be closed. Following a series of severe storms and spurred by the pleas of Clinton, Admiral Arbuthnot reluctantly prepared for a second action. On April 8, in fair wind and driving rain, nine British warships proceeded in single file down the middle passage some eight hundred yards from Fort Moultrie, white ensigns snapping aloft. Passing the works under full sail, the warships exchanged cannon fire with the fort but never hesitated, pushing on into the inner harbor. Fort Moultrie's gunners found their targets early but soon smoke from cannon fire became an impediment to accuracy. All the British vessels, save one transport that ran aground and was burned, passed the fort, suffering only twenty-seven total casualties in the process. Clearing the Middle Ground, and amid cheers and yells of the Hessian grenadiers from atop their newly completed redoubt, the fleet turned left to find anchor near the ruins of Fort Johnson. The British naval squadron that now lay just outside the guns of the city had effectively completed the circle of English guns around Charles Town. Whipple had again failed Lincoln, refusing to engage the British ships and falling back to a position between Shutte's Island and the mainland. There he sank seven vessels, interlocking their masts with chains to block British naval excursions up the Cooper, dooming and immobilizing his remaining few warships.

Clinton decided to issue a summons for surrender to the

now almost surrounded city. His carefully worded letter afforded terms for the besieged and, as usual, included a somewhat veiled threat for nonacceptance. General Lincoln rejected the summons on advice from the Charles Town governors, and the guns again began to fire. Clinton realized that the still-open access route up the Cooper River must be definitively closed to ensure the city's capitulation.

A plan was developed to eradicate that opening by launching a column up the left bank of the Cooper some thirty-two miles to Moncks Corner, where the American cavalry was reportedly based. On March 12, he summoned one of his favorite subordinates, the capable Lieutenant Colonel Webster, whose reputation would steadily grow until his untimely death of wounds following the battle of Guilford Court House. Assigning Webster a column of fourteen hundred troops including the Thirty-third Foot, Sixty-fourth Foot, Patrick Ferguson's American Volunteers, and Banastre Tarleton's combined British Legion and Seventeenth Dragoons, he issued orders for an assault upon the last line of American egress to Charles Town. Major Ferguson's Tories advanced through Dorchester to Middleton Plantation at Goose Creek, where they were united with Tarleton's green-coated dragoons. Webster followed with the infantry, sweating heavily in the heat and humidity. After a lengthy rest, at 10 P.M. on the thirteenth Tarleton and Ferguson undertook the eighteen-mile night ride to Moncks Corner, hopeful of surprising the Colonial horsemen.

Encamped at Moncks Corner, unsuspecting and unprepared, were a variety of American units, mostly cavalry, under Gen. Isaac Huger. Col. William Washington's one hundred riders had been joined by the remnants of Pulaski's Horse, whose commander had fallen at Savannah, under Maj. Peter Vernier as well as the light horsemen of Col. Peter Horry. A detachment of South Carolina militia completed the five-hundred-man force. Sometime between 4 A.M. and daybreak the British raiders struck the Colonial camp. Undeterred by the fatigue of an all-night ride, they rode down the Colonial pickets and spurred into the camp at Biggin Bridge. The punishing night march was followed by an immediate all-out attack on the Colonial force, featuring use of sword and bayonet, and continued without mercy until the outcome was clearly decided. In the ferocity of the attack a regrettable incident occurred. Major Vernier, badly wounded, attempted to surrender and requested quarter, but his appeal was refused and his attackers bayoneted him. He died cursing his assailants and the Americans who deserted him. The ferocious assault was a preview of future onslaughts orchestrated throughout the south by the twenty-six-year-old Tarleton, whose name would resound in fame and infamy following the campaign. The outnumbered British riders, supported by Maj. Charles Cochrane's Legion Infantry, slashed into and through the awakening Colonials, leaving more than forty killed or wounded and over one hundred captured, and the remainder, including most of the officers, scattered into the swamps and woods. More than fifty wagonloads of supplies were taken and hundreds of excellent horses were secured as remounts for the British dragoons.

The sudden victory brought significant results. The principal route of communication to Charles Town was severed. British troops could now cross the Cooper to the east, driving on Point Pleasant and completely surround Lincoln's garrison. Furthermore the American cavalry, routed and badly scattered, was unlikely to reappear as a factor for some time. The appearance of Tarleton and Ferguson's men and riders, now with decent mounts, would offset the previous advantage of the American cavalry.

On the fourteenth, as the victors collected spoils, a second incident occurred on a nearby plantation that became a precursor for the vicious campaign to follow. At Fair Lawn, the estate of prominent Tory John Colleton, his wife and a number of ladies were gathered. Three Legion dragoons led by Henry McDonugh entered the house and after looting valuables attempted to force their attentions on the females. A spirited resistance followed in which several ladies were bruised and Mrs. Colleton sustained a saber cut. The culprits fled. A forced entrance on a neighboring estate by the same trio resulted in criminal assault charges. On the following morning, after treatment by a Dr. Johnson, the ladies involved in both incidents identified their assailants. Major Ferguson, furious, demanded immediate execution for McDonugh, and Tarleton agreed; however, Colonel Webster had the three men chained and shipped to Charles Town for flogging and incarceration.

On Sunday morning the British cavalrymen filed east to Strawberry Ferry, crossed an arm of the Cooper River, and proceeded via Bono Ferry to St. Thomas Church on the Wando River. There they united with the hard-marching Thirty-third Foot. Erecting a blockhouse at the bridge over the Wando, Webster encamped his troops in the trees around the church in an attempt to allay the oppressive heat and humidity. Small detachments were deployed to capture Colonial batteries and small piers, scooping up sloops, military supplies, and cannon. On the twenty-fourth, Lord Cornwallis crossed the Cooper and took command north of the river, bringing with him the Twenty-third Foot and the Volunteers of Ireland. Soon redcoats were marching into Mount Pleasant, opposite Charles

Town, and the batteries and redoubts north of the Cooper were in their possession, including the significant work at Lampriere's Point. Fort Moultrie on Sullivan's Island was now completely isolated. When Major Ferguson led a reconnaissance toward Fort Moultrie, he was shocked to discover the British navy in residence. Capt. Charles Hudson had stormed ashore with three hundred sailors and marines and captured the fort, its garrison, and forty-three guns.

Even as Cornwallis and Webster completed the encirclement of Charles Town, the dirty, dangerous game of siege warfare continued on the "neck." Shovelful by shovelful the parallels and saps advanced each evening, permitting the heavy guns to be manhandled ever closer to their targets. The wind blew constantly, creating stinging projectiles of flying sand particles accompanied by always-present mosquitoes and sand fleas. When the deadly storm of musket and cannon balls was added, life was difficult and unpleasant for sappers and gunners as well as the jaegers and light infantry who afforded them protection. General Clinton paced the parallels each evening, his presence noted by sweaty, tired soldiers who never learned to love him but, nevertheless, admired his ability and courage. Zigzag trenches or saps snaked forward from the first parallel to an advanced gun position then to a second and a third. Soon a communications trench, rapidly enlarged into the second parallel, connected this network of batteries. By the thirteenth, twenty-two 24-pound guns were in place, as well as numerous 12-pounders, mortars, and howitzers.

Each night sweating lines of sailors, soldiers, and slaves hauled shells forward to the small magazines dug into the trench walls. Ewald's jaegers were positioned near the head of the new parallel, experimentally loading their short, octagon-barreled rifles with 1½ loads of powder, which enabled the green coats to fire effectively into the American gun embrasures at fully five hundred yards distance. While the results of this long-range sniping were inconclusive, American gunners scoured the trenches with grape in angry retaliation. The roar of the heavy guns continued day and night, forcing attackers to live in the sandy trenches, sleeping, when possible, on the firing steps. Although casualties were low in the redoubts and batteries, fatigue was a constant enemy, some soldiers even declaring their preference for a quick solution of assault, despite the probable bloody results. Firing quickly and with great effort the British guns could not establish superiority over the Colonial weapons in the hornwork. An inspired Moultrie instructed his gunners to fire *en ricochet,* bouncing solid shot into the newly erected British sand trenches, with results more symbolic than deadly. A British ball fired from James Island severed the arm of a statue of William Pitt at Broad and Meeting Streets; the revered statesmen thus became a victim to his inability to mediate the disagreement.

By April 22 three new saps were inching forward from the second parallel. On the twenty-fourth a surprise sortie of two hundred South Carolina and Virginia Continentals led by Lt. Col. William Henderson burst into the closest parallel. A vicious hand-to-hand fight exploded between American bayonets and Hessian short swords, resulting in substantial casualties on both sides and twelve Hessians taken captive. Maj. Peter Traille, Cornwallis's artillery commander, issued case shot to gunners in anticipation of further night sorties, but on the following night Lincoln, also concerned about night attacks, had barrels of turpentine ignited in front of his works, removing the threat of further American sorties.

At this point, the third parallel was almost abutting the first defensive ditch, requiring the heavy guns to again be dragged forward to fire at point-blank range. A divergent sap crossed the ditch and abatis reaching the dam. When pierced, the dam began to release the water in the second defensive ditch and wooden galleys were constructed to cross the mud. A final assault seemed near.

Early on the morning of May 8 Clinton sent a second summons of surrender to the garrison. He agreed to a truce for a day, extending the offer to twenty-four hours while Lincoln and his officers pondered the terms. When the Colonials submitted counter terms totally unacceptable to Clinton, the truce was concluded and the guns began to fire in frenzy. The American fire, exploding from 180 to 200 barrels, seemed so tremendous, it was as if they were determined to exhaust their shell supply. On the tenth the British began pushing the sap forward, inching to within twenty-five yards of the American parapet. The jaegers continued to sustain their effective fire at any head that showed above the walls.

On May 12 a lone American drummer suddenly beat a parley; both trenches grew silent. An American officer appeared with a letter from Lincoln to Clinton, seating himself in a lodgment to share a bottle of wine with Captain Ewald, and awaited a reply. Lincoln was persuaded by his aides and Charles Town politicos to accept Clinton's terms, though they were considered unusually harsh. Charles Town was surrendered.

Two grenadier companies, one English and one Hessian, picked a route through the wreckage to take possession of the hornwork, while three regiments, the

Seventh, Forty-second, and Sixty-third paraded into Charles Town along Meeting Street, flags flying and bands playing. The American Continentals marched out to heap their weapons in an area between the two abatis lines while militiamen were disarmed inside the city. Lincoln, his officers, and his men were considered captives, the enlisted soldiers to be incarcerated first in the Charles Town barracks and eventually moved to fetid, damp prison hulks in the harbor while the officers were confined in the old city barracks. Clinton intended to hold the Continental soldiers only until they could be exchanged for Burgoyne's veterans, now in captivity in the Valley of Virginia, but the exchange never materialized and many of these Charles Town captives died of disease. Significantly, the victory removed the Continental contingents of Virginia, North Carolina, and South Carolina, totaling 3,465 experienced soldiers, from the chessboard of war along with more than four hundred captured guns. The British commander paroled the South Carolina militiamen despite objections from men such as Captain Ewald, who stated, "We will surely face them again." Casualties were actually relatively light for the amount of gunpowder expended. American losses of about 100 killed and 150 wounded were comparable to British and Hessian casualties of 75 killed and 135 wounded.

The surrender of Charles Town marked the pinnacle of Henry Clinton's military career. His careful, plodding approach had isolated and pounded Lincoln's hard-fighting American army into surrender. The Queen City of the south was Clinton's, accompanied by the largest bag of prisoners of the war—almost the entire army of the South. Clinton used well the aggressive skills of his subordinates:

Webster, Tarleton, Ferguson, Ewald, Moncrief, Elphin-stone, and even Cornwallis. Where efforts lagged, such as in the naval actions of Admiral Arbuthnot, Clinton begged, prodded, cajoled, and ultimately demanded obedience so that adequate naval action occurred. Two key events—the crossing of the harbor sand bars by the fleet and the early-morning amphibious assaults to establish position on the "neck"—keyed the ultimate capitulation of Charles Town. Only a rash direct assault could have altered the sequence of events once the harbor was secure and the siege underway. Despite his many disagreeable personal qualities, Henry Clinton was too bright and too patient to disrupt the steadfast progress toward surrender.

Lincoln, on the other hand, was less ably served but did not manage his forces as badly as later argued. Early, his militia were unprepared to leave the city and meet the Hessians and redcoats on the sea islands where some measure of success was possible. Once the Continentals arrived, Lincoln's lines were already encompassed. However, he offered a stubborn resistance, aligning his troops well to repel an expected British attack that never came. He was poorly served by Whipple and the naval defenders who avoided combat only to manage to be captured totally, adding nothing to the city's defense. The negligence of Isaac Huger, William Washington, and Peter Horry in permitting the rout and scattering of the American cavalry removed Lincoln's only clear advantage. In retrospect, perhaps Lincoln's only chance for success was to abandon the seaport and retreat inland, similar to Washington's strategic commitment to the preservation of his army over all else. But Lincoln could not exert the necessary leadership to convince local political forces that retreat was a real option. In any case, Clinton's unexpected crossing of the Ashley effectively eliminated the possibility of a strategic withdrawal.

On the eighteenth, some six days after the siege, a tremendous explosion created a casualty list that surpassed that of the siege. As surrendered muskets were thrown into a powder magazine on Magazine Street near Archdale Street, a loaded musket fired into a powder cache and the building erupted. The magazine, a nearby brothel, as well as numerous houses were destroyed. More than two hundred persons were killed, including sixty to seventy British soldiers, many burned horribly. Fortunately, the larger powder magazine at 79 Cumberland Street, about two hundred yards distant, did not ignite, possibly saving the city. Captain Ewald, the noted jaeger leader, was about to enter the magazine when he suddenly and impulsively decided to visit a sick friend, Captain Bissenegrat of the Hessian grenadiers. Fifteen minutes later the magazine exploded. This fortuitous decision preserved the experienced light infantryman to achieve fame in the revolution as well as with the army of Denmark, rising to the level of lieutenant general in Danish service.

Once the myriad details of securing the city, mustering or paroling the prisoners, and inventorying the spoils of battle were complete, General Clinton anxiously began preparing for his return to New York, fearing French intentions on the Hudson River. Appointing Lord Charles Cornwallis to command of the southern army, he spent hours instructing his Lordship in the manner of protecting his newly won prize and consolidating the British position in the southern colonies. He left a considerable force for Cornwallis, including the Seventh, Twenty-third, Thirty-third, Sixty-third, Sixty-fourth, and Seventy-first Regiments of Foot to be accompanied by Loyalist units from New York, New Jersey, and North and South Carolina. Hessian regiments von Dittfurth, von Huyn, and d'Angelelli, garrison regiments of militia status, were also assigned to duty. When joined by a battalion of Royal Artillery, Cornwallis commanded a total force of sixty-four hundred capable soldiers. On May 30, long lines of Hessian and British grenadiers began filing aboard transport vessels moored to the Charles Town piers. Light infantry battalions and Hessian jaegers followed. Soon the escorting warships filed across the bar and gathered at sea awaiting the June 8 sailing of the transports. The fleet of more than one hundred vessels sailed north, enjoying a smooth voyage to New York.

With Cornwallis's army set to move west into the Carolina interior to consolidate their prize, and the southern army of Continentals helpless, the defense of the region seemed now in the hands of the partisans.

CHAPTER 5

The Battle of Camden

"Take care less your northern laurels turn to southern willow."

Charles Lee to Thomas Gates

The chirp of crickets, the thump of bullfrogs, and the mournful screech of a hunting owl, typical sounds of a southern summer night, were interrupted by furtive movements on the sandy Waxhaw Road a few miles north of Camden, South Carolina. The jingle of rein traces and the rattle of sabers synchronized with the steady beat of horses' hooves as green-jacketed Lt. Edward Donovan of the British Legion and twenty of his dragoon outriders rode northward on a moonless night, the lead element of Lord Charles Cornwallis's British field army. From just ahead the faint sounds of opposing riders could be distinguished, gradually becoming louder. A challenge was issued and suddenly pistol shots emitted bright cones of flame as Donovan's horsemen drew sabers and spurred up the roadway. Opposition momentarily vanished until a ragged volley from Lt. Col. Charles Porterfield's Virginia Light Infantry emptied several dragoon saddles, including that of the squadron commander. Quietly, several dragoons retrieved and carried their wounded officer rearward, reassured by the steady voice of Lt. Col. James Webster to the rear, deploying his leading light infantry companies from column to line astride the road. A desultory exchange of musket fire continued, then an uneasy quiet fell over the participants. It was 2:30 A.M. on August 16, 1780, and the leading units of Maj. Gen. Horatio Gates' Colonial army had unexpectedly collided with Cornwallis's redcoats. A few prisoners were taken, but, unable to accurately identify their opponents, both forces were unsure what lay in their front. Certainly, however, daybreak would bring a fight.

The appearance of an American force moving southward into South Carolina so soon after the devastating surrender of Charles Town and Gen. Benjamin Lincoln's field army seems unbelievable and almost irrational. Only an unusual sequence of largely unconnected occurrences produced this collision on the night march to Camden. During the long siege of Charles Town, George Washington had frantically dispatched Continental regiments to bolster the defenses of that key southern seaport; however, now most of the members of those Virginia, North Carolina, and South Carolina Continental regiments that had marched to protect Charles Town were incarcerated in unhealthy prison hulks in that city's harbor. In April the harassed American commander in chief, in a final relief attempt, had sent a unit of his very best soldiers south under a proven and capable field officer.

Washington's relief detachment consisted of two infantry brigades: the first included the First, Third, Fifth, and Seventh Maryland Continental regiments of Brig. Gen. William Smallwood, while the second was comprised of the Second, Fourth, and Sixth Maryland and the Delaware Continental regiment, led by Brig. Gen. Mordecai Gist.

The First Colonial Artillery Battalion of eighteen guns accompanied the two brigades, bringing the column to a total of fourteen hundred soldiers. Commanding this independent little battle group was an energetic, bold Bavarian soldier of fortune, Baron Johann De Kalb.

Born in Huttendorf of humble parents, De Kalb, at a young age, had volunteered for service with the victorious armies of France. He earned a commission as lieutenant in the French army and soon was advanced to the rank of lieutenant colonel for his conspicuous accomplishments. Marrying well, he added the aristocratic "De" to his title and seemed poised to assume a prominent position in French society. Colonel De Kalb was requested to accompany the Marquis de Lafayette in a mission to America, partly to serve as a guardian for the bold and impulsive young French nobleman. He was commissioned a major general in the American service and the fifty-eight-year-old De Kalb proved a pleasant exception to the bevy of brash, egocentric young French officers seeking high rank in American armies. Soft spoken and serious, he possessed enormous physical endurance. His habit of marching thirty miles a day alongside his column and his propensity for dealing openly and fairly with Colonial officers and men enhanced his popularity. He abstained from alcohol, ate sparingly, and slept on the ground with his cloak for cover. Having led a division in Washington's army with dependable consistency, he also shared the cold, hungry winter camps of Valley Forge and Morristown. De Kalb seemed an ideal choice for an independent and perilous expedition.

The selected brigades broke camp near Morristown, New Jersey, on April 13, striding out first for Philadelphia. Resting a few days in the Quaker City, the column turned south to Head of Elk on the Chesapeake, where the marchers found waiting transport vessels. Sailing comfortably down the Chesapeake Bay the fleet turned up the James River to disembark at Petersburg, Virginia. While awaiting the artillery, forced to travel by road, De Kalb searched in vain for baggage wagons and supplies. When he learned that Charles Town had surrendered, the Bavarian nonetheless determined to continue his march southward, arriving in Hillsborough, North Carolina, on June 22. Lack of adequate food supplies and rations promised by the governments of Virginia and North Carolina became a serious problem, and soldiers were authorized to requisition or forage needed foodstuffs from local farmers. Crops were not yet ripe, livestock well hidden, and green corn and unripe peaches the only foodstuffs visibly available. De Kalb was aware that only a small step existed between requisitioning supplies and looting, and he worked hard to control his hungry soldiers. De Kalb was also disappointed by the absence of promised local militia reinforcements. Maj. Gen. Richard Caswell refused to join the Colonials with his North Carolina militia, preferring to remain independent. Brig. Gen. Edward Stevens with seven hundred Virginians was reported to be en route, but he had not yet arrived. Slowly proceeding southward while always searching for rations, the little army camped at Buffalo Ford on Deep River, joined there by the remnants of Pulaski's Legion cavalry, commanded by Col. Charles Armand. Only sixty riders were present and many of this number were Tory or British deserters, considered unreliable by De Kalb. The army was now located about seventy miles from the South Carolina village of Cheraw, where a British outpost was garrisoned by a unit of the Seventy-first Highlanders. The Colonial army (the only armed force in the south, save partisans or militia) was too weak to proceed further.

Meanwhile, Congress, recognizing the importance of the little command encamped on Deep River, decided to appoint an American commander in hopes of enticing militia volunteers. Horatio Gates had been successful in drawing together militia troops in New York prior to Saratoga and they hoped his appointment would result in similar actions. On the thirteenth of July, without consultation with General Washington, the congressmen appointed Maj. Gen. Horatio Gates to assume command of the southern Colonial army, a rash political decision that marked the promotion of vanity and arrogance, with near fatal consequences.

Gates began his journey south from his estate, Traveler's Rest, in northwestern Virginia, arriving at Deep River about July 25. A man of modest talent whose most consistent attribute was an inflated estimation of his own abilities, Gates assumed command from the cordial De Kalb in a stirring little ceremony of artillery salutes. Dismissing the assistance of Francis Marion and William Washington, he listened only to the estimates issued by Thomas Sumter of the enemy's strength. Immediately he announced his intention of moving south toward Camden, where he had discovered the British were constructing a large supply base. Despite the scarcity of food and ammunition, an inadequate cavalry presence, and minimal knowledge of the disposition and placement of his enemy, Gates persisted in advancing.

Often described as a first-class snob lacking in charisma and military skills, Gates would prove in a few short weeks that he was possibly the most inept American field commander in an army not always distinguished by outstanding leadership. Appointed to exalted rank on the basis of his lackluster performance while serving in the prewar British army, his most salient trait was a knack for deft political maneuverings. Gates achieved immeasurable fame from fortuitous leadership during the battles fought about Saratoga, New York, in the late summer and fall of 1777. This remarkable expedition, contested in the wilds of upstate New York, resulted in the surrender of an entire British army and contributed greatly to the introduction of French troops to the continent. Many described the battle at Saratoga as the turning point of the revolution. Gates shrewdly gained command of the army that enveloped Burgoyne's forces there and his reputation was magnified from the significant outcome. But in truth, Gates was the benefactor of an incompetent opponent, John Burgoyne, and the assistance of two of the finest field commanders in the American Revolutionary army, Benedict Arnold and Daniel Morgan.

The Colonial army of General Gates at Camden contained no subordinates of the ability of Arnold or Morgan, save possibly De Kalb. The force lacked cohesion and the inexperienced militia units were highly undisciplined. Gates, however, was not totally without competent subordinate leadership, though he hardly knew his brigade officers well enough to ascertain their military value. The Continental regulars from Maryland and Delaware, who had marched south with the gallant De Kalb, contained some excellent officers, at least two of whom would become renowned in the critical months to follow.

Capt. Robert Kirkwood, a native of New Castle, Delaware, was a veteran soldier of remarkable revolutionary experience, having fought at many northern battlefields. Educated at Newark Academy and possessing the social skills of a gentleman, he was revered by his men and fellow officers. In any other army he would have been transferred and promoted, but he refused to leave his beloved Delaware troops and he remained a captain for the remainder of the war. Kirkwood performed admirably at Cowpens and during the following numerous clashes in the south. Moving to Ohio after the war, he fell victim to an Indian ball while fighting the Northwest Tribes under the incompetent leadership of Maj. Gen. Arthur St. Clair. Kirkwood, then in the Second U.S. Infantry, was still a captain.

Lt. Col. John Eager Howard of the Maryland line emerged from the war as one of the Colonial army's exemplary officers. He was fearless, intelligent, and remained free of criticism from others. So well did he perform at Cowpens that Congress voted Howard a medal and sword for leading a stirring bayonet charge that routed the Seventy-first Highlanders. Howard continued his outstanding performance at Guilford Court House, Hobkirk's Hill, and Eutaw Springs. Nathanael Greene summed Howard's contributions to the patriot cause: "Howard is as good an officer as the world affords combining great ability with an amiable disposition."

The militia officers who followed Gates reflected a wide range of ability and experience. Col. Otho Williams was a tall Marylander who initially joined the rifle company of Capt. Michael Cresap, marching to the relief of occupied Boston. Williams served with the riflemen until captured during the surrender of Fort Washington in the Battle of New York. Upon his exchange he was promoted to colonel of the Sixth Maryland. Gates appointed the young officer to the position of adjutant general, and he performed well in that beleaguered and unappreciated position. Following

Camden he served for a time in command of the army's light infantry. Soon, Maj. Gen. Nathanael Greene again made Williams adjutant general. A friendly, well-educated, but rigid officer, Williams performed his duties in a conscientious manner and expected the same effort by others. Refusing to become involved in intrigue or politics and avoiding the criticism of his superiors, Williams was an ideal staff officer. He died in 1794 of pulmonary infection.

Brig. Gen. Edward Stevens, a rotund, friendly gentleman of limited military ability, led the Virginia militia. When his troops broke in action at Camden he was overwhelmed and embarrassed, writing Gov. Thomas Jefferson to offer his resignation. Jefferson declined and at Guilford Court House, Stevens wisely scattered a cordon of riflemen behind his line of battle, ordering them to shoot the first man who ran. They stayed and fought, but Stevens was wounded by a musket ball in the leg. He was so large that five men were required to carry his three-hundred-pound frame from the field. He was forced to retire from military action but remained popular with troops and compatriots.

Brig. Gen. Griffith Rutherford was a popular old Indian fighter, having led the North Carolina contingent that razed the Cherokee villages during the 1776 Indian Wars. He led a brigade of North Carolina militia to Camden, keeping his inexperienced troops in the fight through his relentless will until he was shot down in the roadway. Unable to walk he was abandoned and was fortunate to have survived the British bayonets. He rode by wagon to Charles Town, where he received medical attention from his foes. However, the crusty old campaigner was so critical of British occupiers and complained so loudly about the abominable prison hulks that he was shipped to a dungeon in St. Augustine, Florida. Rutherford again survived, although his health was broken. In 1781 he was exchanged. Rutherford was not a great military commander, but he was a leader of focus and will, valuable to the patriot cause.

Lastly, Gates inherited the services of Maj. Gen. Richard Caswell of the North Carolina militia. Caswell was basically a politician playing at soldier, his actions constantly betraying his lack of ability. He had served three one-year terms as the governor of North Carolina and when ineligible for reelection he requested that his successor, Abner Nash, appoint him a major general based on his success earlier in the war at Moore's Creek Bridge. Reluctant to unite his militia with Gates' force, he finally made contact on August 7. When his militia fled he also ingloriously ran, joining Gates on the road to Charlotte. There he was instructed by his commander to rally the survivors while Gates continued north. Caswell remained in Charlotte for a day, followed Gates to Hillsborough, and gradually faded from military service.

Upon the surrender of Charles Town in early May of 1780, Sir Henry Clinton issued instructions for the investiture of the remainder of the province of South Carolina. Within a few weeks, snaking columns of troops were marching inland, spreading like locusts across the rebellious province. Clinton, anxious to return to New York, entrusted Lord Cornwallis with completion of the operation, leaving his estranged assistant with a substantial force of six British regiments, three Hessian regiments, six provincial Loyalist regiments, and a contingent of Royal Artillery, a total of about sixty-four hundred soldiers. These units included the Seventh, Twenty-third, Thirty-third, Sixty-third, Sixty-fourth, and Seventy-first British Regiments of Foot and the von Dittfurth, von Huyn, and d'Angelelli Hessian regiments. In addition the American Volunteers, the New York Volunteers, the Prince of Wales, the Volunteers of Ireland, the British Legion, and the South Carolina Royalists were Loyalist units in his army.

Cornwallis officially took command on June 5, a few days prior to Clinton's departure. A short, thickset aristocrat with a visibly injured eye suffered while playing at sports while in college, he was an unimposing physical figure. But his friendly, easy manner quickly earned him the full confidence of his men. He commanded divisions in New York, Philadelphia, and on the Delaware with commendable talent, demonstrating some tactical skills and a personal fearlessness. When he assumed command in South Carolina another talent emerged, a trait by which he stood above most British officers in America. He possessed an absolute and total ability to focus on the job at hand. He would determine his objectives and drive forward toward those goals, eliminating or disregarding all interference. This powerful concentration and accompanying aggressive energy made his Lordship one of the most effective British officers in the Colonies.

In addition to the crack troops in his command, Cornwallis was fortunate to have several superb field commanders. While he considered Lt. Col. John Hamilton of the Royal North Carolina Regiment a "blockhead" and Col. Morgan Bryan's North Carolina Volunteers as unreliable, his Lordship's army contained a trio of professional officers who were destined to attain considerable acclaim in British service. Lt. Col. James Webster of the Thirty-third Foot or West Riding Regiment was undoubtedly one of the finest field commanders to serve the king in North America. Lt. Col. Lord Francis Rawdon was an Anglo-Irish officer of long experience, and Lt. Col. Banastre Tarleton was an energetic, ambitious cavalryman. The three were well positioned in the little army and enjoyed the confidence of Cornwallis.

In his revealing diary, Hessian captain Johann Ewald discussed at length his relationship with Lieutenant Colonel Webster during the army's drive to encircle Charles Town. He unequivocally writes that "James Webster was the most meritorious of all British Officers." Flattery from such an excellent soldier and habitual critic of British leadership was truly noteworthy. Son of an eminent Edinburgh minister, Webster was already well known in the British army for his steely courage and his ability to think on his feet. His reputation was greatly enhanced during the southern campaign when his Thirty-third Foot and Ewald's jaegers led the difficult advance across the sea islands toward Charles Town. Both Clinton and Cornwallis constantly assigned Webster the critical post or key duty, a tribute to his courage and ability. In postwar writings Webster was the only British officer praised by Cornwallis, Clinton, and Banastre Tarleton, an unusual and highly unlikely occurrence in itself, for the threesome seldom agreed. By the morning of deployment at Camden, Webster was considered Cornwallis's right arm, reliable and relentless. This trust would increase as the southern campaign unfolded. His glittering reputation grew by leaps and bounds at every river crossing and battlefield assault until he was fatally wounded at Guilford Court House while standing alone in the swale before the third American line urging his "brave fusiliers" forward. Carried on a litter between horses for miles, Webster died quietly at Waddell's Mill near Elizabethtown, North Carolina, and was interred in a now unknown grave, forgotten by a nation he served so well.

Lt. Col. Francis Rawdon, later to become Earl of Moira and First Marquis of Hastings, was a young, politically connected, capable Irish officer. While serving on Clinton's staff in Philadelphia, he was delegated to form a corps of Irish immigrants to be entitled the Volunteers of Ireland. Rapidly developing this unit to reliable status, Rawdon became well esteemed by American Loyalists. He was a close friend of Tarleton at Oxford, and their upward progress in the army was somewhat parallel, although marked by envy. A hard-line officer on rebellion, he permitted his Tories their just measure of revenge but was equally stern when dealing with deserters. He issued a bounty for the head of proven deserters, and he favored whipping or deporting those who abetted them.

Not a brilliant or inspiring soldier like Webster, Rawdon was a capable, reliable military performer. On Cornwallis's move north he was left to administer the military governorship of South Carolina and Georgia, a thankless task that gradually saw his perimeter shrink into defense of the port cities. Rawdon soon became ill and sailed for England, only to be captured by a French man-o-war. Lord Rawdon attained considerable esteem after the revolution, being promoted to general during the Napoleonic Wars and serving a term as governor-general of India.

The third subordinate, Banastre Tarleton, has, over the decades since the revolution, enjoyed much print declaring both his fame and his infamy. He was a skilled leader of cavalry, audacious, ambitious, energetic, and merciless. But he also was reckless in battle, egocentric, and headstrong, attracting the enmity of his foes and brother officers. Like Rawdon, Tarleton advanced primarily in command of Loyalist troops, the British Legion, which he trained to elite status and with whom he enjoyed a trusting relationship.

He was also a hard-liner, spreading the terror of his merciless horsemen and outspokenly vocalizing his dislike of "rebels." Tarleton laughed quite openly when informed that the Colonials planned his execution upon his capture, claiming their fears of his Legion outweighed the threats of his death.

Tarleton forged favored relationships with superiors, and many officers considered him a sycophant always seeking personal gain. He was not particularly tactically gifted but rather a straight-ahead, hell-for-leather, hard charger in the tradition of George Patton's World War II tankers. Tarleton insisted that the bayonet and saber were the key to British victory and that Americans would not stand and resist these weapons. He applied them liberally and often. Tarleton's serious defeat at Cowpens, months later, would evoke a cascade of criticism from his fellow officers. The Seventy-first Highlanders, in reserve alongside him at Camden, would lose their First Battalion at Cowpens, and the Second Battalion blamed him and refused further to serve under Tarleton. Two of their officers were unrelenting in postwar criticism of Tarleton. But no one could question his courage. As he stood to horse in the roadway, he was what he was, the finest British cavalry officer in North America.

With his three favored officers, Cornwallis fanned columns into the South Carolina upcountry, establishing an arc of fortified outposts about 150 miles from Charles Town. This line stretched from Augusta, Georgia, on the Savannah River, to the northern South Carolina seaport of Georgetown. Garrisons, often of trusted Loyalist units, were assigned these posts, endowing a Crown presence throughout the province while hopefully facilitating recruitment. Lt. Col. Thomas Browne, a Loyalist who had been mistreated by his Whig neighbors, commanded the post at Augusta with his Florida Rangers. He constructed two strong earthworks, named Fort Cornwallis and Fort Grierson, which commanded the flatlands on the Georgia side of the river. In the back country at Ninety-six, so called because its location was supposedly ninety-six miles from Fort George on the Keowee River, a strong star fort of two hundred yards diameter was erected. Lt. Col. Nisbet Balfour, an experienced British officer, commanded this garrison of three battalions of Royal Provincials that were sometimes reinforced by British light infantry companies. The third and most important post was established at Camden on the Wateree River. This supply base was constructed to amass equipment for the advance into North Carolina. The base seemed permanent with its log barracks, warehouses, and large hospital. Lord Rawdon, the twenty-six-year-old Harrow and Oxford graduate, commanded at Camden while Maj. Archibald McArthur with a portion of Simon Fraser's Seventy-first Highland Regiment advanced to occupy Cheraw, near the North Carolina line. Other garrisons held less important positions at Rocky Mount, Orangeburg, and Georgetown.

In attempting to occupy such a large area Cornwallis's resources were stretched and he depended heavily on experienced officers such as Rawdon, Tarleton, and Patrick Ferguson. Tarleton and his green-clad British Legion and a portion of the Seventeenth Dragoons were the only reliable cavalry unit available to Cornwallis in a country well suited to the use of cavalry and soon to be swarming with partisan mounted infantry. The British army in America consistently suffered from a lack of mobile troops, particularly in the south, but cavalry units were expensive to transport from England and even more difficult to maintain. Despite some distracting personal habits, Tarleton was a strong, aggressive cavalry commander. In his desperate search for glory he gained and maintained the respect of his Loyalists. Major Ferguson, another capable officer, was assigned the task of recruiting and training loyal recruits in the area. While he clashed with Balfour and other Loyalists, no one questioned the courage and bravery of this Scottish officer who died and lies buried atop Kings Mountain.

As he learned of Gates' arrival and the boastful statements of the new American commander, Cornwallis anticipated the massing of American militia and a rapid advance toward his supply base at Camden. Leaving his comfortable lodgings at Drayton Hall, across the Ashley from Charles Town, he dashed north, riding over 140 miles in three days. En route he summoned four light infantry companies from Ninety-six and recalled McArthur and his Highlanders from Cheraw. When Tarleton arrived with his Legion, his Lordship could field a stout little army of 2,339 experienced soldiers. Although well aware through scouts and spies of the size of Gates' force, Cornwallis was nonetheless determined to fight, for he could not give up his supplies or invalided troops. He had great confidence in his intelligence gatherers who informed him not to fear the quality of Gates' army or the skills of its commander.

Thus in the early-morning hours of August 16, in almost total darkness, two small armies moved toward one another, each unaware of the other's approach. They traversed a sandy roadway through fields of broom straw and scrub pines bordered by deep swamps on either flank. Any clash of force would require a straightforward attack, for flanking movements were impossible.

Col. Armand with his horsemen led the Colonial column, Porterfield's light infantry marching in single file

Battle of Camden, August 16, 1780. (*National Archives*)

some two hundred yards to his right and Major Armstrong with a similar force of North Carolinians on his left. Lt. Col. James Webster's division, composed of four light infantry companies, the Twenty-third and Thirty-third Regiments, followed the British vanguard of Donovan's dragoons. Suddenly colliding, the cavalry units recoiled as infantry supports opened fire in the darkness. Colonel Porterfield was fatally wounded in this confusing exchange. After wheeling to present fronts in varying directions and firing into their own units, both armies wisely formed blocking columns and awaited first light.

Both commanders soon realized that they faced a formidable opponent and not just a raiding party, as they initially had suspected. Gates called his senior officers together in council and requested their recommendation: should he fight or retreat? Inexperienced but feisty old Edward Stevens spoke for the majority when he exclaimed: "It is too late now to do anything but fight." Gates had planned to continue south to Saunders Creek just above Camden. There he could fortify a position and await attack. That plan had flown away with the musket flashes in the dark night and disengagement really seemed impossible. After deploying his troops he issued no further orders but awaited daylight. His confidence never wavered, however. He is credited by tradition with stating, "I will breakfast tomorrow in Camden with Lord Cornwallis at my table." Fortunate he was that that statement was not reversed.

Cornwallis intended to force the action from the moment he departed Camden. He convened no council and saw no reason to change his intentions. His best field officer, Webster, was in front and could be counted upon to counter any emergency. He allowed rest of his army to stand easy and rest alongside the roadway, awaiting first light. Confident in his men and unafraid of his opposition, Lord Cornwallis rode from one flank to the other, checking his position. He would deploy at dawn, if necessary.

Well before daybreak, Gates' army formed in the mile-wide field split evenly by the Waxhaw Road. He divided his force into two front line divisions and held a third unit in reserve some two hundred yards north. The experienced Maryland and Delaware regiments of Brigadier General Gist were arrayed on the Colonial right under the watchful command of General De Kalb. Opposite, on the Colonial left, were placed fourteen hundred North Carolina militiamen led by General Caswell and seven hundred Virginians under the rotund but feisty General Stevens. The First Maryland Brigade formed the reserve line alongside Armand's riders. Capt. Anthony Singleton's eight Colonial guns, many of which were captured British ordinance, were scattered between the various positions. Both contingents of militia

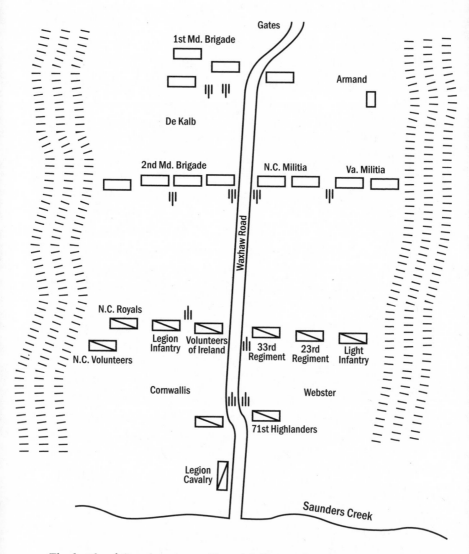

The battle of Camden. An accidental collision of cavalry units during the early morning of August 16, 1780, led to a sharp, brief battle on the Waxhaw Road north of Camden, North Carolina, an encounter that culminated in a rout of Gates' Colonial army.

were green as grass, neither unit having fired a shot in battle. Steven's Virginians had been issued bayonets the day prior to the battle, but most could not attach the weapons to their muskets. These backwoods troops would see more shining steel on the morrow than they could believe existed. Gates seemed to forget that British armies traditionally fought right-handed: their best units were placed in the post of honor on the right. When Gates arrayed his troops he placed the militia units, his weakest troops, on the left, opposite these red-coated veterans. Gates took personal station just north of the reserve unit and as he had done at Saratoga, he calmly and quietly awaited the battle's outcome.

Cornwallis set his troops in motion at first light to the thunder of drums. Lord Rawdon, who would command the left, filed his Loyalists off the roadway. The Royal North Carolina units were followed by the infantry of the British Legion and the 303 members of Rawdon's own Volunteers of Ireland. Morgan Bryan's North Carolina battalion was placed in close reserve. Seven hundred Loyalists made up the left wing.

On the right, Colonel Webster wheeled his redcoats from column to battle line in an awesome display of martial prowess, intimidating to the watching American militiamen. The four light infantry companies filed right and were followed by the Twenty-third Regiment in red coats, blue facing, and white breeches, then the Thirty-third in solid red uniforms. The 648 redcoats formed two lines in the field on the right and as the drums fell silent stood in attentive formation. Governed by the eighteenth-century linear tactics of movement and combat, the soldiers marched to the combat zone in columns of two or more files of men, a maneuver best suited for mobility. Once on the battlefield, the troops were deployed into ranks, each facing front with men standing shoulder-to-shoulder to form their line of battle. This formation provided concentrated firepower as well as easy application of the second British weapon, the bayonet. Ranks could charge with the bayonet, a shock instrument, to carry the point of impact. The speed by which an army deployed from column to line was critical, providing an important edge to the best-disciplined units.

Lt. John McLeod galloped two 6-pound guns up the roadway and unlimbered between the British wings. Major McArthur with 250 Highlanders attired in red coats, white breeches, and clan bonnets stood steadily in reserve on the roadway, their drummers and pipers alongside at the ready. Finally, Banastre Tarleton and his green-coated dragoons stood to horse in the roadway beside McLeod's two 3-pounders. Cornwallis, resplendent in a scarlet coat with gold lace and epaulets, took position on the roadway, just in rear of his initial battle line, poised to observe and adjust. Few could display or deploy an army like his Lordship, and on this morning he proved his mettle.

As Cornwallis deployed, Col. Otho Holland Williams, Gate's adjutant general, imagined the British lines to be confused and vulnerable, although his perception of the motion was largely a sign of his own inexperience. He spurred north to Gates' post on the roadway and proposed an assault on the British regulars by the untrained militia. Gates listened attentively and while not commenting, nodded his consent. Williams galloped back to General Stevens' position and attempted to personally lead an advance to harass the British deployment. However, he could convince only a few bold men to follow; most of the troops uneasily remained in their ranks, staring in awe at the redcoat lines.

The double ranks of redcoats stood still. Only the faint keening of a piper from the Seventy-first down on the roadway could be heard in the distance. Time seemed suspended.

In the odd quiet, redcoats held their Short Land Muskets tightly at order arms, their forty-two-inch barrels elongated by bayonets. Short Land Muskets were labeled the Second Brown Bess, for they were copies of the earlier forty-six-inch-barreled muskets. Bayonets were fitted in right-angle sockets over the muzzles and locked firmly in place. Noting the mass of Colonial militia on his right, Cornwallis altered his attack plan and immediately sent forward Webster's redcoats.

Suddenly, like hornets, the British drummer boys exploded, beating their strident cadence of advance. With a loud "huzza" and the presentation of arms, a glittering wall of steel appeared, the British line stepping off as one man, marching in measured tread. Proceeding to within about forty yards of the Colonial line, the redcoats halted, dressed their ranks, and presented muskets, firing a rolling volley, left to right. Accuracy was not a high priority. Maj. George Hanger, Tarleton's deputy commander, wrote that "a musket, if properly bored, will strike the figure of a man at 80 yards, but a soldier is truly unlucky if wounded at 150 yards by someone aiming at him."

On this steamy, humid morning large billows of smoke rolled low across the field, obscuring visibility. But lack of vision was immaterial; the fight was over on the American left. The Virginia militia broke and ran in an irresistible panic, a sympathetic rout, throwing aside arms, cartouche boxes, and accouterments while springing rearward and fighting for running space. Officers bold enough to inter-vene placed themselves in great peril. Stevens wrote later to Governor Jefferson lamenting the rout: "It was beyond the power of man to rally them." The Virginians, unfamil-iar with the area, stuck close to the Waxhaw Road, fleeing north in a wave, irresistible. They rallied primarily in Hillsborough, North Carolina, 180 miles north.

The North Carolinians aligned alongside copied their Virginia counterparts except for their routes of departure. Fleeing North Carolinians scattered, headed for homes or other places of refuge. Within seconds the entire left wing of the Colonial army evaporated. Otho Williams estimated that two-thirds of the army fled without firing a single shot. Only a small unit of Lt. Col. Henry Dixon's North Carolina troops moved across the roadway and attached themselves to the Delaware Continentals and continued the fight. Webster wisely halted his pursuit and wheeled his veterans left onto the left flank of De Kalb's Continentals, the British emerging from the heavy smoke in a bayonet charge. Closely behind, Cornwallis turned and dispatched his aide, Capt. Alexander Ross, to locate Rawdon and order his left wing forward.

Rawdon spied Ross approaching and waved his lines in. But the struggle on this British left side of the road would develop in an entirely different manner. The Second Maryland Brigade stood firm, repulsing Rawdon twice, and led by De Kalb, they charged bayonets into the Volunteers of Ireland near the roadway, a maneuver that threatened to split the British army. Cornwallis rode into the melee to rally the Volunteers. Smoke rolled so thickly that De Kalb was unaware of the fate of the militia and continued to resist furiously. So close were the combatants that reloading was difficult and the contest became a bayonet fight, a forte of the well-trained redcoats. Most of the Colonial prisoners who were wounded displayed bayonet cuts only. Farther up the roadway the First Maryland Brigade was forced back by Webster's wheeling line and could not penetrate to unite with Gist's brigade, despite the repeated urging of Otho Williams. Brig. Gen. William Smallwood had left the battlefield.

Cornwallis sent for Hanger and Tarleton and launched his riders forward in two cavalry charges around the swirling action to fall on De Kalb's rear. This quickly executed maneuver pinned De Kalb to the swamp, surrounding and assaulting his force on three sides. De Kalb fell with three musket balls in his chest and shoulder and was also bayoneted eight times in cruel, senseless vengeance. Lt. Col. Johanne Du-Buyson, his aide de camp, attempted to protect the baron but was himself seriously injured. The redcoats seemed to particularly resent the participation of French officers with American troops. Cornwallis discovered the brave Bavarian lying prone in agony and had De Kalb carried back to the Logtown Hospital at Camden. He succumbed of his wounds some three days later. On that same day, General Gates rode into Hillsborough, 180 miles north.

The surrounded Continentals were forced to surrender, save for a small number who braved escape through the swamps. General Gist gathered over one hundred Continentals who retreated by wading waist-deep thought the mire, the only substantial group to escape by this manner. Tarleton turned his riders north on the Waxhaw Road in pursuit of fleeing Americans. Green coats thundered up the pike swinging their heavy sabers until they were arm weary. Exhausted, they halted at Hanging Rock, some twenty-two miles from the battlefield. Guns, wagons, muskets, and camp followers were taken, but the dragoons were irritated by the paucity of American spoils.

Cornwallis carefully compiled his casualties. He listed 68 British soldiers killed and 250 wounded or missing, certainly much less than the Americans, but still an expensive price to pay from regiments already eroded by disease and campaigning and lacking the means of recruiting immediate replacements. Colonial losses were more difficult to compute, for rosters of militia units disappeared as well as any reports of dead or wounded. A figure of 250 slain and 800 wounded or missing was released by Gates, but this figure probably underestimated militia losses. Many of these volunteers fled to their homes and never reassembled. British figures list seven guns, two thousand muskets, and 1,000 men captured.

Horatio Gates, major general in the American army, has garnered much of the blame for the Camden debacle, and in truth much of this criticism is fairly awarded. Accepting, even lobbying, for the political plum of army command, Gates, upon that appointment, began ambling south in his usual pompous and arrogant manner, determined to rekindle the fame and adoration that had followed his Saratoga triumph. His so-called military abilities were largely a label of his own imagining, and Gates took counsel from few, relying on his reputation to frighten and scatter his foes. He never demonstrated in any campaign or action any intellectual or military skill beyond those of a basic organizational nature. His highly praised British army background, the basis of his rapid advancement in rank, was the work of a staff officer and not a very accomplished one at that. Gates' overwhelming arrogance, a trait of many British officers, probably masked an inferiority complex dating back to his humble early childhood in servants' quarters.

Arriving in North Carolina to assume command, Gates found his army to consist of a few understrength Continental regiments and a mob of North Carolina and Virginia militiamen who had never experienced hostile fire and in many cases could not discern how to attach their newly issued bayonets. Nathanael Greene later remarked that Gates' primary error was not his mismanagement of the Camden battle but rather his decision to move south and fight at all with such an undisciplined force.

When the two forces collided in the darkness, a shaken Gates deployed his units poorly, arraying the militia in an exposed fashion. He then waited for dawn. As had been his practice at Saratoga, he took no further part in the next day's combat, relying on his reputation, his subordinates, or Providence to deliver a victory. No rally points or positions of regrouping were enumerated, and when the battle went against him, Gates fled west and north on one of the fastest horses in the Colonies. His oft-recalled comment— "A man may pit a cock but he cannot make him fight"— revealed his disrespect for his troops. Gates took no active role in the battle, made little attempt to rally fleeing troops, and disassociated himself from the outcome. Almost criminally, he raced for Charlotte, then Hillsborough, abandoning De Kalb and his still-resisting Continentals to their fate.

In other armies, other wars, and other times, Gates' behavior would have produced charges of court-martial, certain conviction, and serious punishment up to a death penalty. Generals do not run away and leave their armies to destruction. Widespread criticism of Gates swept through the army and flowed north to Washington and Congress. Gates halted in Hillsborough and began to reorganize the survivors, principally Continentals and Virginia militia. However, Washington was directed by Congress to appoint a successor and Nathanael Greene was so named. Upon relieving Gates near Charlotte, Greene was requested by the now maligned general to convene a court of inquiry concerning Gates' conduct at Camden. Greene wisely declined, claiming a lack of sufficient general officers present, referring the matter to Congress, and postponing a trial, which never occurred.

In August of 1782, after a two-year leave at his home in Virginia, Gates was restored to army duty and assigned to Washington's headquarters. He soon became involved in the near treacherous Newburgh Conspiracy whereby a group of officers threatened Congress for back pay. His wife died and Gates began searching for a successor. Marrying a wealthy young lady, Gates moved to New York and enjoyed the social scene. In 1806 he died and was buried in Trinity Churchyard near Wall Street. He lies forgotten there today. No tombstone or monument exists to one of the revolution's most inept military leaders.

Initially the significance of the Battle of Camden seemed almost cataclysmic to the fortunes of those of a patriotic bent in the south. A British army had defeated, actually routed, the lone remaining Colonial force in the Carolinas, its survivors scarred by the terror of total uninhibited flight before phantoms wielding bayonets and sabers. Following so closely upon the capitulation of Gen. Benjamin Lincoln's major field army and the surrender of the leading center of trade in the south, Camden seemed a possible death knell of the revolution, or at least of the independence of the southernmost provinces.

Colonial strategy seemed uncertain, indecisive, or perhaps nonexistent. Tactical battlefield leadership since Sir Henry Clinton's investiture of Charles Town had been lethargic and weak, Colonial units consistently outmaneuvered by British tactics and energy. The performance of American troops had been generally poor with the militia even deplorable, actually fleeing at the first sight of redcoat bayonets.

Lord Charles Cornwallis evaluated the situation in euphoric terms. Initially tied by Clinton's orders to occupy and consolidate the Crown position in Georgia and South Carolina, he now utilized his newly found freedom to communicate directly with London, undercutting Clinton's plans. Through a series of communiqués and the ardent work of his hard-traveling aide, Capt. Alexander Ross, he convinced the ministers that victory lay within his grasp, a dramatic triumph that would conclude the long revolution in North America. He insisted on aggressively marching north to pursue, catch, and destroy the remnants of the American army. Cornwallis reasoned that by merely holding the two provinces, the Americans would benefit, for they could return and attack when the circumstances were to their advantage. Thus he and his army must strike at once, following the sensible course to victory, the elimination of the Colonial army.

The easy success of the British army presented the proud English general with a deceptively simple solution, and he ignored other options that held results beyond his immediate comprehension. Cornwallis was a battle commander of the first order, a leader of soldiers, a maestro at setting a battlefield, and he possessed the courage, tenacity, and charisma to successfully conduct a battle. But his Lordship's strategic gifts were questionable; some portion of his military personality was impatient, his actions often lacking proper caution. Cornwallis identified his enemy and focused on bringing his opponent to heel. His overwhelming need was to push on to battle, to decide irresolutely the issue. Patience to Cornwallis was a vice.

The strategic helm in the southern theater passed into the hands of Cornwallis, enjoined with high expectations by king and ministers. Concurrently, a new complex set of circumstances evolved, factors that would have challenged the abilities of a strategic genius. Ultimately a fine British gentleman and field officer would become ensnared in these fast emerging factors.

The revolution had evolved into a full-fledged world war with French assistance progressing far beyond the initial material assistance to the Colonies. Spanish forces had emerged from the Gulf of Mexico to assail and capture British garrisons on Florida's western coast. A large French army was encamped at Newport, Rhode Island, and fleets flying the French flag cruised the Atlantic coast while Dutch vessels challenged the British navy in the Channel. Although the newly captured southern ports appeared easily defensible, it was no longer possible for British columns to move freely throughout the provinces without attention to French naval actions that might disrupt communication or supply lines.

The supply of British field armies had become a logistical nightmare, a difficulty that increased exponentially with the distance a column journeyed from their seacoast supply centers. British forces in North America derived the bulk of their provisions from the British Isles, the supplies channeled through the port of Cork in western Ireland. Commissary generals were appointed in each province to obtain supplemental goods from American sources, usually through purchases from Loyalists. Armies on the move also utilized foragers to search for cattle, swine, horses, fodder, and grains, including rice. As more provisions were needed locally and searches less successful, the fine line between foraging and looting became indistinct. Carts, wagons, and trucks, accompanied by horses and oxen, were utilized to convey provisions for moving columns, using local drivers; however, mismanagement and corruption were rampant in provisioning and transporting supplies for the armies. Cornwallis issued an order on December 23, 1780, in which he forbade the quartermaster general from transporting personal property in wagons used by his army.

The area contemplated for invasion by Cornwallis created further problems. It covered a vast and rugged area and was best described as an incomplete map. Distances between points were tremendous, roads deplorable, bridges nonexistent, and the large expanse was thinly populated and cultivated, thereby providing scant supplies for an army. North Carolina did not enjoy the seaports or transportation resources of Virginia and South Carolina. De Kalb had remarked to associates that most British officers did not understand what war is about in America or how to contend with obstacles of nature which appeared so readily in the provinces. Brig. Gen. Henri Bouquet, a Swiss soldier of fortune, perhaps best described campaigning in North America: "In America everything is terrible, the face of the country, the climate, the enemy. There is no refreshment for the healthy, nor relief for the sick. A vast desert, unsafe and treacherous where victories are not decisive, but defeats are ruinous." In addition the province had little back country history of established government or social systems. To march into such a wild, unknown area was awe-inspiring to an army of British soldiers. The task was more difficult than that undertaken by Burgoyne's comparable force in the woodlands of New York, an expedition of disastrous results.

That such a field army of slightly more than three thousand men—redcoats, Hessians, and Loyalists—would undertake such an enterprise attests to their confidence in the leadership of Charles Cornwallis. Concurrently the fact that this hard little force marched great distances in downpours and freezing rain, sustained itself on local foodstuffs such as pumpkins and sweet potatoes, and fought wherever challenged confirms their strong esprit de corps, their evolution into an elite fighting unit. They followed the British flag as truly as professionals all over the world have created their own loyalties in foreign legions or in near impossible expeditions such as those portrayed in the *Anabasis* of Xenophon, a member of the Greek mercenary army known as the Ten Thousand, which marched the length and breadth of the Anatolian Peninsula.

Further complicating the goals of Cornwallis were the changing sympathies of those loyal Colonists whose support the British needed. Despite the recent defeat of Gen. Thomas Sumter at Fishing Creek, inklings were appearing of a significant partisan eruption in South Carolina. In a parallel fashion the flow of Loyalist recruits to British militia units was shrinking to a trickle. Indications of weak support of the Crown in North Carolina, indeed lackadaisical support of either combatant, were already apparent to Cornwallis, a matter which should have garnered immediate investigation. Extravagant claims of Loyalist support upon arrival of a redcoat army proved invalid.

The seeming pinnacle of British success and unlimited opportunities presented by the Battle of Camden were based on soft underpinnings caused by overall strategic needs. That Charles Cornwallis would not recognize these limitations is unsurprising and a realistic measure of the man. That the British government would place its strategic trust in Cornwallis and allow his pursuit of a dream was idiosyncratic, initiating a trail that led slowly but surely to American independence.

CHAPTER 6

The Rise of
Partisan Warfare

"Good Lord, our God who art in heaven, we have reason to thank Thee for the many favors received at thy hands, the many battles we have Won. The great and glorious battle at Kings Mountain where we kilt the great Gineral Ferguson and took his whole army, the great battles at Ramseur's and Williamson's, and the ever memorable and glorious battle of Coopens where We made the proud Gineral Tarleton run doon the road helter skelter, And Good Lord, if ye had na suffered the cruel Tories to burn Billy Hill's iron works, we would na have asked any more favors at thy hand. Amen."

Prayer of John Miller, Presbyterian elder

Following the surrender of Charles Town in May of 1780, celebrations were conducted in London by the firing of volleys of Household Artillery, and in Dublin, Ireland, candle illuminations rivaled the displays of Christmas season. British military forces enjoyed their domination of the principal cities of South Carolina and Georgia, relaxing in the pubs, enjoying the social graces of the balmy climate, and paying minimal attention to the small groups of patriots that were organizing along the North Carolina-South Carolina border.

Anxious to depart South Carolina and return to New

York, Sir Henry Clinton unwisely issued a sweeping proclamation on June 3 demanding that all South Carolinians support the cause of their lawful king, despite previous paroles, truces, or agreements, and insisting that none could remain neutral. They were even to serve in Loyalist militia units when requested. In this attempt to increase Loyalist participation and recruiting, he enticed many to take the oath of allegiance, but others were induced to resist and join the evolving patriot resistance groups. Instead of increasing the base of a pacifying Loyalist militia, Clinton's action brought divisiveness and retribution. Meanwhile, a number of British hard-line officers, in attempting to support Tory units, allowed their foraging parties to virtually become looters and plunderers, carrying off livestock and slaves and torching the homesteads of any persons suspected of supporting the rebel cause. Combined with the increased foraging and raiding of British troops that visited dire consequences on both Whigs and Tories, farmers in the back country began casting their lot with the rebels.

On the twenty-ninth of May, just days prior to Clinton's edict, a catalytic event occurred on the North Carolina border. A detachment of Virginia troops led by Col. Abraham Buford were overtaken near the Waxhaws area by Lt. Col. Banastre Tarleton and his British Legion. In a vicious attack, the British declined to offer quarter. The legionnaires killed 113 and wounded 150 of Buford's men while suffering only minimal losses. The Scotch-Irish settlers of the area labeled the cold-blooded attack a massacre, decrying the treachery of Tarleton's attackers and coining a rallying cry of "Tarleton's Quarter," indicating that the cavalryman and his followers should not expect mercy if captured.

This highly exploited action and other excesses by Tory units bent on local retribution greatly encouraged the swift formation of patriot bands, usually led by prewar militia leaders of some esteem in the community. As they grew and merged into larger units, leadership fell upon those individuals who achieved successes, thus warranting their following. Membership was fluid in that many individuals joined a group for one raid or action, returned home, then reported for duty with another unit in a future expedition. Additionally, large numbers of deserters who fought for one side then another brought about widespread distrust, hangings, and retribution slayings, each instance of which increased the atmosphere of violence and terror.

Initially these infant bands of riders concentrated on protecting themselves or exacting a measure of revenge on local Tory organizations, but as the northern provincial regiments and British troops increased assistance to southern Tories, the patriot groups targeted Tory camp-sites, supply trains, couriers, and small English columns whenever possible. Soon Cornwallis was forced to assign large escort forces to move his supplies and troops about the countryside. Guerilla war had begun.

The American Revolution was, in its time, a new kind of war, truly one of revolutionary tactics and style. At no location did these radical changes occur as often and as rapidly as in the southern provinces. No longer was the war a contest for cities, forts, river crossings, or geographic strong points, for whenever these sites were contested American defeat was imminent. The object of the contest evolved into a goal, not of the overthrow of England or the English Empire, but a stripping away of part of that empire, an expansive and economically well-developed part. As the war progressed it became obvious that partisan activities would become a critical part of that effort in the lower south.

As soon as the neophyte partisan captains assembled riders and military equipment and established hidden or secreted campsites, they initiated the first stage of guerilla war, scattered terrorism. British attempts to erase these efforts by heavy-handed retaliation proved counterproductive, much as similar American tactics would reveal in Vietnam. Historian George Bancroft postulated correctly that "brutality, fear, and the resulting chaos work only for the guerillas, no matter who initiates the practice." Redcoat attempts to intimidate produced, in fact, the opposite effect than that intended. Instead of being cowed, numerous patriots lashed out at their oppressors.

As organized military resistance subsided in the south, the first hints of partisan warfare appeared. In many localities, due to religious divergence, population settlement patterns, and economic relationships with English traders, latent Tory or Whig sentiments emerged into first political then military support. Quick successes by British armies followed by rapid Tory activation produced a Whig response triggering civil war.

Religious divergence between Tories and Whigs reinforced differing political alliances. Church attendance in the Colonies was not necessarily high, but the broader local influence of religion was pervasive. Dissenting Protestantism developed as a key factor in spurring the breakaway of the Thirteen Colonies and the maturing of their political and civic culture. However, these religious divisions between Tories and Whigs were extremely complex and varied greatly between the various colonies. Whig support was generally greatest among Puritans and Presbyterians. King George III once angrily labeled the revolution a "Damned Presbyterian War." Catholics and

High Church Anglicans tended to support the Loyalist cause. Nevertheless, these divisions were never absolute, for economic- or immigration-based factors could easily replace religious divides. In Virginia many Anglicans resided who supported the patriot cause due to the more important economic factor of tobacco sales, thereby trumping adherence to religious causes.

In Mecklenburg and Rowan Counties in the North Carolina Waxhaws region, Scotch-Irish Presbyterian ministers dissented to British rule with such vehemence as to declare all authority of the king or Parliament annulled. Colonel Tarleton, whose cavalry operated in that area often, declared these counties to be the most hostile to England in America. Oddly, similar ethnic groups reacted quite differently. Many of the Highland Scots who were exiled or migrated to North Carolina after the Battle of Culloden during the revolt of 1745 fiercely defended the king. Peopling the area of the Cape Fear River from Wilmington to Cross Creek, these Scotsmen lived in tightly organized little settlements awarded as land grants by the English king. Further, they were encouraged to exercise their religious freedoms and to wear their distinctive and colorful Scottish garb.

The enlistment of blacks to the Loyalist cause, initiated by Sir Henry Clinton in 1779, presented a two-headed political weapon. He drafted an order allowing blacks full occupational security while within British lines. A single black cavalry unit was initiated in 1781 to chase deserters, but most ex-slaves were used in support roles, as teamsters, workers, orderlies, or musicians. Landowners who feared uprisings among trained black soldiers vehemently opposed this policy. British administration of the policy was almost criminal, abandoning black families in many

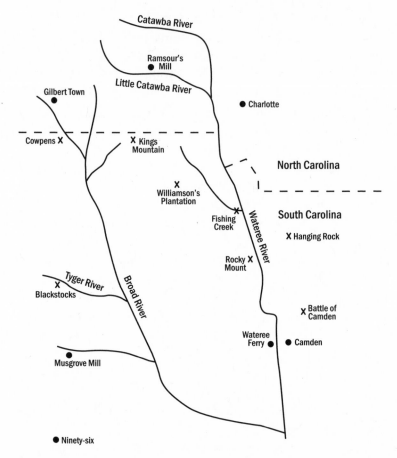

The South Carolina back country. The partisan uprising of 1780 centered initially in the area of the Carolina back country, south and west of present-day Charlotte, North Carolina.

instances. When British forces moved on, blacks were forced to find their own methods of sustenance.

The emerging scope of warfare in the south, whether revolutionary, guerilla, or civil in nature, quickly produced a style that was vengeful, merciless, and cruel. Men of material greed and large economic ambition or those committed to revenge upon their neighbors attempted to control guerilla groups of both parties by permitting looting. Other men of conviction attempted to control or limit the scope of the conflict while a third group sought neutrality. It was soon evident that this new style of war was in practice, independent of, or in conjunction with the standard military conflict.

Ramsour's Mill

The first clash of substantial proportions between organized Tory and Whig forces took place on June 20 at Ramsour's Mill in North Carolina (present-day Lincolnton). Lt. Col. John Moore, a Tory of Col. John Hamilton's North Carolina Royal Volunteers, was dispatched by Cornwallis to scout the area about his home, near Ramsour's Mill, some thirty-five miles northwest of Charlotte. Cornwallis had become adeptly involved in intelligence gathering concerning Crown support in North Carolina as he prepared for an anticipated march northward. He assigned Moore to measure Loyalist support and pass on his Lordship's message of patience to the faithful adherents of the Crown, a dangerous task in such volatile times. Cornwallis had consistently warned the area Tories to remain inactive until he began his expedition and to simply gather provisions that would be needed by his redcoats when the march began.

His instructions received, Moore donned his faded old red regimental coat and trusty saber, for if captured he hopefully would be considered a prisoner of war. He safely reached the area on the eighteenth of June and assembled a group of about forty loyal followers, spreading Cornwallis's anticipatory messages. Soon he was joined by Maj. Nicholas Welch, a mysterious character resplendent in a new red coat who began dispensing newly minted gold coins to those who would take an oath to the king. The word spread rapidly and within days some thirteen hundred Tories or potential Tories were encamped on a low ridge near Ramsour's Mill. They enjoyed an old-fashioned camp-style meeting with impassioned speeches, not of a religious tract but complimenting the recent victories of the British troops. Many of these interested attendees were German farmers without weapons who avowed neutrality but agreed to listen to the Tory speeches.

Such a large gathering could not go unnoticed by Whigs, and information was relayed to Charlotte. There, militia general Griffith Rutherford had about seven hundred North Carolina militiamen quietly observing the activities of Lord Rawdon's force at Camden, South Carolina. Rutherford had a minimal force, but he dispatched Col. Francis Locke and Maj. Daniel Wilson toward Ramsour's Mill with orders to gather whatever Whig troops they could find and disrupt the Tory camp meeting. Locke's force was joined en route by small units under Captains Falls, Thomas Brandon, and Charles McDowell, the rebel force growing to almost four hundred men and camping at the Glades, a site about sixteen miles from Ramsour's Mill. Eager for action but aware of the numerical advantage of their opponents, the Whig leaders hesitated. Finally, after much discussion, they decided to march at night and initiate a dawn attack when, perhaps, their foes would be unprepared.

Locke's little army moved silently through the moonlight, following a dark, winding road through heavy woods. The riders of Falls, Brandon, and McDowell led the column while the infantry followed two abreast. As the column approached Ramsour's Mill, a band of twenty riders led by Adam Reep appeared in the roadway. Reep, a local farmer and avid patriot, provided Locke with a detailed and accurate description of Tory numbers and deployment. The Tory force was well positioned, camped on a ridge about three hundred yards east of the mill. From the summit they enjoyed a two-hundred-yard field of fire down to the roadway.

As Falls' riders advanced, they encountered a Tory picket force of twelve some six hundred yards from the camp. Alert, they began firing and falling back to warn the encampment. The rebel riders pursued the pickets at a trot, wheeled right, and started up the ridge. Believing that they faced a confused enemy, Falls and his men spurred up the slope, but they soon encountered more fire than they expected. Captain Falls and several men and officers were slain. The remainder of the riders turned and fled downhill, passing through the now deploying rebel infantry. Tory fighters, excited and exhilarated, charged wildly downhill in pursuit of the rebel horsemen. Colliding, the two lines of opposing infantry spread out and settled into two roughly straight lines of combatants, firing into each other at near point-blank range. Little organization was evident, as each man conducted his own fight in conjunction with friends on either side. The only marks of identification were pine tops worn in the hats of the Tories and paper squares on the lapels of the rebels.

As the lines grew closer there was no time to load and, lacking bayonets, the opponents fell on each other with gun butts, knives, rocks, or even fists. The ferocious hand-to-hand combat was unrelenting as the slain and wounded scattered across the field were sometimes trampled underfoot. In instinctive backwoods style, Captain Hardin, an experienced patriot Indian fighter, led a party of Whigs down a fence line and emerged on the Tory left flank to unleash a galling fire. Pushed to a stalemate in the center and now turned on their left, the Tory line fell back to the crest of the ridge, continued down the reverse slope, and crossed a creek to an encampment where many of their unarmed comrades were waiting.

The Whig force pressed the retreat to the top of the ridge but upon looking down the hillside saw a new line facing them. They redeployed and totaled up their numbers to find that only 110 rebels remained. More than 170 of Locke's force were now casualties and many others were widely scattered. Realizing their numerical disadvantage, Locke and his officers decided to hold their newly won position and dispatch riders to Rutherford, who was rumored to be approaching. Riding seven miles rearward the couriers discovered the dragoons of Maj. William Davie approaching at a gallop, but before Davie could arrive the Tories retreated, Locke too weak to pursue. Requesting a truce to bury the dead, the Tories secretly disbanded and most headed for home. Colonel Moore and Major Welch escaped with thirty riders and by a roundabout route arrived at the British camp in Camden. Moore found himself in disfavor and was threatened with court-martial for his role in the unauthorized uprising. At length Cornwallis relented and released Moore, deeming it impolitic to hold him to trial.

This brief, extremely vicious clash north of Charlotte was a limited success for the rebels. But in truth the encounter was less a battle than a fight between two armed mobs characterized by the ferocity of its participants. It is difficult to measure the strength of political convictions of the fighters or if the level of physical violence was a measure of the commitment of the backwoods persona to a cause. At Ramsour's Mill, Locke's four hundred rebels encountered an active force of seven hundred Tories, with both groups demonstrating a willingness to fight despite inept leadership. Casualties are hard to ascertain, save through the memoirs of participants. Patriot losses were declared to be 70 slain and 150 wounded while Tory losses were deemed about equal, bolstered by almost 50 captives. This compilation of more than 400 casualties from 1,100 men in action was more than 28 percent and in many cases exceeded the rate of losses in revolutionary battles between trained troops, where contests were often decided in favor of the better-trained and supplied participants. As better trained men fought, the level of combat casualties escalated.

On the morning following the battle, friends and neighbors of both parties gathered to locate the wounded and bury the slain. Fifty-six bodies were recovered from the ridge upon which most of the hand-to-hand action occurred. A long trench was dug on the hillside, into which the remains of both Tories and Whigs were placed, the rites performed by representatives of both sides. Captain Falls' wife rode twenty-five miles in an old wagon to find her husband's remains and wrapping his body in a quilt, conveyed him home for burial.

The defeat curtailed Loyalist support in western North Carolina for a time, a fact lamented by Cornwallis. He remarked angrily that the folly and impatience of his Loyalist friends in their premature actions would cause him unpardonable difficulties in later campaigns. As if a prophet, his assessment would prove correct. Months later when his army moved north he received little support from the German and Scotch farmers who had fought so long and so well at Ramsour's Mill that day. While the brawl had little long-term military significance, it should have illustrated to the British command through its quickly magnified size and ferocious intensity that this partisan civil war was growing in scope and would prove more and more difficult to control by conventional forces.

Huck's Defeat

A second significant, although smaller, confrontation between Whigs and Tories followed, occurring on the twelfth of July at James Williamson's Plantation in York County, South Carolina. Involving limited numbers of participants, this onslaught gained significance by pitting troops from well-trained British provincial units against Colonial partisans, escalating the level of combat and expected casualties. In an effort to destroy the Aetna Iron Works, located in the Catawba Valley and a major source of musket balls for rebel use, British colonel John Turnbull, in command at Rocky Mount, decided to send a mounted raiding column into the valley to burn the works and its surrounding outbuildings. This legitimately justifiable military target, however, became an excuse for the expedition's commander, Christian Huck, to conduct a terror raid.

A wealthy Philadelphia Tory lawyer, Huck was ruined when the British withdrew from his native city in 1778. His extensive real estate holdings were confiscated and the Pennsylvania Supreme Executive Council charged Huck with treason. This turn of events forced the avid Loyalist to find service in a provincial unit, and he attained a commission in Emmerick's Chasseurs. Soon he was dispatched south, attached to Lt. Col. Banastre Tarleton's British Legion although he was never officially a Legion officer. Huck proved to be an intelligent, hard-driving leader, but his experiences had left him bitter, impulsive, and vindictive, all qualities that compromised his ability to command.

Operating in the chaos of the back country, Huck, a devoted Quaker, openly displayed his intense hatred for the Scotch-Irish populace and their Presbyterian church.

Impeccably uniformed and spouting profanity, he led a column of riders down into the Catawba Valley, intent on his mission and also determined to push the rebels as far as possible. His raiding column was small, consisting of thirty-five British Legion dragoons, twenty mounted infantrymen of the New York Volunteers, and about sixty Tory militiamen. Marching on June 16, he arrived at and incinerated Hill's Iron Works on the eighteenth, finding the site truly a tremendous supply of musket balls. Plumes of smoke from burning houses soon marked the progress of his column, for the angry Loyalist torched every house along the route. Horses and beeves were confiscated, food, clothing, and valuables appropriated. Many male residents were arrested, incarcerated, and threatened with hanging. On one occasion, Huck torched the church of rebel Presbyterian minister John Simpson, an event later depicted in the movie *The Patriot,* but thankfully there were no communicants inside. Huck constantly debased local religious leaders and rounded up a number of hostages in an old corncrib, attempting to intimidate their wives and kin in order to acquire information under threat of executions. Riding a few miles farther, he reached the abandoned plantation of James Williamson, and there he decided to camp for the night of July 11, before applying the torch.

Carelessly, Huck permitted his column to bivouac alongside a wide lane between split rail fences paralleling the impressive entry lane to Williamson's house. The soldiers erected their tents in the area, while the officers took possession of Williamson's stout, two-story log house. No opposition had materialized so Huck detailed only a quartet of sentries, and his remaining Loyalists sought their blankets. This gross inattention to military safety would lead to unceremonious interruption between 4 A.M. and dawn.

The seeming lack of pursuit was misleading, for riders had galloped far and wide along Huck's route seeking rebel partisan bands. Numbers of men were gathering under leaders such as William Bratton, John McClure, and Edward Lacey, Jr. Incensed by viewing the smoking ruins of homes and barns, riders massed in wooded glens, intent on retribution. As usual in partisan fights, though, cooperation was difficult to obtain, for rumors and false information abounded. As many as five hundred riders were marshaled during the late afternoon, but there was so much confusion that only about half that number reached the scene of Williamson's Plantation.

First Bratton's men arrived about dark, and he reconnoitered the Tory camp, shocked to discover the inadequate level of alert. Before midnight two additional Whig bands appeared and the leaders developed a well-conceived strategy. Two of the parties would approach the split rail fences from opposite directions, catching the Tories in a cross fire, and the third unit would infiltrate a nearby orchard, charging into the farmyard about the house. Silently Bratton's men reached the rail fence line and laid their weapons across the wooden ramparts about seventy-five yards from the tents of their enemies, the sentries sleeping peacefully and unaware. When daylight broke a point-blank volley was poured into the tents. Soon, McClure's men arrived and Lacey's force sprinted through the orchard and infiltrated the barnyard. The Tories were neatly surrounded and could only surrender or flee.

Captain Huck refused to consider capitulation. Rushing to the doorway of the log house, he ordered a bayonet charge but received no support. Throwing on his blood red coat, Huck dashed into the yard, drew his sword, and mounted his horse, arrogantly commanding, "Disburse, you rebels!" A number of rifle flashes followed with Thomas Carroll, a backwoods rifleman, being credited with firing the ball that struck the Loyalist captain behind the neck, killing him instantly. As his sword flashed across the yard and his body heavily hit the ground all resistance ceased, although many Tories sought escape, every man for himself. Rebels recovered their mounts and the chase began in every direction. Casualties were heavy among Huck's column, for vengeance for the burning of homes and barns was uppermost among the minds of the rebels. Tarleton reported that only twenty-four survivors reached his camp, implying that ninety or more were killed or captured. This figure may be high, as turncoats or deserters were common and often not tabulated until later. Pursuit was eager, however, and rumors of Tories being hung were possibly accurate.

The battle at Williamson's Plantation was a signal triumph for the rebels. It marked an improvement in the organization of and cooperation among the rebel units. In addition, the partisans demonstrated they could stand battle against Loyalist troops regarded as almost the equivalent of redcoats. William Hill, owner of the ironworks, remarked that "it had a tendency to inspire the Americans with courage and determination that the enemy was not invincible." Lord Cornwallis openly stated, "The unlucky affair that happened to Capt. Huck had given me great uneasiness." The assessments of both men should be modified by consideration of the foolish, inept leadership of the blustering Huck. His decision to encamp in hostile territory without adequate sentries being posted was completely unsupportable. Nonetheless, the psychological effect of Huck's defeat proved of great value to rising partisan forces in the south and became highly celebrated in the back country.

Rocky Mount and Hanging Rock

Encouraged by rebel success at Williamson's Plantation, another South Carolina militia veteran began to increase a cadre of followers along the North Carolina border. Having served ably in the revolutionary army that defended Charles Town in June of 1776 and marched across the state to assist in pacifying the Cherokee, Col. Thomas Sumter had achieved considerable reputation in back country militia circles. Bored, he returned home to the High Hills of the Santee during the shadow war that followed, intent on mending his suffering business ventures. Sumter did not return to defend Charles Town in 1780, perhaps contemplating maintaining his guarded neutrality, but in the spring he received a warning that a squadron of Tarleton's dragoons were crossing the Santee River, searching for his plantation. Sumter donned his old Continental coat, buckled on his sword, and rode north, prepared to fight again.

Capt. Charles Campbell and his dragoons galloped up to Sumter's home at Great Savannah on May 28, 1780, only to discover that their quarry had recently flown. Frustrated, the British officer determined to gain some measure of revenge by torching the Sumter property. Dragoons carried Sumter's invalid wife, Mary, who was seated in a rattan chair, outside and into the yard. The buildings were then torched while she and eleven-year-old Tom, Jr., observed. The enmity earned for that afternoon's work would prove extravagant to the king's cause. Intimidating tactics applied to men such as Sumter constantly backfired, for his rage and desire for retribution overcame all fear or hesitation, a fact constantly misunderstood by many British officers.

An egocentric overachiever, Sumter was a prima donna of the first order, but he was also a recruiter of partisans without peer, utilizing every ploy, including revenge, plunder, and loot to inspire men to follow his lead. Sumter's operational techniques were less successful, for his expeditions were often characterized by impatience, rashness, and costly frontal assaults. However, his tireless energy, unlimited personal courage, and ability to inspire others made Sumter a most dangerous opponent to British invaders of South Carolina. Subsisting on plunder and completely self-determined, Sumter was analogous to the twentieth-century warlords of China.

In late July, Sumter gathered several hundred riders and, fortunately, recruited the services of Maj. William Davie. The two men determined to assail the outposts of Lord Rawdon that were scattered north of Camden. Sumter plotted an attack with five hundred men on a Tory detachment posted at Rocky Mount, while Davie, the young Princeton graduate, would demonstrate toward Hanging Rock to prevent possible Tory support. Riding in the rear of Davie's column was a skinny thirteen year old destined to become the seventh president of his still unborn country, Andrew Jackson.

Lt. Col. George Turnbull and his 150 tough veterans of the New York Volunteers were encamped at Rocky Mount. Small in number, they devised defenses in a group of log buildings that were skillfully surrounded by an abatis of sharpened tree limbs. When Sumter arrived on July 30 and launched a direct assault, he was rudely repulsed with heavy casualties by the plucky old Yankee Tory and his men. Without benefit of artillery, Sumter attempted to fire the wooden buildings, but a severe, sudden rainstorm stymied that effort. The eight-hour siege that followed was primarily a sniping contest with few casualties and an embarrassed Sumter was finally forced to retreat. Meanwhile, Davie arrived at Hanging Rock some fifteen miles east and quickly realized he was outnumbered and outgunned. While conducting a reconnaissance he noted a column of Col. Morgan Bryan's North Carolina Volunteers approaching. Skillfully, Davie cut off the new arrivals and attacked, cutting them to pieces in full view of five hundred Tories. He captured sixty horses and one hundred weapons and adroitly led his eighty riders and military plunder to join forces with Sumter.

Sumter and Davie regrouped. Further volunteers had swollen their ranks to eight hundred and the garrison at Hanging Rock, although numerous, was unfortified and vulnerable. Tory units camped at Hanging Rock included the Prince of Wales Loyal American Regiment, the infantry of the British Legion, Browne's Florida Rangers, and the survivors of Bryan's North Carolinians, all commanded by Col. John Carden. Sumter planned a night march and a dawn surprise attack with three separate columns utilizing a mounted infantry style by which columns would approach mounted, then form and attack on foot. The plan fell apart, as all three units intermingled, but the large mass of troops drove through the dispersed Tory camps. As the Tories fled from their encampments, Sumter's men who had charged with such stern bravery fell victim to the lure of loot, plundering the enemy camps and liquor supplies, losing all sense of discipline. As threatening British forces approached, only the inestimable efforts of Davie and his riders rescued Sumter's mob. The Loyalist Prince of Wales Regiment was destroyed as a fighting unit and more than two hundred casualties were absorbed by the Tories. Sumter's casualties were much fewer, although the valuable Captain McClure was slain. This significant set of actions concluded unpleasantly but could have presented a serious setback to Lord Rawdon, save for the interruption of demon Jamaican rum.

Fishing Creek

As the American southern army of Maj. Gen. Horatio Gates prepared to move south on its ill-fated journey to Camden, the independent-minded Thomas Sumter rode down the opposite side of the Catawba River searching for plunder amid Tory camps that were emptied as Rawdon consolidated his troops. Sumter dispatched Colonel Taylor to invest Carey's Fort, a small redoubt located at Wateree Ferry, whereupon a colonel, thirty troopers, and thirty-six wagons of rum, clothing, and food fell into rebel hands. Taylor learned from his prisoners that a large provisioning column was approaching from the British post at Ninety-six and decided to ambush this reinforcing unit. Successful in his surprise ambush, he added another fifty captives and an invaluable herd of beef cattle to his booty.

Sumter and his contingent joined Taylor on the river road, suddenly hearing the roar of artillery fire from the direction of Camden but unaware of the battle's outcome. Presently, three riders splashed across the Catawba and Capt. Nathaniel Martin approached Sumter with disturbing news of the Colonial defeat. The vigilant Davie, aware of Sumter's vulnerable position, had sent Martin to inform Sumter of the rout and his own exposed danger. Tarleton's Dragoons had been unleashed by Cornwallis to find

Sumter despite their exhaustion from pursuing Gates' flee-ing army. Tarleton gave his riders no rest, urging them on to scatter Sumter.

Beginning to retreat, Sumter was encumbered with pris-oners, wagons, and cattle; therefore, his progress was slow in the heat and sun, but he resolutely refused to abandon any of his plunder. Increasing the pace, the column marched all day and night and into the next day. Slowly, Sumter's force crossed Fishing Creek at Cow Ford and at noon he encamped, reasoning that he was safely removed from the battlefield. Allowing his men to light cook fires and bathe, Sumter removed his blue and red-faced regi-mental coat as well as his boots and crawled under a wagon to fall asleep. Capt. John Moffitt's riders arrived at Sumter's camp, and James Collins, a sixteen-year-old cavalryman, recalled that "the men were greatly fatigued. . . . many fast asleep and scattered in every direction."

Sumter had badly misjudged the aggressive Tarleton. The British cavalryman had many faults, but relentless energy in pursuit was one of his primary attributes. Once the bit was in his cheek, he would never relent. Tarleton had begun pursuit with 350 men and a single three-pound gun. He pushed rapidly forward, advancing to the Catawba, and made a cold camp to avoid alerting his quarry. Crossing the river, the British force followed Sumter's easily visible trail up the west side of the Catawba. At Fishing Creek, Tarleton was surprised to find few challengers. His infantrymen were exhausted, so he emplaced them in an advantageous posi-tion on a hilltop and continued on with 160 riders—100 dragoons and 60 light infantrymen, most riding double. His 160 men would soon face Sumter's almost 800. British scouts collided with rebel outriders, whom they scattered, and a sergeant and four privates proceeded to the crest of a nearby hill. Excitedly, the scouts returned to summon Tarleton. He rode forward and found the rebel force encamped, arms stacked, sleeping, eating, and resting: an unprecedented opportunity. The British commander never hesitated despite the large disparity in numbers. Forming his riders into one line he charged the rebel camp, bugles blowing and sabers hacking. Many patriots were cut off from their weapons and horses and forced to run for the woods. The attack generated a perfect rout, an indiscriminate slaughter with no quarter given as the Americans scattered. Only minimal fighting occurred near the captured supply wagons as Sumter fled on a wagon horse without a saddle, abandoning coat and boots.

Tarleton recovered the captured British troops and numerous loaded wagons of stores. Inflicting 150 American casualties and capturing more than 300 militiamen, his exhausted riders finally curtailed their pursuit. Only 15 British casualties were reported, although, oddly, Capt. Charles Campbell, the officer who had burned Sumter's home, was slain near the wagons. Tarleton and his legionnaires returned to Camden on the twenty-first with their recovered booty, to the plaudits of Cornwallis and his army. His lordship wrote: "Lt. Col. Tarleton executed this service with his usual activity and military address." Young James Collins and his American comrades, like their commander, slept in the woods for days, finally making their way to Davie's camp near Charlotte.

Occurring immediately after the rout at Camden, the clash at Fishing Creek reversed the growing rebel power in South Carolina. British assumptions that insurrection and commotion in the province would subside seemed more reasonable. Sumter's reputation suffered greatly from the surprise attack at Fishing Creek. With a five to one numerical advantage, he had ignored proper security and been routed and chased by aggressive enemy forces. But soon the resilient partisan was again recruiting and organizing his militia unit, surprisingly finding ample volunteers among rebels who overlooked his liabilities in light of his spirit and determination.

Musgrove Mill

As Cornwallis routed Gates at Camden and Tarleton scattered Sumter's raiders at Fishing Creek, Col. Charles McDowell was nervously fencing with a Tory column under Lt. Col. Patrick Ferguson some miles westward. One of a pair of brothers from Quaker Meadows, North Carolina, McDowell was never very successful as a military commander, but he served patriot aims well through his ability to organize back country forces. In this instance, somewhat panicked by a rapid British advance, he dispatched a message over the mountains to his friend Isaac Shelby in modern East Tennessee, begging for support in resisting the enemy. Shelby, an experienced militia soldier, raised a small force of about two hundred volunteer mounted riflemen and crossed the Alleghenies to join McDowell at Cherokee Ford on the Broad River. Upon arrival Shelby found a third compatriot already in camp, the tough Col. Elijah Clarke and his Georgia rebels.

McDowell, deciding to act as a theatre commander, dispatched the two, Shelby and Clarke, on a series of missions against local Tory strong points, with some success. On June 30, Thicketty Fort, a strong, well-manned Tory redoubt, was invested and captured by the duo, who acquired many weapons and a large supply of powder. Soon Clarke and Shelby led another foray into South Carolina that culminated in a pitched fight at Cedar Springs with Major Dunlap of Ferguson's command. An inauspicious charge by Dunlap resulted in his abrupt repulse by the patriots, who pursued and were in turn countered by Ferguson. Shelby and Clarke returned to McDowell's camp tired and hungry but anxious for continued action. In contrast, Shelby's men were desirous of returning home, fearing that Indian uprisings might threaten their homes and families, but Shelby convinced them to remain for one more fight before their enlistment period expired.

On August 17, McDowell sent Clarke and Shelby on another mission. Joined by Col. James Williams and a militia company, the patriot officers silently led their riders out before nightfall, headed toward an enemy encampment reported near Musgrove Mill. The shadowy file of riders rode all night on narrow trails through heavy woods, arriving near the Tory camp about dawn. Shelby deployed five scouts forward across the Enoree River, and when they drew fire from alert enemy sentinels, he prepared to attack. Suddenly a nearby farmer rode into Shelby's camp, informing the rebels that Col. Daniel Clarey's Tory garrison had been reinforced the previous afternoon by the arrival of Col. Alexander Innes from Ninety-six with several companies of the New Jersey Volunteers and Delancey's New York Battalion. He estimated the combined enemy force in excess of five hundred men, rather than the anticipated two hundred.

Shelby and Clarke conferred quietly, considering their newly acquired information. Their horses were dead tired following the forty-mile overnight ride, but the enemy seemed too strong to attack. In addition, Ferguson was camped only fourteen miles away, and the aggressive Innes had discovered their presence through Shelby's probing. Their only recourse seemed to stand fast and fight rather than flee. Withdrawing a few miles to Cedar Shoal Creek, the rebels began construction of a semicircular, chest-high defensive line of brush and downed logs. The horses were picketed in the rear and the riders deployed: Shelby's riflemen assembled on the right, Williams' South Carolina militia held the center, and Clarke's Georgians massed on the left. A small force of twenty horsemen was concealed on each flank, and Clarke appointed a forty-man reserve force.

Now prepared to fight, Shelby sent Capt. Shadrach Inman, an old Georgia partisan, with twenty-five riders on a probing mission in hopes of enticing Innes to fight. Inman succeeded, with the hard-pursuing Tory column charging into American lines. Bugles blowing and drums beating, the Tories shouted and charged with bayonets, and a tough hand-to-hand fight developed about the hastily constructed rebel barricade. Gradually, enemy numbers forced Shelby's riflemen to give ground, and matters became grave. Clarke then sent in his reserve to boost Shelby's line. Heavy smoke hung close to the ground, limiting visibility to twenty feet or less. Suddenly a fortunate incident changed the course of the entire contest. Colonel Innes, a brave and capable officer, was up front on the rebel right where the battle was fierce. A rifle ball fired by one of Shelby's riflemen wounded him. William Smith declared, "I've killed their leader." The Tory line hesitated, confused and uncertain. Sensing the indecision, Shelby ordered his line to charge and sent forward the horsemen on his flank. Clarke then charged from the opposite wing, unleashing a fierce Indian yell. A panic ensued, precipitating a rout as Tory infantrymen threw away their weapons and fled. Many were turncoats, having served previously in patriot militia, and they knew their fate if captured. The brave Inman was shot seven times, a rifle ball to the forehead sealing his fate.

As Shelby and Clarke prepared to pursue, a courier, Francis Jones, arrived on a lathered horse. McDowell had learned of Gates' defeat and sent word to his subordinates to retreat to Gilbert Town. The rebel expedition was now dangerously exposed and must rapidly react to extract itself. Aligning their seventy prisoners, the rebels began to withdraw in a northwesterly direction, close to the friendly mountain ridges. Constantly they were pushed by a detachment of Ferguson's troops. After a bone-jarring ride of sixty miles without stopping, living on green peaches and raw field corn, the exhausted riders reached McDowell's camp, ill and exhausted.

In forty-eight hours the rebel column had completed two marches totaling almost 120 miles and fought a tough stand-up encounter. Rebel losses were never accurately ascertained. Tory casualties included sixty-three killed, ninety wounded, and seventy captured: severe losses from a five-hundred-man force. Certainly these losses would have been heavier if the rebels had pursued the fleeing troops. At Gilbert Town the patriot leaders agreed on a plan for reassembly to confront Ferguson if he advanced farther. Links of communication were established and Colonel Williams escorted the prisoners to Gates' camp at Hillsborough. Clarke and his Georgians left on the mountain trail south, while Shelby's riflemen began the return climb over the Appalachians.

Marion at Black Mingo

Somewhat east of Camden, in the swamp country formed by the rivers Black, Lynches, and Pee Dee, another partisan leader was emerging, one who would be considered the most gifted in American history. Any narrative on the southern revolutionary campaigns would be remiss without mention of the mysterious Francis Marion, the "Swamp Fox" of the Carolinas. Without the benefit of social position or education Marion rose to mythological status in American folklore through innate intelligence, courage, character, and tactical abilities. During the nadir of Colonial hopes following Camden, his reputation evolved into the model of a guerilla leader, soaring and exaggerated in the pantheon of popular beliefs.

Francis Marion was reared in a French Huguenot family of modest means, receiving his initial military experience in the South Carolina regiments that participated under British command in the Cherokee Indian wars of the 1760s. He was assigned the command of a fifty-man company and performed conspicuously although appalled by the policy of burning the towns and fields of the Indians. He commented afterwards that he found such destruction a shocking sight and could scarcely refrain himself from tears as the very staff of Cherokee life sank under the swords and torches of his men. Those in authority noted his abilities, and Marion was advanced in militia rank when the South Carolina army was established in 1775. He was assigned to command an artillery section during the British attack on Charles Town in 1776, directing the fire of his guns from the sand and palmetto fortress of Fort Moultrie. Ever the practical warrior, Marion learned to skip the fire from his smoothbore guns into the wooden sides of the British warships, a practice that increased accuracy and damage. When Breach Inlet could not be crossed, the Colonial gunners achieved a solid little victory. Marion marched to Savannah in 1779 to fight in the terrible assault of Spring Hill Redoubt where hundreds of Colonial and French lives were wasted. Marion followed Col. John

Laurens into the ditch before the redoubt, planting the flag on the berm, but miraculously he was unhurt.

In late July of 1780, accompanied by twenty oddly attired swamp dwellers, Marion arrived at General Gates' camp at Rugeley's Mills, North Carolina, to offer his services to the Colonial army. Unimpressed, Gates sent Marion and his men south to burn boats and bridges over the Santee River, ostentatiously trapping Rawdon's forces, which he was about to attack. Some days later, as he rode downstream, Marion was informed of the American debacle at Camden, an event he probably expected, for he issued no comment. Suddenly he was isolated, alone in command of a tiny detachment of virtual outlaws without sources of support or information. Gradually he began to assimilate a small group of followers, but his force was always subject to wide fluctuations. At times he scarcely could muster twenty troopers, while on other occasions he rode with seven hundred men at his back. Marion realized he must win the minds of his unpaid volunteers by providing them with successes, yet still sparing their lives. He opposed firmly the burning of Tory homes, whippings, and hanging, practices that had rapidly became common in the chaos of uncivil partisan warfare. Conversely, he was sometimes forced to punish the turncoats and informers that abounded to appease the anger of his men.

Marion rode first into the swamps and bogs of his rivers searching for secure bases from which to launch his personal war against Tory militia and British supply lines. A geographic triangle formed by lines drawn between the villages of Cheraw, Kingstree, and Georgetown formed the heart of his operational zone, the marshes provided refuge, and families and residents freely gave assistance and alarm. His favorite encampment was on Snow Island, a high, dry ridge between the Pee Dee and Lynches Rivers. This five-mile-long island was the property of William Goddard, whose fields marked the only cleared area amid heavy woods and tangled thickets. The partisans constructed lean-to shelters and dry caches for powder and supplies in the woods. Bridges were stripped of boards, fords obstructed, and boats sunk or hidden. Eventually, Marion erected so many swamp camps that he could move nightly from one to another. His camps were well picketed, as Marion was the lone southern partisan whose emphasis on security was so severe that his enemies never surprised him.

He began his military endeavors by pursuing a guard force under Capt. Jonathan Roberts that was escorting prisoners captured at Camden to Charles Town. Surprising and capturing the marchers he turned his column and disappeared into nearby swamps, leaving no trace of his passage. Emerging some miles away, he sparred with and scattered the Tory militia units of Micajah Ganey and Jesse Barfield, producing panic among local Loyalist residents. Maj. James Moncrief, the garrison commander at Georgetown, organized two columns to entrap Marion. He dispatched a force of redcoats and Hessians under Maj. James Wemyss and another of Tories led by Col. John Bull to surround and entrap Marion. Wemyss was a vigilant, aggressive, and ruthless officer, having burned more than fifty homes in a swathe from Kingstree to Cheraw. However, by these hard-line efforts, Wemyss became Francis Marion's most successful recruiting officer, angering residents into supporting the rebel leader.

Marion circled first around Wemyss and then drove Bull's Tories in panic into the streets of Georgetown. Such impertinence brought a rapid response from Lord Cornwallis, who was reluctant to march north with Marion across his supply line. He dispatched his best cavalry unit, the British Legion of Tarleton, to disperse Marion, setting up one of the most famed encounters in Colonial partisan history. Tarleton collected a number of local Tory units to support his green coats and developed a shrewd scheme to surround and capture the rebel force. Establishing a Tory camp in plain view, Tarleton concealed his men in anticipation of a night attack. But when Marion arrived to view the force so innocently encamped in the open, he instantly recognized the trap, turned, and retreated. Tarleton began a frustrated pursuit. His sweating, hard-riding dragoons pursued Marion's riders for seven hours in a chase that covered twenty-seven miles, until the rebels disappeared suddenly into Ox Swamp. Tarleton drew rein and staring into the trackless morass, called off the chase, muttering, "As for this damned old fox [Marion], the devil himself could not catch him." From this oft-repeated statement Marion's nom de plume as the "Swamp Fox" was born.

The partisan war was escalating, growing in ferocity and scope, as Marion, Sumter, and others did not hesitate to confront Cornwallis's professionals. The rise in numbers and successes among partisans was reflected in the numbers of back country fighters who reported in militia units and participated in later battles. From a position of seeming invincibility, the vastly superior southern army of the world's primary military power was gradually surrendering the initiative to a ragtag conglomeration of guerilla fighters. During the last five or six months of 1780, British armies absorbed heavy losses in almost constant encounters with back country partisans. Every supply column, every payroll delivery was contested. More than 1,200 British soldiers were killed or wounded and an additional 1,286 captured and marched north to Colonial prison camps. These valuable troopers would not be easily replaced. Rebel militia leaders, always politically inspiring, were developing the skills to conduct military operations successfully. Soon a new commander, Nathanael Greene, would arrive, a leader with an outstanding strategic gift: the ability to weave marauding partisan raiders into a coherent pattern of coordination with a field army. This unlikely combination would prove deadly to British goals. A liaison was also established with those mythical frontiersmen who resided over the mountains in the wilderness valleys of Tennessee and Kentucky. This lifeline, these hard, serious men whose purpose was the tracking of human game, would offer assistance soon.

CHAPTER 7

Battle at Kings Mountain

"Kings Mountain was the first link in a chain of evil events that followed each other in regular succession until they at last ended in the total loss of America."

Sir Henry Clinton

The brightly uniformed soldiers dispatched by George III to subjugate the rebellious citizens of his North American provinces were, at that particular historical juncture, possibly the world's best soldiers. Tempered in constant European warfare while accustomed to coolly cowing native insurrections with a show of bright red coats in disciplined alignment, the soldiers assumed an easy arrogance bred of success that often fostered a dangerous underestimation of the fighting prowess of their enemies. Nowhere in the British army was this attitude more pervasive than among the pampered young officer caste that led the elite regiments of the monarch. Purchasers of their rank, these arrogant sons of the gentry were often insufferable in barracks and boorish amid the drawing salons of London, but just as likely unbelievably brave and daring in combat. Throughout history, however, gross disrespect for the peculiar abilities of one's opponents has led to startling military reversals. This consistent miscalculation of the determination and fighting qualities of rebel back country settlers was the principal cause of the disastrous defeat of a proud little Loyalist army at Kings Mountain, South Carolina, on October 7, 1780, and the concurring demise of one of the most outstanding officers in service in America, the personable and brave Maj. Patrick Ferguson.

Thin, oval-faced Patrick Ferguson was a handsome, intelligent, rather impulsive officer of twenty years' military service to the Empire. But in 1777 he proved as guilty as his compatriots in assessing American military abilities. On one occasion he was heard to comment, "A volley and a dash of cold steel was just the dose to cause rebels to break and once on the run such troops would never rally." Ferguson and his fellows misunderstood the impetus for reactionary violence possessed by the settlers of the southern Appalachian uplands. Schooled in intermittent combat with marauding Indians, these backwoodsmen learned how to expertly handle their weapons, the value of adroitly fighting from cover, when to retreat—even flee headlong—and to always exercise unmerciful vengeance on a vulnerable foe.

Of Scottish heritage, young Ferguson was born on May 24, 1744, and grew up amid the bustling, exciting city of Edinburgh, Scotland, where his solicitor father, James Ferguson, Lord Pitfour, served as Lord Commissioner. His mother, Anne Murray, was of an equally noble Scottish family, and her brother, Brig. Gen. James Murray, who replaced the dying Gen. James Wolfe on the Plains of Abraham during the French and Indian War, advocated a military career for his nephew Patrick from birth, leaving orders that the youngster be enrolled in military school at Woolwich. Patrick and his five brothers and sisters were reared in physical comfort amid an atmosphere of intellectual culture and learning. With his summers spent exploring the city, young Ferguson was especially enthralled with the great stone castle frowning down from its lofty perch. He witnessed the pomp and panoply of the Scottish regiments parading daily behind their pipers from their Edinburgh Castle barracks and, an impressionable youth, he listened breathlessly to fanciful tales of battles won and lost, as spun by bearded old campaigners. Patrick attended the Royal Military Academy at Woolwich and enlisted in the Royal North British Dragoons, later the Scots Greys, as a sublieutenant when he was barely fifteen. Soon the slightly built youngster joined his regiment in Germany, fighting boldly against the powerful French cavalry at Minden. Commended for bravery on two occasions, Patrick fell seriously ill, as did much of his regiment, from the effects of foul drinking water. He probably contracted a mild case of typhoid and was posted back to Edinburgh Castle in 1762. When his illness persisted he was forced to resign his commission.

In 1768 at age twenty-four, his health much improved, Ferguson again joined the king's service, on this occasion purchasing a captain's commission in the Seventieth Regiment of Foot, where he served as company commander under his cousin, Lt. Col. Alexander Johnstone. Performing admirably in tours in Grenada and Tobago, Ferguson enjoyed the tropical climate and lush vegetation. He also campaigned against the fierce Caribs on the island of St. Vincent. Contacting yellow fever he was assigned pleasant duty in Halifax, Nova Scotia, but again fell ill due to a flare up of arthritis and was posted back to London in 1773. Extremely frustrated, Patrick feared his army career, even though marked by exemplary service, was doomed by the continual relapses of his health.

While assigned to barracks duty, the industrious Ferguson, who enjoyed both books and fiddle, became bored and began experimentation with a remarkable breechloading rifle originally of French invention. Isaac de la Chaumette, a Frenchman of inventive talent, had designed the breechloading weapon in 1704 but fled to England for religious purposes and never completed the weapon. Ferguson altered the original weapon's breech-block, reconfiguring the breech in such a manner as to increase the containment of gasses and accuracy of the weapon. The ramming step was eliminated, thereby increasing speed of firing and permitting the weapon to be loaded while kneeling or even prone. Ferguson demonstrated this rifled gun at Woolwich Arsenal on April 27, 1776, before a highly skeptical British military audience. He began his demonstration by firing at a rate of four shots a minute, which he increased to seven. Marching toward a target, he proceeded to fire and reload while in movement. Of course, Ferguson's skill with rifle or pistol presented an advantage, for he was widely considered the best marks-man in the king's service—many even credited him as among the best marksmen living, claiming that his loading and firing ability surpassed even the best of American frontiersmen—but his weapon far outshone the conventional Brown Bess musket then standard issue to all British regiments. Ferguson's evolutions were performed at a target range of more than two hundred yards, well over twice the range of conventional guns. The fifty-inch-long weapon weighed 7½ pounds, some one-third lighter than the Brown Bess, and carried a twenty-five-inch razor-sharp bayonet. So impressed were the king and his ministers that one hundred guns were ordered and Ferguson was assigned to supervise their production. Patrick also experimented with an artillery piece of breechloading capacity, a small, easily maneuvered one-pounder of extended range. Summoned to active service in North America, he never completed this model.

During the winter of 1777, a company of one hundred light infantrymen was organized, outfitted with unique green jackets, and instructed by Ferguson himself in the use of the newly manufactured rifle. In March, Captain Ferguson led his new command aboard ship for transport to America and service in Sir Henry Clinton's army. The newly developed rifles would be field-tested in the forests of America against rebels who would demonstrate they also had a firearm of long-range accuracy.

Ferguson's company scouted from Head of Elk northward as British general Robert Howe's army approached Philadelphia. But it was September 11, 1777, at the Battle of Brandywine before Ferguson's breechloaders were first tested in actual combat. Near Chad's Ford the green-clad riflemen were engaged as skirmishers in a tough, hard-contested delaying action. The company absorbed heavy losses, a musket ball shattering Patrick Ferguson's right elbow. So serious was his wound that he was compelled to argue vociferously with attending physicians determined to remove his limb. While he succeeded in retaining his arm, the limb was forever useless. Such a handicap was a severe liability to an outstanding marksman, swordsman, and horseman, handicapping the physical prowess of which he was so proud. While he was convalescing over a period of almost seven months, Lord Howe reassigned the company of riflemen. Only Patrick Ferguson and several of his subordinate officers retained the potent breechloading weapons.

An eerie tale involving Ferguson and a chance encounter with a grandly uniformed and unidentified American officer spread rapidly through the army. Ferguson and several of his riflemen were concealed in heavy woods near

Germantown, Pennsylvania, when two Colonial officers attired in blue and green rode into view, approaching to within about one hundred yards. One of the officers, a large man astride a bay horse and wearing a large cocked hat, seemed of commanding presence, so Ferguson stepped forward from concealment, challenging the intruder to surrender. The American, motionless, stared at Ferguson for several minutes, then deliberately turned his back and rode slowly away. Despite the pleas of his riflemen Ferguson disdained the easy shot and forbade his men to open fire. Later it was determined that American general George Washington had reconnoitered the area that morning and may have been the officer whom Ferguson observed. Had the Britisher taken the rifle shot, one can but wonder on the outcome of a conflict that at times was almost sustained by the strength of the American general's convictions. When told of the possibility that his encounter was with the commander of the rebel army, Ferguson remarked, "I am not sorry that I did not know at the time who he was."

Despite the serious nature of his wound, Ferguson refused to resign his commission, instead teaching himself to write, fire his pistols, and handle his Spanish blade left-handed. Soon he was assigned command of a unit of Loyalists raiding privateer bases along the New Jersey shore. In a raid on Little Egg Harbor, long a hot bed of American activity, Ferguson demonstrated his ability to conduct a combined land-sea operation, employing tactics of unusual and innovative style. In an attempt to control the area, he also became accustomed to dealing with deserters, turncoats, and double agents. Ferguson zealously attempted to avoid causing hardship to innocent individuals but was equally unrelenting in his punishment of those openly defying the Crown. He developed a strong rapport with New Jersey

Loyalists and on October 25, 1779, was promoted to major in the Second Battalion, Seventy-first Foot. He continued, however, on detached duty with Loyalists, for he proved fair, considerate, and personable in dealings with Americans. He was one of a handful of British regular officers who earned the respect of those ill-fated Colonials who remained loyal to King George III.

Late in 1779, the conflict changed drastically. Sir Henry Clinton, the British commander in chief, became frustrated with the stalemate in the New York area and decided to open a new campaign in the southern colonies. The British high command was desirous of forcing a separation of the three southernmost colonies of Georgia, North Carolina, and South Carolina from the remainder and recovering these provinces for the king. The principal southern seaport, Charles Town, South Carolina, was captured after a siege and Maj. Gen. Lord Charles Cornwallis was assigned to command the British southern army. While not provided a large force of British regulars, the numbers of southern Loyalists flocking to his colors initially encouraged the commander. Patrick Ferguson, with his reputation as a respected leader of loyal Americans, was ordered south to assist Cornwallis, accompanied by his Loyal American Volunteers, a unit composed of several hundred riders from New York and New Jersey. Ferguson was promoted to provincial lieutenant colonel and ordered to raise a legion of southern Loyalists. In April, Clinton promoted Ferguson to the permanent rank of major in the Seventy-first Foot, or Fraser's Highlanders, and he was forced to surrender his provincial rank, although the soldiers still addressed him as colonel.

The initial fight of Ferguson's little corps occurred at McPherson's Plantation and nearly proved fatal for the major. He and his men carefully approached an enemy encampment after nightfall. Finding it deserted, they decided to await the return of the occupants, carefully concealing themselves and planning an ambush. At dawn another British force, the infantry of Tarleton's Legion under Maj. Charles Cochrane, suddenly charged the camp and a spirited clash occurred between the Legion and Ferguson's men. Ferguson, fighting desperately with three assailants, was slashed in his left arm and would have been slain except for Cochrane's belated recognition. With both arms now useless, Ferguson was forced to sit his horse with reins in his teeth. Refusing to abandon the campaign, Ferguson developed a command system wherein he issued orders to his Loyalists through a series of shrill notes from a silver whistle worn on a lanyard about his neck.

Cornwallis was undoubtedly pleased to have the gentlemanly Ferguson join his command, even though he was fully aware of the Scotsman's impetuous and independent nature. Ferguson was affable, witty, and socially gregarious. Irresistible and courtly to the ladies of Charles Town, he developed a reputation as somewhat of a rake. He would encounter Colonials willing to converse and then he would spend hours trying to convince the listeners of the dangers of their rebellious position while attempting to inspire continued loyalty to their lawful sovereign. Ferguson's successful recruiting of Loyalists was based on his personal magnetism and his application of stern, fair military discipline, traits that earned respect and influence among local Tories.

Cornwallis slowly consolidated his position in South Carolina by fortifying strong points in strategic locations about the colony. Establishing a command center near Camden, he utilized Ferguson and Tarleton as leaders of flying columns that attempted to offset the success of American guerilla leaders such as Thomas Sumter and

Francis Marion. When Cornwallis routed Gates at Camden and Tarleton surprised and defeated Sumter at Fishing Creek, momentum swiftly swung to the redcoats. Cornwallis decided to pursue his initial gains with an invasion of North Carolina. Ferguson was ordered west to the critical fort at Ninety-six with his American Loyalist Volunteers to recruit local militia units. He was also assigned responsibility for screening Cornwallis's army from surprise forays from the western mountains. Ferguson worked feverishly to train his new recruits as rumors of raids by patriot militia forming in the mountains became more frequent.

While Patrick Ferguson earnestly strove to make competent soldiers of his recently enlisted Loyalists, a phenomenon occurred in the southern backwoods. In the borderlands of Virginia, North Carolina, South Carolina, and Georgia, as well as in over-the-mountain and unorganized areas of Kentucky and Tennessee, a shadow army was forming. Stung by the challenges of Ferguson, Tarleton, and Cornwallis and convinced of the complicity of the British and hostile Indian tribes, frontiersmen were at last ready to apply their unfelt but considerable power to the rebel cause. Masters of the preemptive strike, they disdained awaiting an invasion of their mountain valleys by redcoats or Indians, preferring to assail the source of their perceived threats, confident in the power of their long rifles to eliminate those who would endanger their freedoms.

As the call to arms circulated among the valleys and hills, frontier leaders of many Indian fights took down their Dickert flintlocks, summoned their followers, and began to move toward the announced rendezvous. While leadership was unordained, unadorned, and tenuous, gradually the companies were organized into battalions or regimental units under accepted commanders. While none of these officers were strategically knowledgeable, all understood and espoused the back country, open-order style of combat where each man was his own captain and shirkers were not tolerated.

From this massing of volunteers, the leadership of four meritorious colonels emerged, four who would form the command group that held together this temporary army and delivered its terrible firepower on Kings Mountain. The two initial instigators of the gathering were neighbors and close friends, John Sevier and Isaac Shelby. A third, William Campbell, added the power and prestige of his Virginia revolutionary militia service, while Benjamin Cleveland was typical of the North Carolina mountain rebel clan, uncompromising, unrelenting, and somewhat brutal. All were self-made men, hardened and tempered on the frontier and determined to complete whatever task they undertook. While of varying ancestry they all had recent immigrant roots. Their personal courage and dedication had been long attested on many an Indian trail, as was their devotion to freedom in the American style. Col. William Campbell of Washington County, Virginia, assembled 400 rifle bearers, the largest contingent, while Col. Isaac Shelby of Sullivan County, North Carolina, and Col. John Sevier of Washington County, North Carolina, each added about 240 combatants. These three units assembled at Sycamore Shoals and force-marched over the mountains, arriving at Quaker Meadows, near present Morgantown, North Carolina, on September 30, 1780. At that juncture, a 350-man contingent from the eastern slopes of the Appalachians, led by Ben Cleveland, joined the assembling army.

Isaac Shelby was making his second journey across the divide, having supported Col. Charles McDowell's North

Carolina militia several months earlier, and was perhaps the first to recognize the serious threat offered by Ferguson's continued presence. The son of Evan Shelby, Jr., a tough old fur trapper of Welsh origin, Isaac was reared as a cattle herder. Born on December 11, 1750, in Maryland, he had moved in 1771 to a claim on the Holston River near present-day Bristol, Tennessee. Isaac had marched to Point Pleasant as a lieutenant in his father's company, taking over command when Evan replaced the slain Col. John Field as regimental commander. His contributions proved critical to the survival of Col. Andrew Lewis's army. Despite an absence of rudimentary education, Isaac quickly demonstrated his innate leadership. Tall, heavily muscled, with dark eyebrows and a strong chin, he rose rapidly in Virginia militia ranks. Promoted to captain by Patrick Henry, Isaac performed so effectively as commissioner of supplies for the Virginia forts that Thomas Jefferson elevated his status to major.

In the spring of 1780, upon return from a journey to survey Kentucky land claims, he received an urgent appeal from Charles McDowell to raise a force and march east to assist in the repulse of bands of Tories, then overrunning the North Carolina foothills. Shelby responded with two hundred select mounted riflemen, the first organized response of southern backwoodsmen to the conflict now entering the southern provinces of North America. After a series of fights from Thicketty Fort to Cedar Shoal Creek, and informed of the rout at Camden, Shelby withdrew into the mountains. He and his riders returned to their homes promising to return when an expedition was formed to entrap Ferguson, now identified as the primary enemy. Shelby, the tireless, reserved frontiersman served his country well. After the revolution he became first governor of Kentucky and in 1813 led four thousand volunteers to join William Henry Harrison's army in Canada. He died of apoplexy in 1826.

Shelby's close compatriot, John Sevier, was almost like a brother although the two were quite different personalities. While Shelby was reserved and aloof, Sevier was possessed of great charisma. Short, stocky, and well muscled, Sevier claimed he could outride, outshoot, and out curse most of those who followed him. He was brave, fearless to the point of rashness, but also enjoyed a frolic or party and could become quite wild while in his cups. Sevier was born on September 23, 1745, in the Valley of Virginia, his father, Valentine, of Huguenot lineage. Valentine married Joanne Goade and they settled near New Market, Virginia, where John was reared. John was married at seventeen to Sarah Hawkins and moved to a plot on the Holston River, residing only miles from the Shelby clan. He volunteered for service with Col. William Christian's Cherokee war force, performing well as both a company captain and a scout. In time Sevier participated in over thirty Indian fights, more than almost any of his contemporaries. When Sarah died in 1780 he married Catherine Sherrill, a young lady whose life he had once saved. When John Sevier rode to Kings Mountain his brother, Robert, was alongside but not destined to survive that day. After the revolution and numerous Indian campaigns, Sevier became deeply involved in politics, serving twice as governor of Tennessee, although he became a sworn political enemy of future president Andrew Jackson. Called Nolichucky Jack for the river on whose banks he ultimately settled, Sevier was a born adventurer and much-admired frontiersman. He lived to age seventy, perhaps the most popular of men on the frontier.

Benjamin Cleveland, the rotund roughneck who raised the eastern slope frontiersmen to action against Ferguson, was a hard-nosed fighter and an obstinate individual. Born in Bull Run, Virginia, on May 26, 1738, he became a hunter, a long rifleman while in his teens. Like many, he detested the drudgery of farming, preferring to follow the yell of the hounds, gambling in the taverns, and straight-line horse racing. He moved with his wife, Mary Graves, and her father to the Yadkin Valley of North Carolina, erecting a cabin he called a "roundabout" in a bend of the Yadkin River. Appointed an ensign in the Second North Carolina militia, Cleveland found his calling in campaigns against the Cherokee. Later he pursued Tories with identical vengeance, not averse to dispensing summary justice on those occasions when he saw fit. He was appointed colonel of the Wilkes County, North Carolina, militia, raising 350 volunteers to join the rebel cause at Quaker Meadows. His speech prior to the Kings Mountain battle, in which he challenged each rider to step out three steps if not willing to fight, was legendary. No one responded, whether from patriotism or from fear of Cleveland. Called "Old Round-about," denoting his extreme girth, Cleveland carried almost 300 pounds to Kings Mountain. He later gained to more than 450 and was unable to perform his role as a county judge, spending his final days sitting in a special stout chair on his piazza where he discussed any relevant topic with passersby. Cleveland was a man of good humor, loyal and faithful, but also brutal and uncompromising, never able to reconcile with any man whose leanings had been Loyalist.

The fourth colonel was a Virginian, William Campbell, of Scottish lineage via Ireland. The best educated of the command council, Campbell was awarded overall command at

Kings Mountain by vote of his contemporaries. A large man, almost six foot six and stout, Campbell was of a ruddy complexion with light reddish hair and bright blue eyes. Kind and considerate, he also could be quick tempered and impulsive. His father, Charles Campbell, married a Miss Buchanan and moved to Augusta County, Virginia, from Pennsylvania and in 1745 was blessed with one son, William. He was educated at David Robinson's quality academy and when his father died, William relocated his mother and four sisters to the Holston River near Wolf Hills, or present Abingdon, Virginia. At twenty-two he was head of the household. In 1774, Campbell marched to Dunmore's War in Col. William Christian's column as a company commander. But Christian's men arrived too late to fight at Point Pleasant and Campbell was sorely disappointed. When the revolution began, Campbell volunteered for duty in the First Virginia Regiment under Patrick Henry, but again experienced little action save for assisting Andrew Lewis at Gwynn's Island. William returned from that campaign with a bride, Elizabeth Henry, sister of the Virginia governor. Increasing involvement in militia affairs, William led a number of expeditions to suppress Tory activities in the backwoods, even venturing down into North Carolina in alliance with Benjamin Cleveland. When the call to assemble was issued by Shelby and Sevier, he and his cousin led four hundred followers to Sycamore Shoals, William carrying the family broadsword strapped across his back. Following the battle at Kings Mountain, Campbell fought stoutly with Nathanael Greene at Guilford Court House, but became involved in a serious controversy with Light Horse Harry Lee that caused Campbell to resign from the American army. Campbell reentered service to serve under Lafayette in Virginia but died of a heart attack in 1781 at age thirty-six.

Though these back country leaders were gathering force, following Cornwallis's victory at Camden, Ferguson's forays into western South Carolina began to achieve significant results. Loyalist enlistments rose and patriot activities seemed subdued. Ferguson rounded up beef cattle and swine wherever possible, in Tory and Whig fields. He burned the barns and houses of a few turncoats as this civil war grew increasingly bitter. But remaining in character, the dapper British officer was gallant and polite in his contacts with females, even the wives and kin of known rebels. As volunteers flocked in, large numbers of camp followers joined the column. Two of these became servants of Ferguson: Virginia Paul, who assumed the cooking chores, and Virginia Sal, or Salter, a comely, buxom redhead who washed his uniforms, among other duties.

Ferguson moved into North Carolina, establishing his headquarters at Gilbert Town. Penetrating to Davidson's Old Fort, deep in the mountain foothills, only about fifty miles from the Holston Valley, he issued a proclamation more provocative than intimidating. Concerned with persistent rumors that backwoodsmen intent on his demise were gathering in the valleys west of the mountains, Ferguson issued an edict designed to cow those who might oppose his forces. Paroling Samuel Philips, a relative of Isaac Shelby, he sent a message to the over-the-mountain men. Ferguson proclaimed: "If they do not desist from their opposition to British arms, I will march my army over the mountains, hang their leaders, and lay waste their country with fire and sword." Arrogantly he addressed the mountain men as he thought proper in dealing with rebels. But the effects of his threats were diametrical in that the results served as a catalyst increasing American opposition. Seldom in military history has such a statement of bravado, impossible to complete, produced such catastrophic results. The proud, fiercely independent frontiersmen received his warning as a gauntlet flung down to challenge each of them to a personal duel, and such it became. Patrick Ferguson, an outstanding British officer, thus made his first serious mistake in a campaign destined for failure: he seriously misjudged those he was about to fight. He, like most British officers, identified these backwoodsmen as nuisances to be easily scattered by organized, trained professional soldiers. None of these experts envisioned the sudden formation of a ghost army, assembling in the vastness of mountain valleys and led by hard, merciless, violent men tempered in Indian warfare. It was an army more numerous than Ferguson's force and would suddenly appear, armed with superior weapons and more violently vengeful than any could imagine. Ferguson's bombastic threat created a response with a united battle cry: find and kill Patrick Ferguson.

On Monday, September 25, Col. William Campbell rode into Sycamore Shoals on the Watauga River with two hundred Virginia volunteers to find Isaac Shelby and John Sevier already encamped with hundreds of riflemen, accompanied by their wives and children. The message to gather had swept swiftly through the mountains, much as the circulation of a fiery cross gathered Highlanders in Scottish history. Scores of campfires twinkled in the night alongside the Watauga as this largest gathering in memory took on the character of a religious camp meeting. Backwoodsmen smoked their pipes, swapped tall tales, and awaited the order to march.

On the twenty-sixth, Rev. Samuel Doak, a Princeton graduate and Presbyterian minister, delivered a long sermon invoking divine protection and declaring the little army "the sword of the Lord and of Gideon." Kissing their wives and mounting rawboned horses, the riders, serious in demeanor and purpose, turned east and began to ascend the mountains. Armed with long-barreled, lovingly protected Pennsylvania or Dickert rifles, knife and tomahawk in belt, and provisioned with bags of parched corn and maple sugar, they the long file rode slowly up Gap Creek, camping that first night at Shelving Rock, where care was taken to protect their powder from the rain. On the following day the column waded up Toe River and began the long, hard pull up Roan Mountain, crossing at 4,582 feet the Yellow Mountain Gap. Atop Roan Mountain snow was falling and the bald spot was white as the shivering riders dropped over the crest before lighting their campfires. On the following morning they discovered that two of their number, James Crawford and Samuel Chambers, had deserted to join Ferguson, informing the Loyalist army of their intentions. To prevent an ambush the column split, William Campbell leading the Virginians down into Turkey Cove while the riflemen of Shelby and Sevier filed into North Cove. The two factions reassembled at Quaker Meadows, where locals had accumulated provisions.

Ferguson had abandoned Gilbert Town upon receiving warning of the back country army's approach. He repositioned his Loyalist command at Denard's Ford on Broad River, uneasy but much too proud to retreat. Without doubt, Ferguson's concerns were realistic. His command was not a strong force, a fact of which the seasoned campaigner was well aware, though his army contained an excellent company of redcoats calling themselves Ferguson's Corps, about 110 men strong. These reliable troops had journeyed south with their commander and were originally from units such as the New Jersey

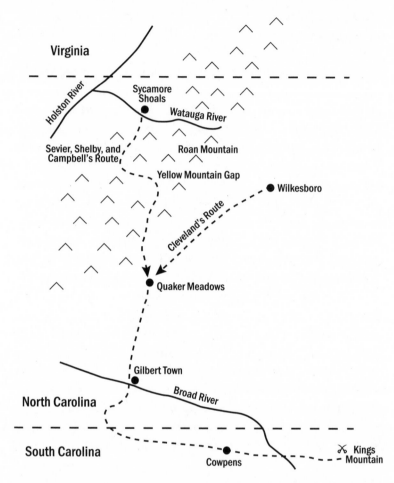

Line of march, September 26–October 7, 1780.

Volunteers, Queen's Rangers, and King's American Rangers, stout Loyalist units with proud, lengthy fighting records. They were armed with Long Land Pattern muskets called Brown Bess, castoffs from British regiments, whose .75-caliber, forty-six-inch barrels were lengthened by a socket bayonet of nineteen inches. Two veteran officers, Capt.

Abraham De Peyster and Capt. Samuel Ryerson led these solid Loyalists while Lt. Anthony Allaire served as adjutant and Dr. Uzal Johnson as surgeon.

In contrast to Ferguson's Corps the remainder of his force was made up of southern Tory militia, recently recruited and hardly trained. A North Carolina battalion of 430 to 450 men commanded by Col. Ambrose Mills was joined by a South Carolina contingent of about 340 men under Maj. Daniel Plummer. These militia units were rather indifferently armed with rifles, shotguns, fowling pieces, and muskets. In accord with Ferguson's insistence on the use of cold steel, all were equipped with long knives, the butts of which they whittled so as to fit into the barrels of their guns. While this 950-man force seemed adequate to confront any partisan force expected in the back country, Ferguson surely recognized the he was too weak to fight a rebel army.

In an attempt to gain local control, Ferguson issued another proclamation, widely distributed to local residents and designed to encourage their support of his forces. He addressed the barbaric nature of the approaching over-the-mountain men, describing possible results if citizens allowed these ruffians to transgress their lands. He continued: "If you want to be pinioned, robbed, and murdered and see your wives and daughters abused by the dregs of mankind . . . If you choose to be pissed upon by these mongrels say so at once." The mountain men surely must have wondered at this desperate statement by a king's officer.

On October 6, Ferguson marched his force sixteen miles and camped atop a steep hill known locally as Kings Mountain. More confidently, he dispatched a message to Cornwallis stating, "I arrived at King's mountain and have taken a post where I do not think I can be forced by a stronger enemy than that against us." The Kings Mountain ridge on which Ferguson encamped was the summit of a stony, isolated ridge about six or seven hundred feet in length. The width at the crest varied between sixty and two hundred yards and was roughly shaped like a human foot. The crest, clear of trees and underbrush, was scattered with lichen-encrusted stone outcroppings, while the hillsides were forest covered and composed of great, tall trees extending almost to the crest on each side, a factor noted with trepidation by Captain De Peyster. Believing his force in a near impregnable position only thirty-five miles from Cornwallis's main army, Ferguson arrogantly committed his second and final grievous error. He placed his largely raw militia army on a mountaintop more easily assaulted with rifles than defended with bayonets.

Meanwhile, the patriot force cautiously advanced south through Gilbert Town and by October 4 was camped at Ferguson's old campsite at Denard's Ford. By October 6, the frontiersmen assembled at Cowpens, receiving reinforcements from local militia under captains such as Frederick Hambright, William Graham, and William Chronicle until the force numbered almost sixteen hundred. Col. William Campbell, who was elected to lead the rebel army until a general officer appeared, learned that Ferguson was at Kings Mountain and decided to pursue and attack at once. Streamlining the force for rapid movement, Campbell and his officers culled out those who were ill, equipped with improper weapons, or possessed tired horses. More than nine hundred riders, almost all riflemen, prepared to take up the chase, although perhaps a hundred determined footmen followed. Initiating the advance about 9 P.M. in a pelting rain, black felt hats pulled low and gunlocks protected by shirts, coats, or bags, the shadowy line of gaunt, thin riders pressed into the night. By sunrise on the seventh the horses were worn and the men hungry, with little to eat but jerky or parched corn. A halt was considered but Shelby desisted, stating, "I will not stop until night, if I follow Ferguson into Cornwallis's lines." Struggling on in a steady rain, the leaders encountered a young girl who, pointing, informed the rebels that Ferguson was on a ridge three miles away. Soon a messenger was captured with dispatches for Cornwallis. The messenger related to the riders that Ferguson was the best attired officer on the mountain but his uniform was covered in a checked shirt or duster. The word spread down the column: search for the checkered shirt. Within a mile of Kings Mountain the frontiersmen dismounted, hitching their horses in the wood. Forming into two lines of two columns, the detachments began to move, filing right and left, silently surrounding Kings Mountain.

The contrast in weaponry employed by the two contending forces would prove decisive on this overcast afternoon, particularly in light of tactics and terrain. Rebel leaders were intent on maximizing their weaponry advantage, employing long-range rifles effective at three hundred yards from open-order, individually concealed formations, their tactics ideal for the heavily treed slopes. Ferguson, ironically, was an excellent and experienced rifleman, but he committed his force to utilizing volley fire of their Brown Besses, with one-hundred-yard ranges, complemented by bayonet charges calculated to disorder the bayonet-less riflemen. While little choice was available to either commander by the afternoon of the fateful conflict, the terrain of Kings Mountain decidedly favored the American riflemen.

By 3 P.M. the rain halted and faint sunlight filtered

through the wet leaves onto the forest floor. William Campbell issued open-ended orders to the various unit leaders, requesting that they reach their assigned positions and then race for the mountain crest when they heard the Indian war whoops of his and Shelby's men, who would initiate the attack. Quietly the frontiersmen slipped through the rain-soaked woods, capturing Tory pickets wherever discovered. Ferguson's picket line encompassed the entire mountain at its foot; men were stationed on all possible approach trails. Capt. Alexander Chesney, an alert militia officer, rode the forest trails, checking the outposts. As he returned to the mountaintop and prepared to dismount, a single shot rang out, then a number of others, and Chesney heard the *zip* of rifle balls and the eerie, keening cry of the mountain foxhunter. Remounting, he started back downhill, but his horse was hit and Chesney pinned under the animal. Concurrently, Captain De Peyster recalled the loud war yells he had heard at Musgrove Mill and turned out his redcoats to the staccato roll of drums. Gradually the arc of rifle fire increased and spread around the mountain.

Campbell's and Shelby's men crept up the slope of Kings Mountain Indian style, moving from tree to tree, on opposite sides of the mountain's narrow heel. As the rebels neared the crest, Ferguson spurred his white horse along the length of the mountain, his Spanish sword aloft in his left hand. A volley of musket fire rolled at a shrill blast from his silver whistle and suddenly his redcoats launched a bayonet charge that drove Campbell's Virginians into undignified flight. Those riflemen of agility escaped unhurt, but many of the slow or stubborn were overrun and cut down by flashing blades. As the running mountaineers reached the foot of Kings Mountain, Colonel Campbell and Maj. William Edmondson were among them,

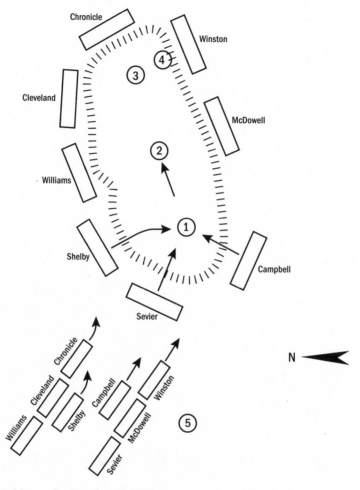

Kings Mountain, October 7, 1780.

1. Sevier and Campbell initiate the battle. Repulsed until Shelby closes on Tory rear.
2. Tory defense regroups until rebel groups attack from all sides of mountain.
3. The British surrender.
4. Ferguson slain in escape attempt.
5. Colonials file into position surrounding Kings Mountain.

yelling, cursing, and threatening, rallying the lines to return and fight. While their charge had produced a near rout, the Loyalists halted on Ferguson's whistle blast as rifle fire erupted from the opposite side of the mountain. Shelby's men had arrived at the crest.

Meanwhile, Cleveland's and Sevier's boys were scaling the rocky slopes and, assisted by various smaller units, were surrounding the broader toe of Kings Mountain where the wagons and tents of the British force were located. The volume of rifle fire increased, yet few rebels were visible from the mountain crest. The fringe-coated backwoodsmen needed no tactical instruction in such broken terrain, simply seeking good cover and getting close enough for the deadly long rifles to speak. This fluid, skirmish-style combat was

Hillside at Kings Mountain. Colonial riflemen advanced up the hillside at Kings Mountain utilizing the available heavy tree cover. (*Photo by Penny Swisher*)

natural to men reared fighting Indians. The mountain seemed wreathed in smoke as the fighting became savage. Long-accumulated passions found outlet in violent fashion, some among neighbors or within families.

As the swell of battle increased, the indomitable Patrick Ferguson was everywhere, spurring from crisis to crisis. He lost two steeds and mounted a third, a dapple gray. With his whistled commands he repeatedly organized volley fire and charges, certain that the backwoodsmen would not long stand against the cold steel. Each bayonet assault drove the rebels pell-mell down the slope, but when the chargers halted and began to rescale the slopes, the *ping* of balls sang about them. On three separate occasions the attackers cleared the hillside, mercilessly bayoneting wounded rebels, but in each case they suffered heavy losses when struggling back uphill from a foe surely not adverse to shooting their enemies in the back.

Benjamin Cleveland, his huge frame astride an equally large stallion, led his followers along with those of Maj. William Chronicle and Maj. Joseph Winston around to the northeast end of Kings Mountain. He dismounted and struggling heavily began to ascend the slope. Sixteen-year-old Robert Henry followed the bold Chronicle, transfixed when his leader was shot down by a Tory volley. Even without Chronicle, Cleveland and his compatriots reached the crest at the northeast corner, and the obstinate German, Frederick Hambright, continued to inspire his men despite a boot full of blood.

When Ferguson recalled his redcoats following a third assault, confusion broke out on the mountain crest. His recall command was interpreted as a retreat summons by the Tory militia, and they suddenly broke from the heel of the mountain. Campbell's, Shelby's, and Sevier's men met

American monument, Kings Mountain. The American monument at Kings Mountain is located on the site of the Tory wagon camp, the point of last resistance. (*Photo by Penny Swisher*)

on the crest and began to drive north toward the Tory camp. After the prolonged British defense only two sergeants and twenty privates remained in action from Ferguson's elite company of redcoats. Many Tory militiamen were cowering amid the wagons, some even refusing to return fire. De Peyster witnessed the militia giving way and crowding into a mass, hiding behind rocks or wagons, completely unmanageable. All his efforts to rally them failed and he began to think there was no option but to make a break, lest they all be killed.

As De Peyster attempted to gather a mobile breakout force, several militia members erected white flags only to have Ferguson, still clad in his checkered coat, spur among them slashing down their surrender markers with his blade. The proud Scotsman exclaimed loudly "that he would never yield to such a damn band of banditti," clearly demonstrating his frustration at seeing the battle swing to the backwoodsmen. Several horsemen, including Maj. Daniel Plummer and Col. Vezey Husbands, joined Ferguson in a desperate charge to break through the rebel cordon. Starting downhill on a woodland path, the riders were fired upon by dozens of long rifles. Plummer and Husbands were shot down immediately and Ferguson was struck in the arm, hip, and chest, but still maintained his seat. Reeling, the British commander was hit in the forehead by a ball fired by Robert Young of Sevier's command. As he tumbled from his horse a foot stuck in a stirrup and the commander was dragged for a time parallel to the patriot line, as if a target in a shooting gallery. Scores of rifle balls found their mark; some claimed more than fifty shots were lodged in his body or clothing. Ironically, the only British professional soldier on the field, an officer of training and experience, was chased down, entrapped, and slain by the very rabble he had treated with such contempt. Perhaps realizing the severe straits of his little force after one hour's fighting, Ferguson rejected the dishonor of surrender for glorious death in a desperate last charge. In writing to his mother earlier, Ferguson had proclaimed, "The length of our lives is not at our command, however much the manner of them may be." The inordinate pride and stubborn arrogance of Patrick Ferguson, assisted by plain misfortune, precipitated those fatal miscalculations that brought defeat and death on a wilderness peak to this honorable soldier of the king.

De Peyster assumed command of the remnants of the army upon Ferguson's fall, recognizing at once the futility of further resistance. Lt. Anthony Allaire of Ferguson's Corps stated he could get no more than six or seven men in line to resist the frontiersmen. The remaining Tories had been driven into a space of sixty by forty yards and were ringed by frontiersmen, so De Peyster, although later heavily criticized, caused white flags to be hoisted as high as possible. Captain Chesney, wounded and helpless, recalled that De Peyster's signals were initially ignored as riflemen yelling "Buford's Play"—referencing the supposed massacred of Buford's Continentals by Tarleton's British Legion several months earlier—continued to load and fire into the mass. Through the efforts of Shelby and Campbell the firing was gradually halted, although Shelby admitted later that it took some time and many were shot down. Red-headed, red-faced, and soaked with sweat, William Campbell ordered the surviving Tories to sit down while he interposed his bulk between them and the riflemen, pleading for an end to the continual firing. Finally the guns grew silent and a huge cheer of celebration rose from the mountaintop. Unexpectedly a single shot toppled rebel colonel James Williams from his horse, sparking another outburst of firing.

Williams had enemies in both camps, but whoever slew him almost caused the massacre of the remainder of the Tory force. When American officers again halted the firing, the casualty rate was found to be staggering. More than 150 of Ferguson's command were slain, 160 or more wounded, and 664 captured, none escaping from Kings Mountain. Patriot losses were much lighter, 28 rebels being slain and 62 wounded. Campbell's Virginians suffered the highest losses among the rebels, almost one-third of the total casualties. Their repeated assaults and retreats in the opening phases of the contest saw thirteen of their officers slain, including three of one family: Capt. William Edmondson, Lt. Robert Edmondson, and Ens. Andrew Edmondson.

As the guns grew silent, the dead lay scattered across the mountaintop. Bodies of slain Tories were wedged amid the rock formations where they had fought their last fight, most shot through the head. James Collins recalled the pitiful cries of the wounded for water that seemed to emanate from all directions. On the field lay a wounded Tory who saw his brother-in-law, a rebel captain, pass by and he pleaded for assistance. "Look to your friends for help," came the cold reply. No physicians accompanied the mountain army, but the unusually dedicated work of Dr. Uzal Johnson, a New Jersey Loyalist who tended and amputated Whig and Tory alike, saved William Moore of Campbell's Virginians as well as a number of prominent Tory officers. Gradually the Tory wounded and captured were gathered and placed under guard, to suffer a long night without food, covered at dawn by a heavy frost. The Tory wounded, abandoned on the forested hillsides without water or medical aid, would suffer horribly during the chilly night, though some few would be rescued by wives and family who appeared as if summoned, searching through the dead and bringing water to the living.

When firing lifted, Elias Powell, a Tory lad who had served as Ferguson's orderly, hurried to clean and wash his commander's bloodied face. Removing the officer's silver whistle, he secreted the relic as large numbers of American riflemen gathered to view the body. Ferguson was stripped, his fine uniform and possessions distributed as trophies by the victors. Pvt. Samuel Talbot appropriated Ferguson's pistol while Capt. William Lenoir claimed his broken Spanish sword. Other artifacts were attained by the patriot commanders. John Sevier received a silken sash, Isaac Shelby a second silver whistle, and Ben Cleveland, whose horse was slain, was awarded Ferguson's gray charger. Numerous other items, including a turnip-sized silver watch and pieces of uniform or braid, would become prized treasures of Appalachian mountain families a hundred years hence. Once the body was stripped, the victorious mountain men, extracting the final measure of revenge in a uniquely crude and vulgar manner, gathered around and urinated on the corpse.

Many biographers and historians have refused to confirm this act, but far too many reliable sources are available for the incident to be denied. Such a deed, unthinkable within the context of gentlemanly accords extended to captured or slain officers on the fields of Europe, occurred in a vastly different milieu. This fight, this vicious clash atop an isolated backwoods peak so very critical to the future of American freedom, was in reality a very personal campaign between two forces, neither possessing any accurate concept of their opponent.

Patrick Ferguson, a conventional soldier detailed to pacify the southern back country and detesting the partisan nature of the assignment, attempted the task in the only manner he knew. He threatened, bluffed, and cajoled the residents to retain or regain loyalty to their lawful king while dismissing the mysterious over-the-mountain men with an arrogance and contempt reserved for those outside the pale of civilization. His edicts described these men as mongrels, barbarians, dregs of mankind and proclaimed the uncivilized nature of these ruffians. Though ignorant of the true nature of the frontiersmen, Ferguson would probably have found their sense of personal honor, fervor in attachment to their cause, and dogged persistence quite similar to his own.

Conversely, the fringe-coated men who gathered at Sycamore Shoals were tough, merciless, unintimidatable individuals who aimed their retribution directly and personally at Patrick Ferguson. Their character of violence— simple, direct, and personal—skewed a military campaign against eastern Tories so that it became a vigilante action, one designed to accord justice to the detested British major. They marched, fought, and slew their Tory foes without knowledge of the admirable soldierly and personal qualities of the man they were pursuing, a person they would have greatly admired in another setting. It is therefore not decidedly so demeaning, either to the victors or to the vanquished, that utilizing the words of Ferguson's own edicts, they defiled his body in gestures of absolute victory.

The triumphant rebels slept that night in the British tents attempting to discount the cries of the wounded. Little food was discovered, for Ferguson's supplies were equally exhausted, the wagons virtually empty. At dawn, an impatient rebel army arose and prepared to march. Colonel Campbell, assisted by a detail of Virginians and captives, remained to bury the dead. Three large pits were excavated on a small elevation some one hundred yards from Ferguson's camp. The first pit was used to inter the patriot dead while a second contained Ferguson's redcoats. A larger one was used to bury the Tory militiamen. However, the rocky nature of the mountaintop prevented a proper depth of construction and the interments were poorly completed. Wrapped in blankets or coats, the bodies were placed in line within the pits and covered with dirt, rocks, tree limbs, or bark. So shallow were the depressions that gravediggers such as James Collins recalled that many bodies were hardly covered. Within days wolves, wild dogs, and other predators had disinterred many of the remains and scattered body parts across the mountain. A few years later, local efforts inspired a gathering of bones from the mountain crest and reinterment in a proper sepulcher, Tory and Whig together. Dr. Johnson remained with Campbell as long as possible to attend the Tory wounded.

Colonel Ferguson's body was washed and prepared for burial by Powell and several Tory volunteers who wrapped the remains in a large ox hide. Alongside his body was buried Virginia Sal. The red-headed mistress had fallen victim to a random shot early in the battle. Her cohort, Virginia Paul, marched into captivity only to disappear from history somewhere around Gilbert Town. Ferguson was interred in a grave pit close to the spot of his ill-fated charge for freedom. A mound of stones was erected over the grave, a cairn honoring a brave, well-respected leader.

Having accomplished their mission, the army leaders found themselves in a perilous position. Early on the morning of the tenth, a bright, frosty day, the patriot army was astir. With limited powder supplies and scanty rations, the frontiersmen were positioned only thirty miles from Cornwallis's main force and Tarleton's hated dragoons. Rapidly the seventeen British wagons were pulled over the campfires and burned while Tory wounded were gathered

Marker to Patrick Ferguson. This marker to Major Ferguson was erected by a collection of funds from British and American sources. (*Photo by Penny Swisher*)

Ferguson cairn. This cairn of stones marks Ferguson's grave. (*Photo by Penny Swisher*)

at Wilson's Farm some four miles away, Dr. Johnson continuing his grisly amputations. The patriot wounded were loaded into slings rigged between horses. Almost seven hundred prisoners judged capable of marching were aligned single file, each man assigned a captured rifle, flint removed, to carry. About 10 A.M. the line mobilized, captives walking between double rows of American riders. In some instances Tory prisoners were treated harshly, several beaten severely as personal vendettas were repaid. Most were stripped of their valuables, including shoes. Capt. Alexander Chesney lamented on his stolen shoe buckles, his most valued personal possession. Colonel Campbell attempted to put an end to such conduct, declaring the prisoners worthy opponents and deserving of fair treatment.

The column covered twelve miles that first day, resting that evening near the Broad River, where captors and prisoners sated their gnawing hunger in nearby sweet potato fields. As the column proceeded north, pumpkins, either fried or raw, became a major source of sustenance. Lieutenant Allaire was so famished that he recalled the orange balls as the "sweetest food he had ever tasted."

At Gilbert Town the column halted and the prisoners were penned, enduring the abuse of townsfolk. Some miles farther, while camped at Bickerstaff's Plantation, North and South Carolina militia officers approached Colonel Campbell to request a trial for a number of Tory prisoners whom they claimed to be assassins, house burners, or parole breakers. While half of each army was probably in violation of some parole, the initial two charges were considered serious enough to warrant a trial. A copy of a North Carolina law was produced that authorized a jury to be appointed by magistrates to judge the offenders. Colonel Campbell convened a jury of twelve officers to try those accused. This quasi court-martial-civilian trial began a procedure that would prove decidedly uncomplimentary to the accounts of such a remarkable volunteer army.

It is unknown just how those to be tried were selected other than by the loud claims of patriot soldiers, principally rebel militia. Shelby wrote later, "The most atrocious offenders were tried first, those who had committed the most enormous crimes." After hours of deliberation, thirty-six offenders were found guilty and sentenced to be hung. Much of the evidence was based on the testimony of those who may have been intent on repaying personal scores. The army command seemed to feel that some summary justice of guilty Tories was deserved and would perhaps discourage the British practice of hanging rebel parole violators in the future. Late on the fourteenth the executions began, a large oak tree providing the gallows base. Pine torches illuminated the tree as rebel riflemen gathered four deep to witness the executions. The Tories were led out three at a time and hung from a stout tree limb. Lt. Col. Ambrose Mills, Captain Wilson, and Capt. James Chitwood were first to die. Capt. Walter Gilkey, Captain Grimes, Lieutenant Lafferty, Capt. John McFall, Sgt. John Bibby, and Sgt. Augustine Hobbs followed. With the conclusion of these nine executions the patriot leaders, perhaps sick of the activity, halted the proceeding and freed the remainder. James Crawford, who had deserted to Ferguson on Roan Mountain, was sentenced to swing and would have certainly been among the first men executed, but Colonel Sevier, his neighbor, intervened on his behalf and he was pardoned. The Tory leaders were left hanging as the army moved on the next day in a driving rain. Mrs. Martha Bickerstaff, whose officer husband had died with Ferguson's troops at Kings Mountain, cut down the bodies and buried all save Chitwood, whose remains were claimed by his friends.

The patriot army broke camp shortly after 2 A.M. the following morning, marching north in a cold, heavy downpour. Rumors of Tarleton's approach sped the march as the long column covered almost thirty-two miles, crossing the flooding Catawba to make camp near Quaker Meadows. Maj. Joseph McDowell generously donated his fence rails to army campfires and hospitably invited the officers for dinner, including the prisoners.

At this juncture the rebel army began to disperse, many militiamen leaving for their homes. Hearing rumors of Cherokee raids, the over-the-mountain men were anxious to reach their unprotected homes and families. Sevier led them up the mountain trail while Shelby turned the remaining prisoners over to the old Tory hater, Ben Cleveland. Quietly, the mountain army vanished into the hills. As discipline relaxed, large numbers of captives slipped into the surrounding woods, also seeking their homes. Virginia Paul, still with the column, was largely ignored by the mountaineers and soon disappeared. Only about 150 prisoners reached Hillsborough, where they were held for exchange.

The astounding American victory at Kings Mountain was complete, absolute, and conclusive, unlike most actions in this long war. The sudden encounter, so unexpected as to appear accidental, shook to the core the British strategy designed to subdue the southern states. The fight initiated by an American force that weeks before did not exist and would not exit weeks hence also undermined the confidence of Loyalist supporters, creating consequences far beyond the scope and size of the encounter. Cornwallis's advance through North Carolina into Virginia was stopped cold, forcing the British commander to assume, temporarily, a defensive posture. The reservoir of Loyalism, a place where the British army would be welcomed amid supporters, slowly eroded as news of the defeat spread. Depression and fear began to permeate centers of Loyalist support throughout the Carolinas. In contrast, American patriots were rejuvenated as the guerilla campaign of scattered terrorism increased in intensity. By this time war in the south was actually civil war, pitting neighbor against neighbor in a cruel, merciless conflict. No clearer illustration of the fratricidal nature of the conflict can be used than the composition of the armies at Kings Mountain. The battle on the mountaintop was contested entirely by Americans, either Loyalists or patriots. Patrick Ferguson was the lone British professional soldier present.

This miniscule tactical setback with gigantic implications has most often been attributed to the miscalculations of Maj. Patrick Ferguson. His errors were certainly critical to the outcome. Ferguson unwisely precipitated the participation of the mountain men by an imperious challenge to his misunderstood and dangerous foe. When he learned of their pursuit of his Loyalist army, he selected disadvantageous ground and utilized tactics reminiscent of Gen. George Braddock's ill-fated backwoods encounter. Ferguson knew well the deadly advantage of the rifle; he was its most earnest advocate in his own army, yet he attempted to recast his American Loyalists as disciplined redcoats, insisting that cold steel would quickly disperse American riflemen.

Many, including Cornwallis and Tarleton, criticized Ferguson but also blamed one another. Tarleton believed that Cornwallis should have dispatched his British Legion to rescue Ferguson. Cornwallis countered angrily by stating that he had ordered Ferguson not to engage and that he had entreated Tarleton to march to his rescue but the dragoon officer pleaded illness from a fever and did not respond. Perhaps none were so damning as Alexander Chesney, Ferguson's faithful Tory subordinate. Chesney blamed the defeat on the terrain and wooded hillsides that favored the open-order rifle tactics of the enemy over the volley and bayonet charges planned by Ferguson. Sir Henry Clinton blamed Cornwallis since he felt the British general should never have allowed Ferguson to advance into the back country without a corps of British regulars to anchor his army. Clinton followed these critics in his memoirs with an analysis that "the American victory at Kings Mountain was the first link in a chain of misfortunes that followed each other in regular succession until they ended in the total loss of America." This explicative narrative, although perhaps designed to transfer blame to Cornwallis, was amazingly perceptive in evaluating the outcome of an action never fully appreciated by historians.

The five and a half month campaign initiated at Kings Mountain on October 7, 1780, encompassed Cowpens on January 17, 1781, and Guilford Court House on March 15, 1781, and slowly and surely led the progress of war in the south down a spiraling path to Yorktown. Kings Mountain swung the impetus of warfare from the steady tide of British success to an uncertainty about how to wage the war in the reality of the opponent they faced. Their strategy arrested, and their concerns over future aims vague, the British high command seemed dazed. No other battle in the American Revolution, save Saratoga, provoked such widespread impact.

In a strange fashion, the over-the-mountain army, so swiftly assembled at Sycamore Shoals, abruptly vanished into American legend. But it was not a myth. It was a fighting force of hardy, physical men that, though lacking in training and discipline and armed with an unproven weapon, vanquished Ferguson's Loyalists, then disappeared into the backwoods from which it had come.

CHAPTER 8

The Fight at Hannah's Cowpens

"I was desirous to have a stroke at Tarleton and I have given him a devil of a whipping."

Daniel Morgan

Richard Hovenden, captain of His Majesty's British Legion Dragoons, cautiously urged a tired horse through the parklike expanse of tall trees that marked the entrance to a South Carolina crossroads junction locally known as Hannah's Cowpens. The pre-dawn grayness, coupled with a raw, cold mist, sharply limited visibility, but the green-jacketed young officer could distinguish a ragged line of fringe-clad riflemen strung across the field to his front, swinging their arms vigorously and clapping hands in attempts to keep warm. Deployed in the frost-covered fields, breath creating vapor trails in the morning air, backwoods Colonial long riflemen awaited British targets. As the mist lifted, Hovenden observed the glint of gunmetal from the weapons of a mass of militia arrayed beyond the aforementioned skirmish line, and he realized that he had located the little Colonial army of patriot brigadier general Daniel Morgan and that the battle would be here. Dropping his reins and removing his plumed dragoon helmet, the cavalry subaltern called forward his commanding officer, Capt. David Ogilive, who in turn dispatched a courier for the twenty-six-year-old chieftain of this British column, Lt. Col. Banastre Tarleton.

The principal British field force under Eton-educated Lord Charles Cornwallis had enjoyed a steady stream of successes in its confrontation with Colonial forces, save for the disastrous setback of Ferguson's defeat at Kings Mountain. In contrast, American fortunes in the southern theater were at a desperate level following the rout of its largest field army at Camden on August 16. Despite the encouraging results of the Kings Mountain victory and the inspired efforts of Francis Marion, Thomas Sumter, Andrew Pickens, and other rebel partisans, British field forces in the south seemed nearly invincible.

In October 1780, George Washington dispatched Maj. Gen. Nathanael Greene, among his most valued subordinates, to take command in the Carolinas. A self-educated ex-Quaker, Greene was intelligent, strategically gifted, and an extremely capable military administrator. Immediately after his arrival near Charlotte, North Carolina, on December 2, Greene met privately with Brig. Gen. Daniel Morgan, the old Virginia backwoodsman who had recently come south to oversee militia and light troops in the area. The fortuitous assignment of this duo of officers to conduct a southern campaign whereupon their complementary strengths would so expeditiously blossom—the astute, meticulous Rhode Islander with gifted strategic skills and the unlettered frontier Virginian of innate tactical gifts and inspiring leadership—seems almost determinative for Colonial purposes. Of such random alliances are battles and campaigns won or lost.

Audaciously, Greene divided his small army on

December 21, dispatching Morgan with 650 soldiers westward across the Broad River to present a threat to the important British outpost located at Ninety-six. Upon discovery of Greene's move, Cornwallis ordered a similar force under Lt. Col. Banastre Tarleton to march westward, countering Morgan's maneuverings. Greene informed Morgan, "Col. Tarleton is said to be on his way to pay you a visit. I doubt not that he will have a decent reception and a proper dismissal." Almost concurrently Cornwallis reminded Tarleton by letter that he must ensure the safety of the fort at Ninety-six and added: "I should wish you to push Morgan to the utmost."

Morgan loosed his cavalry troop under Col. William Washington to boldly harass Loyalist forces in western South Carolina. When Tarleton's strong relief column approached Ninety-six, Morgan began to fall back toward the North Carolina state line, where he could reasonably expect some militia reinforcements. Tarleton appealed to Cornwallis and obtained the services of the Seventeenth Dragoons and the Seventh Fusiliers, substantially strengthening a column that already contained his Loyalist Legion and the First Battalion of the Seventy-first Highlanders. He immediately began an active pursuit. Across the Enoree and Tyger Rivers marched both the pursued and the pursuers. Bridges were nonexistent in the back country, thus fords became valuable possessions during the rainy season. Water temperature was just above freezing, shivering soldiers sometimes marching with icicles hanging from their gaiters. As his column neared the banks of the Pacolet, Tarleton suddenly swerved westward, crossing upstream at Eastwood Shoals in a vain attempt to cut off Morgan, who was encamped at Burr's Mill on Thicketty Creek. The green-coated Legion dragoons almost caught Morgan in camp but the Old Waggoner, as he labeled himself, escaped and rapidly fell back toward the Broad River.

Tarleton became convinced that Morgan was committed to a retreat and would continue to flee across the Broad River, so he awakened his soldiers at 3 A.M. and began a relentless advance despite some disorder among his leading units. When Tarleton's advance guard of dragoons came out of the tall pines at Cowpens, he was both surprised and pleased to find the Colonials calmly awaiting his pursuit. He possessed little respect for the prowess of Colonial militia and was certain that Morgan had erred by preparing to give battle with a river at his back, and predictably, he proceeded to initiate a straightforward attack before the Americans could continue their retreat. But Morgan had garnered valuable time by rapid marching and he had wisely utilized this opportunity to select advantageous ground on which to fight. He had fed his troops and carefully positioned each unit according to his perceived battle plan. It was as if Tarleton's hounds, in full bay, had pursued the Colonial fox, panting and excitedly chasing him to ground, only to discover that their quarry was confidently arrayed before them, arrogantly preparing to resist.

The small Colonial army awaiting battle in the cold mist was led by a true frontiersman, Daniel Morgan of Winchester, Virginia. This forty-five-year-old unlettered, some would even say uncivilized, product of the southern backwoods was bent and scarred in appearance, but physically still perhaps the toughest man on the field. Morgan wore no sign of rank except a sword, but in the frontier tradition he was the easily recognized leader. He lacked the sophistication expected of an army commander although he had demonstrated his military abilities as a militia officer at company and regimental levels. Loud, profane, and uncouth, he was also cunning, woods-smart, and possessed of considerable amounts of

Brig. Gen. Daniel Morgan. (*National Archives*)

plain common sense. Underestimated most of his military career by friend and foe, on this day he would demonstrate conclusively his tactical military skills.

Daniel Morgan was born in New Jersey of Welsh immigrant parents about 1735. Little is known about him until he appeared in Charles Town, Virginia, at age seventeen. About six foot two and 220 pounds, Morgan was a strong, hard worker and quickly earned funds sufficient to purchase a wagon and team. He initiated the operation of a freight-hauling business, the Colonial equivalent of today's long-distance independent trucker, achieving considerable success. As his business grew, so did Morgan's unsavory reputation as a hot-tempered barroom brawler, an uncensored womanizer, and a frequent consumer of local apple brandy. Arrested repeatedly for charges such as horse stealing, assault, and resisting arrest, he conducted a continual feud with the Davis brothers, a family of frontiersmen who were competing wagon drivers, and other frequenters of Battletown's (present-day Berryville, Virginia) infamous taverns. Morgan seemed headed toward long-term incarceration or even worse until he suddenly took up with the sixteen-year-old Miss Abigail Curry. In short order, Daniel Morgan, never fully tamed, was at least partially domesticated.

In 1754 a British army was formed to march against Fort Duquesne, and Morgan obtained a contract as a wagon driver. Following the rout of the redcoat column by French and Indians lying in ambush, Morgan hauled numerous wounded soldiers back down Braddock's Road. Weeks later Morgan found himself the wagon boss of a British supply column near Fort Lewis on the Roanoke River near Salem, Virginia. He was unusually overbearing with his drivers in the accustomed frontier style, sometimes kicking or cuffing the laggards. One old wagon driver named Fisher related a story that was retold so often it almost came to characterize Dan Morgan.

One day Fisher saw Morgan kicking several drivers and swore if he played such a prank on him he would taste the butt of Fisher's rifle. Soon Morgan passed down the line and gave Fisher a kick. The offended arose, followed Morgan, and struck him in the head, driving the bully down onto the ground. With that several other waggoneers ran up and laid into Morgan. A young British Ensign ran to see what was the ruckus and as a dazed Morgan bound up to his feet he grabbed the Ensign by the throat . . . thinking the Ensign had something to do with the drubbing he had received. Within moments a file of redcoats had Morgan in arrest.

He was sentenced to 500 lashes for laying violent hands on an officer of the Crown—300 to be given on the spot until his back was raw as beef—next morning he received the additional 200. Later Morgan joked that the drummer had erred and he only got 499 lashes and that King George owed him another lash. For six weeks, Morgan lay at Fort Lewis, his survival uncertain.

This harsh punishment, although common in British military regiments, would probably have killed many lesser men, and it left Morgan, already a marked individualist, with little toleration for Crown authority.

Returning home to Winchester, he became a respected militia leader, excelling in the persistent pursuit of Indian raiders. In the spring of 1756, while carrying military dispatches, Morgan was shot in the back of his head by a hostile, the ball exiting through his left cheek and removing several teeth. He escaped his assailants through the exertions of a courageous mare that outdistanced his racing pursuers, but Morgan was left with a permanent facial scar, one he wore as a badge of honor.

Morgan married Abigail and they settled on a 255-acre purchase near Winchester, Virginia, where she patiently taught him his letters. When the political differences between colonists and mother country flared into open revolution, Morgan anxiously volunteered for service. Initially assigned to command a Virginia rifle company, he was dispatched with a unit of ninety-six long riflemen on July 17, 1775, to march six hundred miles to Cambridge, Massachusetts, to provide reinforcements for George Washington's growing army besieging Boston. Captain Morgan's reputation skyrocketed when others witnessed the shooting accuracy of his long riflemen. Marching through the snows of Maine to attack Quebec alongside Gen. Benedict Arnold, Morgan and most of his men were captured during the misfired assault on the city, he and his riflemen being imprisoned in the Citadel atop the city. Well treated by his captors, Morgan fortuitously avoided the small pox epidemic that swept the ranks of retreating Colonials. Later released, he and his reconstructed rifle unit enacted a key role in the defeat and surrender of Gen. John Burgoyne's British army at Saratoga. Morgan's frontier leadership skills and courage were clearly evident in each of these fights, but his gruff manner and social skills were considered inadequate for a general officer and he was bypassed for promotion to brigadier general. Suffering badly from sciatica contacted during the march to Quebec, he grudgingly resigned from the army and returned home to Virginia. Bent and seemingly much older than his years, Morgan, grumbling constantly over the political machinations of the American army, was administered icy baths by Abigail. In 1780, as a result of the critical American position in the south, Morgan was activated by Congress, promoted, and ordered south to assume command of light troops. While he had never led an independent force of more than a few companies of riflemen, he was a natural leader, an innately tough, merciless captain, respected and feared by the backwoodsmen. When he aligned his troops at Cowpens, Daniel Morgan possessed basically no credible military reputation, but, more importantly, he was supremely confident in his own ability to lead a fight, which he did brilliantly.

Morgan's little force was a hybrid army of Continental line soldiers, state regimentals, and militia, reinforced by Continental dragoons and volunteer cavalry. His five companies of Continental line troops—three from Maryland, one from Delaware, and one from Virginia—were experienced, steady soldiers commanded by the very capable Lt. Col. John Eager Howard. Dashing and energetic, Howard was fearless and cool under fire. Later, Greene would repeatedly describe Howard as, "as good an officer as the world affords . . . of great ability and agreeable disposition." These blue-coated regulars enlisted and were paid by the Continental Congress although each unit still retained its state regimental number and name.

Morgan's state troops were primarily from Virginia and were of above-average ability and experience since each regiment contained a number of recently discharged ex-Continental regulars. In addition, many of these men were from the western or back country counties of Augusta and Rockbridge and were armed with deadly long rifles. Maj. Frank Triplett led this Virginia battalion of about 150 men. His company commanders were Capt. James Tate of Augusta County, Capt. James Gilmore of Rockbridge County, and Capt. John Combs of Fauquier County. Each company contained about 40 riflemen with a supplemental unit from Burke County, North Carolina, joining the battalion.

Morgan's militia units from North Carolina, South Carolina, and Georgia embraced a wide range of experience and potential military value. They were armed with every possible weapon from rifles to shotguns. When Col. Thomas Sumter refused to report, offended somehow by Greene and upset with his role in the campaign, the affable Andrew Pickens took command of these assorted militia units, perhaps a fortunate circumstance for Morgan. This lean, sinewy, extremely devout Presbyterian had served in earlier campaigns against the Cherokee and Tory partisans and was widely respected in South Carolina as a soldier as well as a fair and honest man. The rotund Lt. Col. William Washington, a kind, lax disciplinarian who turned into an energetic, merciless fighter when the bugles blew, commanded the eighty-two American dragoons to which about one hundred attached militia riders who possessed swords and mounts were added.

Morgan's exact numbers are hard to ascertain. He marched from Charlotte with about 650 men and was reinforced by militia units right up until the night before the battle. Most sources credit him with between 1,000 and 1,100 men; however, historians who have reviewed the pension records feel a reasonable estimate would be 1,300 to 1,400 soldiers. Morgan's men enjoyed soaring morale as Thomas Young recalled, "We were very anxious for battle . . . and Morgan went about among the volunteers all night, visiting their fires and joking of the morning's fight."

Morgan's antagonist, the somewhat arrogant yet genteel Lt. Col. Banastre Tarleton, was the antithesis to the backwoods frontiersman. He was smooth, glib, well educated, and a marvelous horseman. Born in 1754 near Liverpool, England, the third son of the mayor of Liverpool, young Tarleton was reared in comfortable circumstances, attended

Lt. Col. Banastre Tarleton. (*National Archives*)

Oxford University, and enrolled in the Middle Temple, England's finest law school. When Tarleton's father died suddenly, leaving him some inheritance, he dropped out of school determined to live the life of a rake and gambler. Soon his financial resources disappeared and he began frantically searching for a career. His family assisted by purchasing a cornet's rank in the First Regiment, Dragoon Guards for eight hundred pounds, and Tarleton was instantly transformed into an innately capable cavalry soldier. He volunteered for service in the Colonies, where opportunity for promotion seemed ripe.

Initially, he drew service in the New York area and became known for dashing raids, sudden attacks, and all-night rides requiring tremendous physical exertion. Although inclined toward impulsiveness, his natural drive, ambition, and persistence, coupled with talents in intelligence gathering, made Tarleton an ideal cavalry officer. Rapidly he obtained promotion to lieutenant colonel when not quite twenty-four years of age. He was appointed to command the British Legion, a unit composed of Loyalists from Pennsylvania, New York, and New Jersey. The legion, half cavalry and half infantry, wore green jackets faced in black with huge black helmets and green plumes. Tarleton advocated that the primary tactical use of cavalry was in headlong charges or in bold flanking movements causing the enemy to scatter. He would then relentlessly and mercilessly pursue and punish the foe. He developed a successful pattern of raiding: after obtaining accurate intelligence, he conducted a swift march, a surprise appearance, and immediate attack utilizing swords and bayonets. These tactics stood him in good stead against ill-disciplined Colonial militia. While his reliance on shock and pursuit was usually successful, his impetuosity failed

Tarleton on at least two occasions, at Blackstocks and at Cowpens.

Tarleton's genius as a dragoon officer blossomed when his legion was detailed to accompany General Clinton on the second investiture of Charles Town. Upon landing in Edisto Bay, Tarleton found himself without horses, for most had died on the storm-tossed voyage south. He promptly confiscated mounts of every description from nearby farms and plantations and proceeded to cut the American supply lines into the city. At Moncks Corner the legion defeated the American cavalry, gathering good riding stock, while Charles Town's fate was sealed.

Tarleton enjoyed his stay in the Charles Town area, daily appearing at the city's famed bordellos and taverns. Of all the Colonial cities occupied by the British army, the South Carolina seaport seemed favored due principally to balmy climate, cuisine, and beautiful ladies. Short in stature, Tarleton was well proportioned and extremely strong and muscular, cutting a magnificent figure on horseback. Red-haired and dark-eyed with charm and sophistication, Tarleton appealed to women of all ages, social stations, and political persuasions. On one occasion, discovered with the mistress of a fellow British officer, Maj. Richard Crewe, Tarleton barely escaped a duel that would probably have terminated his military career. His amorous successes among American lasses also contributed significantly to the detested status that he rapidly attained among the Colonists.

Dispatched north from Charles Town to capture a regiment of retreating Continentals, he pursued and attacked the Tenth Virginia Regiment in a slashing head-on attack at Waxhaws near the state line. An absolute rout ensued and Tarleton was accused of allowing his dragoons to shoot down wounded and surrendered Americans. He denied these charges, claiming he was pinned under his horse while the action continued, but the ratio of killed and wounded was so inordinately high as to belie this defense. His reputation among his adversaries became extremely negative and Americans proposed to offer him no quarter instead of offering a price for his head and coined the term "Tarleton's quarter." While he may have permitted excesses on occasion, and he gladly burned the properties of patriots and hung several turncoats, Tarleton was probably no better or worse than other cavalrymen of both armies. The bitter, punitive nature of warfare in the south, often among neighbors and amid individuals who changed sides repeatedly, exasperated the efforts of the best commanders. Strangely, Tarleton seemed to pride himself in the hostile threats offered by his foes. He reasoned that fear and demoralization among his enemies caused by his reputation more than offset any real danger to his person.

Tarleton followed his initial success with a victory over Gen. Thomas Sumter at Fishing Creek when he surprised his foe by a rapid, hot chase. Months later Tarleton was repulsed by the same Sumter when forced to engage in a stand-up fight at Blackstocks Plantation. Tarleton's cavalry skills as a drive and slash leader were apparent, but he still seemed somewhat out of his realm when faced with a set-piece fight. Daniel Morgan took advantage of that weakness when he skillfully feigned panic in his retreat, drawing Tarleton forward in a helter-skelter fashion. Then the old frontiersman calmly prepared a trap and presented Tarleton with a set battle.

Tarleton's army was actually a mixed bag of soldiers. Alongside his British Legion of American volunteers, Cornwallis provided him with portions of several light infantry units, unified to form a light infantry battalion of

110 men. Additionally four companies of the Seventh Regiment of Foot Fusiliers, totaling 167 soldiers were included. These recent Irish recruits, wearing red coats faced with blue piping, had no previous combat experience and were designated to serve as garrison troops. His principal strength was in the line companies of the First Battalion, Seventy-first Highlanders, redcoats with white facing, gaiters, and white pants replacing their previous colorful kilts. These splendid soldiers marched to the music of their pipes, 250 strong under command of Maj. Archibald McArthur. Tarleton's mounted troops were portions of the Seventeenth Light Dragoons and the British Legion Dragoons. The Seventeenth retained its red coats while his largest contingent, the British Legion Dragoons, were attired in their distinctive short green jackets with black facings and huge dragoon helmets. Two artillery pieces, 3-pound grasshoppers, accompanied the column with an appropriate contingent of artillerymen. These unique light brass pieces were usually mounted on a Congreve carriage that could be pulled by horses or when equipped with shafts, carried by its crew, either underarm or on the shoulder, even transported by packsaddle if necessary. Gun crews varied from four to eight per weapon, each superintended by a noncommissioned officer.

Morgan's initial dispositions at Cowpens, according to Edwin Bearrs, who studied them carefully, were almost brilliant although highly unorthodox. He placed his soldiers in three distinct defensive lines, each partially screening its successor. This defense in depth was designed to wear down the British attackers by forcing their advance against progressively stronger lines of defenders. The rebels were posted on slightly sloping ground in open grassy fields surrounded by scattered woodlands of hickory, oak, and chestnut trees with mini-mal underbrush. Good defensive ground in that, much like Gettysburg, Pennsylvania, the strengths were not so read-ily apparent and did not appear so strong that an enemy was unlikely to attack. Morgan met with his captains on the evening prior to the fight, carefully explaining the role and expectations of each unit, even drawing explicit maps. But the old frontiersman asked no advice or council; he would make his own decisions. He later claimed that he knew his adversary and was confident of a head-on, straightforward attack. Morgan awoke his soldiers early next morning for a hot breakfast and merrily assured the anxious militiamen that "Bany was coming," but if each man did his duty they would send him running.

The initial American line was actually a strong skir-mish line of North Carolina, South Carolina, and Georgia militiamen under the command of Maj. Joseph McDowell, Maj. Charles Cunningham, and Maj. Samuel Hammond. All were experienced, McDowell a North Carolinian of Cherokee War, Musgrave's Hill, and Kings Mountain com-bat. Hammond, a long-time veteran, had fought at Point Pleasant then moved south to participate in battles at Savannah and Kings Mountain. Samuel Cunningham led the small contingent of Georgia riflemen. In widely scat-tered groups about 150 yards in advance of the second and main militia lines, these riflemen calmly awaited the enemy. The second rebel line consisted of four South Carolina militia battalions drawn up in loose linear forma-tions and aligned left to right under Lt. Col. Benjamin Roebuck, Col. John Thomas, Jr., Lt. Col. Joseph Hayes, and Col. Thomas Brandon. All had fought at Kings Mountain except Thomas, who recently had replaced his ailing father. Roebuck would be wounded in March and imprisoned on a Charles Town prison hulk to die shortly, while Hayes, a

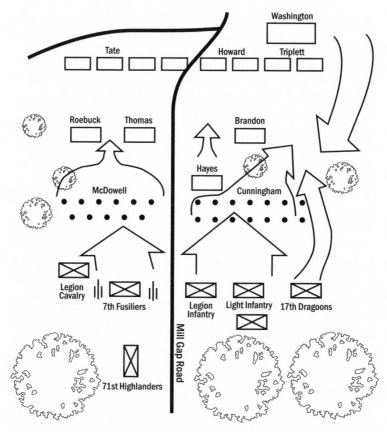

First battle line, Cowpens, January 17, 1781. Tarleton's infantry charged recklessly and dispersed Morgan's skirmish line shortly after daybreak, continuing to confront the second rebel line composed of assorted militia battalions.

bold and rash officer, would be hung and hacked to death by "Bloody" Bill Cunningham. Brandon, a rabid anti-Tory, was an accomplished swordsman and would be credited with slaying three dragoons at Cowpens. Responsibility for the entire line was exercised by the dour-faced but rock-steady Col. Andrew Pickens. A third line, located at the crest of the slight slope, was composed of the five sixty-man Continental line companies flanked on either side by units of experienced Virginia state troops. Tarleton was therefore forced to assault three lines, each progressively stronger than its predecessor. Morgan's cavalrymen, Continental dragoons and mounted militia swordsmen, were grouped behind the third line under Col. William Washington.

The impulsive Tarleton, always searching for a fight, never hesitated. Ordering his leading elements to drop their packs and deploy, he determined to press forward at once. Initially he ordered his Legion Dragoons to scatter the skirmish line, but when that effort failed due to wet ground and lackadaisical effort, the infantry deployed. The light infantry battalion and British Legion infantry were aligned in two-deep ranks to the right of the Green River or Mill Gap Road, which split the field, and the Seventh Fusiliers aligned similarly left of that landmark. A 3-pound gun was unlimbered on the road between these attack units and a second gun aligned in an interval amid the Seventh. The Seventeenth Dragoons were deployed on his right flank and a unit of British Legion Dragoons on the left. As the Seventy-first Regiment, Fraser's Highlanders, arrived they were formed in reserve.

As soon as the British line stepped off to the beat of their drums, American skirmishers began to fire, despite the loud protestations of their officers. Thomas Young, a militiaman celebrating his seventeenth birthday on this day of battle, called the advance "the best line he ever saw . . . they gave a loud British halloo and came at the trot." The American rifles were deadly, and marked officers and artillerymen began to fall. Yet on came the British line, absorbing the rifle fire until, presenting bayonets preparatory to charging home, the American line faded away, the skirmishers moving rapidly backwards and sifting through the gaps of the larger militia line to

Cowpens battlefield. British infantry attacked Morgan's second line through this field. (*Photo by Penny Swisher*)

the rear. Tarleton, riding up front, for he was certainly no shirker, clearly observed the second American line and decided to press on without reforming, speed being essential to breaking the American position.

The skirmishers, after falling back, infiltrated the militia line and reformed on the flanks or in the gaps. Tarleton's infantry, at full cry, continued forward, discharged their two cannon, and repeated their short, staccato cheers. Small groups of expert riflemen fired on the British officers, but upon the urging of Morgan and Pickens, the militia line held its fire until the British formation was thirty to forty paces distant. They then unleashed an aimed rolling volley that seriously injured the attacking line. The British troops were staggered. Some hesitated for a time, in particular the Seventh Fusiliers, stopping cold until their officers applied the flats of their swords to again drive them forward.

Ultimately the redcoats rallied and came on with bayonets shining, intimidating the Colonial militia. Some American units were caught with unloaded guns. The militia line broke first in the center and then folded and dissolved. These temporary soldiers fled at full speed to the safety of their third line, some in obvious panic. British casualties were unusually heavy at the militia line, and the survivors cheered at the abrupt retreat of their opponents while momentarily halting to reform and reorganize their front. The Seventeenth Dragoons on the British right under the ebullient Irishman Lt. Henry Nettles charged the fleeing militia of the American left with great effect, riding in among the fugitives and utilizing their sabers on the heads of the fleeing Colonials. They were countered abruptly, however, by a stern charge of William Washington's Colonial cavalry. James Collins, a militiaman

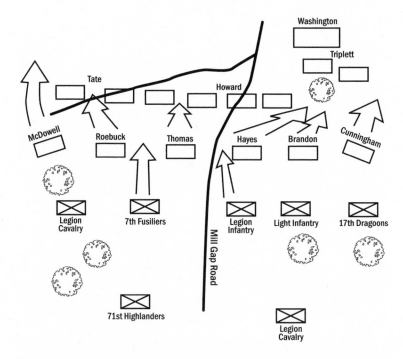

Fight at the second Colonial line. British infantry, despite absorbing considerable losses, broke the second Colonial line, redressed their ranks, and proceeded forward to attack Morgan's third line of Continental infantry.

running for his life, recalled that "we fell back to our horses and then the British cavalry overtook us and started to hack. Suddenly like a whirlwind Col. Washington's horsemen hit their disordered flank and drove them out of sight." Though outnumbered by the British horsemen, the Colonials enjoyed the advantage of superior horseflesh. They rode mounts of thoroughbred-draught-stock mix, strong horses far superior to the confiscated pleasure mounts of the British.

Now, staring at a third American line, the British tightly dressed their lines and awaited orders, the three assault

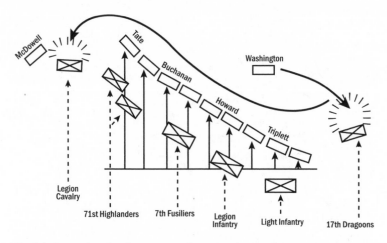

Final fight at the third American line. As the third American line mistakenly retreated, British units sprinted forward in a disorganized manner. Turning, the Continentals fired and charged. With the assistance of Washington's cavalry and regrouped riflemen, the Colonial forces surrounded and forced the surrender of the Seventy-first Highlanders.

battalions compressing to conceal their many losses. Soon the British front again began to advance to the drumbeats, despite continued rifle fire. Halting at close range, the advancers traded volleys with the blue-clad American Continentals. Mounted officers such as Morgan and Tarleton ranged the front, miraculously uninjured. The firefight increased in intensity and for almost fifteen minutes seemed about even in results. Spotting backwoods militia by their distinctive hunting jackets, Tarleton noted and targeted these units, aligned on the American right. He summoned his reserves, the best fighters in his army, the Highlanders of the Seventy-first, to advance on the double, bonnets of black and green plaid appearing from the smoke, accompanied by the Legion Dragoons, to turn the American right flank, an occurrence he expected to precipitate an American rout. McDowell's riflemen, concealed among the trees, disputed this movement with rifle fire until Major McArthur's Highlanders, their shrill pipes keening, broke into a run, shattering their ranks. Again Washington's cavalrymen thundered to the rescue, checking the Legion Dragoons.

Colonel Howard, recognizing the pressure of the Highland advance on his flank, attempted to refuse his right by folding back like a swinging gate his far right elements, the Virginia troops under Capt. Edmund Tate. However, misunderstanding the order, or either ignorant of how to obey the command of "Right wheel, march," the Virginians marched directly to the rear rather than folding to their left. This movement uncovered the adjoining units, which were then forced to follow in succession as each recognized their flank was exposed. This linear withdrawal occurred in a succeeding fashion and not simultaneously, thus producing the effect of an *en echelon* retrograde movement. Morgan, observing the mistake, intuitively reacted. Spurring his horse to the top of a slight rise, with his sword he drew a line in the dirt marking a point at which he loudly ordered his officers to halt and redress their units.

The British infantry, already exhausted from their strenuous efforts, lost all order when they observed the backs of the Americans and sprinted wildly forward in pursuit of what they perceived to be a completely routed foe. Their few surviving officers vainly protested the undisciplined dash, for they noted that the American infantrymen were marching rearward still in their officers' firm control. The Colonials were carrying their weapons at trail arms, loading as they moved.

Upon reaching Morgan's designated line, the American units halted, dressed their line, turned to their front in a slightly oblique fashion, presented weapons, and fired by volleys, right to left. The sprinting enemy pursuers were devastated, as they were caught breathless and largely with unloaded weapons, and absorbed casualties at point-blank range. At that critical moment, Howard ordered a bayonet charge by his Continentals. William Washington's cavalry, having defeated the Legion Dragoons, exploded into the Highlanders' left flank as McDowell's previously scattered sharpshooters reappeared and closed on the British flanks. Only the Scots and the artillerymen fought on, the gunners to the last man. When the Seventh Fusiliers surrendered, Howard wheeled his entire contingent on the Highlanders.

The survivors of the proud Seventy-first were surrounded and John Howard recalled, "They laid down their arms and their officers delivered up their swords." Morgan permitted absolutely no abuse of his captives, to the surprise of the British officers, who openly expressed fear that no quarter would be granted. Vainly, Tarleton attempted to lead his British Legion to rescue the Scots, but this unit deferred. Twice he ordered his dragoons to charge the oncoming Americans, but they turned and fled the field. Alexander Chesney, serving as a leader of Tory scouts, recalled that the British Legion Dragoons had been recruited from American captives after the Battle of Camden and had been uneager to fight. Another source agreed with the nature of such recruiting and felt that these hired sabers of dubious quality, all turncoats, knew what would happen to them if captured. Washington spurred his Colonial horsemen in pursuit and initiated a lively duel with Tarleton and a number of supporters. The two antagonists exchanged sword thrusts, with Tarleton sustaining a slight wound and Washington, whose sword shattered, was perhaps saved by the timely intrusion of his fourteen-year-old bugler.

At this point the fight was finished. British losses were more than 120 dead, several hundred wounded, and almost 900 captured. American casualties are harder to define. Morgan reported 24 killed and in excess of 100 wounded, but his totals are of the Continentals and do not include the various militia commands, for at least another 100 casualties were probably suffered by the militia units, raising rebel losses to more than 200. An embarrassed McArthur remarked to Colonel Howard, "Nothing better could have been expected when troops were commanded by a rash, foolish boy." McArthur's comments, coming immediately after his capture, probably reflect his ill humor at his circumstance, but they cannot be lightly dismissed. The impulsive, hell-for-leather Tarleton, personally brave and always aggressive, did not exhibit nor possibly possess the patience and tactical expertise required to oppose the American alignment. When he faced Morgan's unusual battle lines, Tarleton reacted by launching a direct head-on assault without proper reconnaissance. He neither utilized his artillery advantage nor did he await the arrival from the rear of the marching column of his best troops, the feared Highlanders of the Seventy-first.

The American commander's adroit use of a combined force of long-rifle-equipped militiamen and bayonet-wielding, musket-armed Continentals embraced the strengths of each and countered Tarleton's frontal assault by gradual erosion of his opponent's strength. Morgan's innovativeness in utilizing tactics that combined these diverse units was amazing, for he had no false illusions concerning the militiamen. He was one of them, and while he appreciated their fighting abilities he also understood their weaknesses and reluctance to face the cold steel of British regulars. Yet he found a method to achieve maximum results from militia efforts while concealing their liabilities. For the first time an American army had tactically confronted and defeated a British army of comparable strength on the battlefield. The crude, backwoods saloon fighter had matched wits and bested a suave, intelligent, British-trained officer and achieved a significant victory for his country.

The triumphant backwoodsman consolidated his spoils and, paroling the officers, rapidly started his army and its captives north across the Broad River. Many of the captive Scots would ultimately reach prison camps in Winchester, Virginia. Augusta and Rockbridge County militia, whose members' enlistments had expired, started over the mountains to the Valley of Virginia escorting more than five hundred captives. As Morgan expected, a disappointed Charles Cornwallis was soon in pursuit, anxious to punish Morgan and rescue his Scots before he could unite with Greene, but Cornwallis marched toward Cowpens expecting Morgan to tarry there rather than move north so quickly. Crippled by recurring sciatica, Morgan reached the Catawba River and reluctantly informed Greene that he must leave the field. Unable to stand or ride, he could travel only in a "chair" (a one-horse light chaise).

The soundly beaten Tarleton years later admitted that his defeat, coupled with the demise of Ferguson's force at Kings Mountain, was a catastrophe to British aims in the American south. He was unusually complimentary in his praise of the good conduct and bravery of his Colonial opponents, but he would never admit that Morgan had outgeneraled him as advanced by one of his subordinates, Lt. Roderick MacKenzie. His assessment of Tarleton was blistering: "He led a number of brave men to destruction and then used every effort in his power to damn the same to posterity." Cornwallis declined to reprimand or censure Tarleton, but he commented later that "the late affair has almost broken my heart." However, Cornwallis's commissary officer and a noted British historian, Charles Stedman, was relentless when he wrote, "During the whole period of the war no other action reflected so much dishonor upon British arms."

The limited size of the two armies that clashed at Cowpens has tempted historians to minimize the significance of the action. In such a transient, fluid arena of conflict, militia units—both Loyalist and patriot—formed, fought, dissolved, and reassembled. The sound defeat of Tarleton, who had conducted such an unrelenting, merciless harassment of patriots and their sympathizers, constituted a major morale coup. Each British defeat eroded the Loyalist base in the Carolinas and increased the influence and recruitment of American partisans. Perhaps equally important was its negative effect upon the morale of British soldiers. Isolated in a wild country such as the southern backwoods, and involved in what has been termed a partisan war, a religious war, or even an uncivil war, the British rank and file maintained unshaken confidence in their ability to rout American militia in any clash of arms. The defeat at Kings Mountain could be explained as an ambush by long riflemen and additionally the British force were Loyalists, not regulars. But here at Cowpens, American Continentals and militia bested a British regular field force for the first time, and so completely defeated them that there could be no denial. Despite desperate attempts to cancel the setback, Cowpens was the linchpin of American success that led directly to Yorktown and eventual independence for the American colonies. Charles Stedman accorded that "Cowpens formed a very principal link in the chain of circumstances which led to the independence of America."

The victory at Cowpens also displayed a remarkable example of military leadership, revealing a captain of inexplicable merit who must rank among the greatest of American battlefield captains. While surely benefiting from the stellar subordinate trio of John Eager Howard, William Washington, and Andrew Pickens, and while confronting an overconfident, rash, and somewhat impatient Tarleton, Morgan, nevertheless, controlled the whole. He decided when and where to fight, drew up the plans of engagement, positioned the lines of battle, and carefully committed his troops according to that plan. He steadied his backwoods soldiers with his constant encouragement and visible presence as he rode all three lines. He allowed his subordinates to conduct their portion of the battle under his watchful eye. And he masterfully and intuitively adjusted his battle plans when threatened by the breakthrough of an opponent's shock troops. By all standards of warfare, his actions precipitated a tactical masterpiece.

It is difficult to compare Daniel Morgan with other captains of American military service, for most American generals of note were trained to their task. Few leaders in history have sprung full-blown from such a limited and obscure background. Perhaps Nathan Bedford Forrest is Morgan's closest tactical American contemporary, for surely both men would be deemed illiterate by modern measurements. However, they were highly successful in their own realm, earning the role of back country leaders. Remarkably, without even the rudiments of education, ignorant of the military sciences, and without access to military texts or even the tutelage of a an accomplished soldier, Daniel Morgan developed military skills of a superior level.

William Washington, also no stranger to heavy action in the southern theater of combat, pronounced Daniel Morgan the coolest man under the duress of combat he ever saw. His ability to remain calm in a crisis was probably acquired in skirmishes with Indians, and this attribute proved critical to his success. Using that trait, coupled with an innovative mind that approached problems logically and without bias, Morgan planned the Battle of Cowpens in a manner he understood and could communicate clearly to his followers. When such native ability to tactically plan a fight was merged with his easily identifiable qualities of frontier leadership in managing that fight, a captain for the ages was produced.

Morgan was a product of the frontier, where the social hierarchy was fluid, mobile, and expansive. Little value was placed on wealth and rank. Leaders were physically tough, shrewd, fearless men who could outfight, out drink, and out gamble their contemporaries and were not averse to betting their lives when necessary. It was not the lettered man who could debate a point or explain a principle who emerged a leader, but that tough, physical man who feared no one and felt none alive could "whip" him. As the frontier rolled westward, a civilizing element followed closely, bringing with it vastly different social and civic demands. A new kind of democratic leader arose, one far removed from the aristocracy of the Virginia tidewater or the South Carolina Low Country. Daniel Morgan attained the upper levels of this emerging frontier aristocracy and projected the frontier leader onto the stage of national awareness, preceding later individuals of note such as Andrew Jackson, Sam Houston, and Abraham Lincoln.

His uncanny ability to communicate with the common soldier further enhanced Morgan as a military captain to be followed, to be obeyed by individualistic men who respected few authorities. Though his fiery temper was legendary and his confrontations with those whom he deemed had wronged him was fearful to behold, Morgan possessed that unusual ability to mix freely with common soldiers, using nicknames in a familiar context without endangering the respect necessary for command. He drew from these highly independent men a concerted performance unequalled by any other American revolutionary leader and by few of any era. As with Stonewall Jackson, there is little to suggest that Daniel Morgan was loved, adored, or worshiped by his followers. His exterior was too coarse, too confrontational, too demanding for such. But he was respected, perhaps feared, and conscientiously obeyed. John Henry, who wrote of the terrible march to Quebec, describes Morgan's manner with men: "His manners were of the severest cast; but where he became attached he was kind and truly affectionate . . . Activity, spirit, and courage in a soldier procured his good will and esteem." Morgan the man seemed bigger than life in an era of men who dominated their particular time and place.

CHAPTER 9

Duel in North Carolina

"Another such victory would ruin the British Army."
James Fox, House of Commons

Crusty, bent old Daniel Morgan scooped up a nine-year-old drummer boy, planted a kiss on the lad's rosy cheeks, and loudly proclaimed to William Snickers, "I have given him [Banastre Tarleton] a devil of a whipping. A more complete victory never was attained." Despite this rare self-congratulatory exclamation, Morgan was far too perceptive to allow unlicensed celebration to replace common sense. He recognized that in order to preserve his hard-earned gains at Cowpens he must avoid British attempts at retaliation by conveying his prisoners and spoils northward beyond the reach of redcoat pursuit. On a cold, rainy afternoon immediately following his exalting victory Morgan began his retreat, falling back over the racing Broad River at Cherokee Ford while leaving reliable Col. Andrew Pickens under a flag of parley to tend the wounded, bury the dead, and parole the British wounded. Frank Triplett's Virginians, their enlistments expired, were returning home to the Valley of Virginia, so Morgan utilized the journeying force by having the riflemen escort the bedraggled, embarrassed redcoat captives to Winchester, Virginia, for internment. Interposing his own column between the prisoners and the expected route of Cornwallis's pursuit, he swiftly moved northward. In five days, on roads frozen solid by night and mud filled by day, Morgan retreated one hundred miles, fording the raging Catawba River before daring to make camp.

Lord Charles Cornwallis, comfortably encamped at Turkey River, received notification of Tarleton's defeat at Cowpens with shock and disbelief. Gracious in his public comments about his favorite cavalryman, Lord Cornwallis seethed inwardly over the capture of a battalion of his prized Seventy-first Highlanders, swearing to recover these tough campaigners no matter the cost. Realizing that only rapid pursuit and a crushing defeat of Morgan's army could recoup his losses, Cornwallis increased his efforts to pursue the enemy. Upon the awaited arrival of Gen. Alexander Leslie with reinforcements from Charles Town, including the von Bose Hessian regiment and the Brigade of Guards, Cornwallis reorganized his army and prepared to invade North Carolina. No other option seemed viable since he had lost the initiative in the southern theater, a critical feature in the recruiting of local militia, and he was determined to recapture that edge.

Cornwallis's pursuit proceeded in slow stages, handicapped by a lack of cavalry and weak intelligence. Delaying for several days, Cornwallis mistakenly marched first in the wrong direction, affording Morgan valuable time, which the Old Waggoner adroitly utilized. While Tarleton and other officers were critical of his spasmodic movements, Cornwallis was struggling to ascertain Morgan's exact location and intentions. On January 22, the redcoats crossed into North Carolina, arriving at Ramsour's Mill on the twenty-fifth to find Morgan only twenty miles away but securely located behind the Catawba, then raging at flood stage. Cornwallis had lost the first lap of the chase.

Meanwhile, Gen. Nathanael Greene, the new American commander in the south, received a message announcing the Cowpens victory from a hard-riding messenger, Maj. Edward Giles. Quickly he addressed appeals for militia assistance to the governors of both North Carolina and Virginia. Swinging into the saddle at Hicks Creek, he departed Cheraw and dashed boldly cross-country accompanied by a Major Burnett and a corporal's guard of horsemen, seeking to find Morgan on the Catawba. Gen. Isaac Huger remained behind to marshal the Continental regiments northward. Greene's one-hundred-mile dash concluded on January 30 when he rode into Morgan's camp. Joined by Col. William Washington and Gen. William Lee Davidson, Greene and Morgan strolled outside the encampment and found seats on convenient logs. There, isolated in the woods, they discussed their options in an impromptu council of war. Cornwallis was desperate to bring Morgan to battle before Huger's arrival, but the Colonial commanders agreed to continue their retreat, assigning Davidson and his North Carolina militiamen the unenviable task of contesting the British crossing at the fords of the Catawba. Morgan, almost invalided, was unable to mount a horse and lay on a bed of leaves, shaking with "rheumatism from head to toe." His sciatica, exasperated by constant stress and physical efforts in the cold rain, had reduced the tough old campaigner to a shivering hulk.

Back at Ramsour's Mill, Cornwallis decided to strip his army of nonessential baggage, hopefully increasing their speed and mobility in an effort to keep pace with the Americans. Cornwallis burned the army's wagons, save for

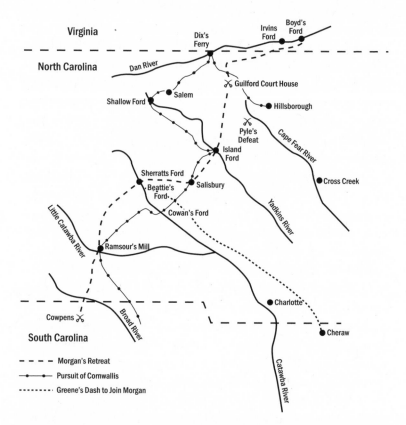

Race for the Dan, January 19-February 14, 1781. Cornwallis pursues Greene across the North Carolina back country.

a few carrying medical supplies, salt, and ammunition, and even destroyed his own baggage to signify the importance of the mission. The army's supply of rum, a treat expected daily by British soldiers, was poured out upon the river-bank. This widely questioned decision compelled the British army to live off the countryside, a dubious method-ology, for the difference between requisitioning and looting was slim and once begun, difficult to control. Even Gen. Charles O'Hara of the Guards, a lifelong supporter of his

Lordship, questioned this calculated risk. "In the most inhospitable, unhealthy part of North America . . . Cornwallis determined to follow Greene's Army to the end of the world," he stated. The army commander, however, recorded the response of his soldiers by reporting that they obeyed his stern directive with a cheerful acquiescence. If so, he was a superbly inspirational leader.

Cornwallis marched cautiously on January 28, approaching the fast-flowing Catawba at Beatties Ford. General Davidson, a confident thirty-five-year-old officer of Continental Army experience at Germantown, awaited the redcoat advance with about eight hundred Mecklenburg County militiamen whom he scattered up and down the Catawba in an attempt to defend the five available crossings. A close friend of Dan Morgan's since their days at Valley Forge, Davidson coolly awaited the enemy as if he still led a Continental regiment. He posted guards at the various fords and began felling trees on the steep approach paths to the four-hundred-yard-wide stream. Cornwallis advanced directly toward Beatties Ford, Col. James Webster's regulars in the lead. Then, in a masterful feint, Cornwallis sent Gen. Charles O'Hara with the Brigade of Guards, the Twenty-third Foot, and the von Bose Hessian regiment in a midnight march downstream to McCowan's Ford, where they stormed across.

A heavy fog hung low over the river prior to first light, but Colonial vedettes faintly distinguished the sound of men wading the river. When the assault column was almost halfway across, the lookouts fired blindly into the mist, alerting General Davidson and his militiamen and causing them to rush back to the river. The Guards light infantry, preceded by three generals on horseback, continued to wade across the raging river, rifles slung, knapsacks and pouches heavy with sixty to seventy pounds of powder and ball, the men utilizing stout poles to maintain their balance in the current. General Leslie was suddenly swept downstream and at almost the same instant General O'Hara's horse was bowled over by the current. Cornwallis continued, his mount shot but still managing to deliver its rider across the torrent before collapsing. As the first British troops waded ashore, they unslung their weapons and opened a scattered fire. In the confused firefight, General Davidson, arriving at the gallop, was struck in the left breast by a musket ball and tumbled from his horse, slain instantly. British casualties were heavy. A Colonel Hall of the British Guards was killed as he stepped from the river, and thirty or more Guardsmen were shot or drowned in the crossing. The British column was fortunate to avoid a loss among the three rashly exposed generals. While Colonial losses were less numerous, the death of General Davidson was akin to catastrophe, creating a panic among his followers, who fled in wild disorder, all thought of further resistance disappearing.

Once across the Catawba, Cornwallis buried his dead on the riverbank and then doubled his pace in a vain effort to force confrontation with Greene or Morgan. But the rains continued to pour, the roads became quagmires, and pursuit fizzled. By February 4 the rebels were across the Yadkin River, nearing Guilford Court House. At that little village Greene took occasion to study the terrain as possible ground upon which to fight Cornwallis. Col. Henry "Lighthorse Harry" Lee rode in with his mixed legion, as did several Virginia militia units, but Greene still felt it best to avoid a confrontation with Cornwallis. On February 10, the pain-wracked Dan Morgan left the army, riding prone in a carriage headed for his Winchester home.

Skillfully, Greene maneuvered his columns to the Dan River, crossing into Virginia at Boyd's and Irvin's Fords, as Col. Edward Carrington, his quartermaster general, secured all available boats up and down the river. Lee's cavalrymen scrambled aboard the final boats, their horses swimming alongside. Unable to cross the flooded Dan without boats, a frustrated Cornwallis fell back to Hillsborough to rally Loyalist support and accumulate adequate supplies. The second phase of the campaign was complete. Greene had masterfully retreated some 230 miles in winter rain, securing his army's safety and further extending his opponent's shaky supply line. His patriot force, now adequately provisioned in Halifax, Virginia, was well positioned to return and fight at a time and place of Greene's choosing. Tarleton, ever slow to compliment his opponent, commented, "Every measure of the American march from the Catawba to the Dan was judiciously designed and vigorously executed."

Lord Charles Cornwallis

Lord Charles Cornwallis, British commander in chief in the south, was a full-blown English gentleman who enjoyed a contrary reputation regarding his military abilities. Often blamed by English historians for the "loss of America" and sometimes hailed as the "Savior of British India," in fact he was neither. Well-educated, intelligent, and socially esteemed, a friend and confidant of King George III, he possessed every advantage of the English elite. Initially, he opposed British policies of a punitive nature toward the Colonies and consistently voted against those measures in the House of Lords. However, once war began he stood firmly to his military duty.

Maj. Gen. Lord Charles Cornwallis. (*National Archives*)

Charles Cornwallis was born in a grand manor house on Grosvenor Square in London on the last day of December 1738, his family of respectable lineage and comfortable means. His father, also Charles Cornwallis, sat in the House of Lords and his mother, Elizabeth Madan, was of an equally esteemed family. Educated first at Eton, then at an Italian military academy in Turin, Charles was commissioned an ensign in the elite Grenadier Guards or First Foot Regiment when war with France was renewed. The promising young officer was married advantageously yet quite happily to Jemina Tullikin Jones, daughter of a colonel on the army lists. He and his wife were close, forming an unusual partnership for that era in that he respected her opinions and she provided important advice on his career. They produced two children, Mary and Charles, before Jemina's tragic death in 1779. Her demise almost destroyed Charles, but he returned to America and immersed himself in military duties, coming to possess a special "love for the serving army in North America."

Colonel of the Thirty-third Foot at age thirty-eight, Cornwallis was promoted to lieutenant general upon his deployment to America. He gained considerable combat experience during the early maneuvering in the middle colonies. Commended for his leadership at the Battle of Long Island where he superbly handled a reserve division, he also fought with aplomb at Trenton, Princeton, Brandywine, and Monmouth. He requested and was permitted leave to return to England upon the illness and subsequent death of his wife, but before departing he became involved in a dispute between Sir Henry Clinton and Sir Robert Howe, a matter which would produce severe consequences for Cornwallis as well as the British army, for it generated severe distrust between the two, interfering with the generals' ability to jointly handle their campaign.

Upon returning to America in 1779, Cornwallis was teamed with Clinton and served as second in command during the campaign to Charles Town. The king adamantly insisted on the unusual partnership despite vehement objections from both officers. Sir Henry Clinton, who was a strategist of some ability, habitually distrusted his subordinates and especially Cornwallis, whom he believed might be conspiring with the king to replace him. Cornwallis, possessing limited strategic skills, was a superb leader of troops and an energetic battle captain; however, he felt restricted and unappreciated by the somewhat paranoid Clinton. The appointment of two soldiers of such complementary merits should have benefited the British army but instead proved a serious liability. Cornwallis accompanied Clinton to Charles Town, participating in the successful 1780 siege and capture of that seaport. Clinton then returned to New York in June, leaving Cornwallis in command, and from that juncture the British southern campaign became his responsibility.

Successful in subduing Georgia and South Carolina, although still harassed at times by active partisans, Cornwallis established an arc of outposts in South Carolina at Georgetown, Augusta, Camden, Cheraw, and Ninety-six. He routed the principal American field army at Camden and by September was poised to move north. His ambitious plans were curtailed by the defeat of Patrick Ferguson's Tory force at Kings Mountain and the rout of Banastre Tarleton's force by Morgan at Cowpens. Desperate to regain the initiative Cornwallis fell victim to his own eagerness, convinced that only rapid pursuit and destruction of Greene's army would lead to a dispersal of the rebel partisans and such a substantial victory would restore the southern colonies to the Crown. Cornwallis actually had little concept of how to suppress a revolution that was now partly a civil war and growing extremely partisan in nature. He wrote: "I am clearly of the opinion that in a civil war there is no admitting of neutral characters and that those who are not clearly with us, must be considered against us as to be disarmed and every measure taken to prevent them doing us mischief."

Determined to catch and crush Greene, Cornwallis prepared to march; however, he was unaware of the strategic skills of his rival, whose survival techniques would rival or surpass those of his mentor, George Washington. Cornwallis, with the arrogance of his caste, neither respected nor attempted to understand the skills of his adversary. The portly Cornwallis was a straight-ahead fighter. He was personally brave, cool, and decisive, an instinctive soldier of reserved temperament. Well liked by his men and officers, he was honest and reasonably compassionate. He avoided the female liaisons so common to British officers in America. He was a man to be admired, to respect, and to follow, although never a gifted soldier.

Following the surrender of the British army at Yorktown, Cornwallis became locked in a public debate with Clinton over responsibility for the momentous defeat of British arms. Maintaining his dignity and with the unwavering support of the king, Cornwallis emerged with his name intact. In 1786 he was appointed governor-general of India, whereupon he reaffirmed his reputation as an administrator of colonial affairs and a military captain of merit. Conducting a masterful campaign against Tippoo Sahib, sultan of Mysore, he emerged victorious, partially upon his logistical accomplishments. Some dozen years later he was asked to mollify a near rebellion in Ireland but his efforts met with little success. Eventually, critical of Crown policy, Cornwallis resigned from the Irish post and surprisingly he retained the good favor of the monarch. Reassigned to India amid a second crisis Cornwallis contracted a fever and died at Ghazipore on October 5, 1805. He was interred in an elaborate mausoleum in that Indian city on the Ganges.

The small army that Cornwallis gathered to pursue Morgan's retiring Colonials was composed of only about two thousand soldiers. But this diminutive force contained the flower of British troops in the south and could be depicted as a hard, tough, professional force. Cornwallis assigned most of his Tory militia to garrison the various South Carolina outposts while he attempted to conduct the campaign with his disciplined regulars. Five infantry battalions made up the core of his army, all composed of experienced veterans. The Hessian von Bose Regiment, in splendid blue regimentals and shiny mitre caps, was led by Lt. Col. Johannes Christian du Puy. An attached company of one hundred jaeger riflemen or skirmishers added firepower to these 320 mercenaries. The green-jacked sharpshooters were equipped with short, accurate German rifles of a style used by foresters in their homeland.

Two decorated British line regiments bolstered the marching column. The Twenty-third Foot, or Royal Welsh Fusiliers, of Lt. Col. Nisbet Balfour contained almost 250 veteran redcoats. This regiment arrived in New York in 1773 and was forwarded to General Gage's force then stationed in Boston, Massachusetts. The Twenty-third marched with the relief force that sallied forth to rescue the English column staggering back from the Lexington and Concord sortie. The Fusiliers had experienced heavy action in almost every northern battle until transferred south to participate in the assault on Charles Town. The Thirty-third Foot, or West Riding Regiment, was a unit of more than 330 strong commanded by Lt. Col. James

Webster, perhaps the best field officer in American service. Experienced and tough, the Thirty-third had once been the command of Cornwallis himself. Participants in the Charles Town attack, the Thirty-third had also anchored the British line at Camden in 1780.

A colorful and spirited unit, the Second Battalion of the Seventy-first Highlanders filed into the roadway in plaid Highland bonnets, following the shrill keening of their pipers. Their green plaid pants had been replaced by more ulitarian garb, captured white breeches. The First Battalion of the Seventy-first had been wrecked at Cowpens, most of its members now imprisoned. Both battalions had been raised in the brooding highlands above Stirling Castle in 1775. Uniformed and issued arms, they were loaded aboard ships bound for New York, learning to handle their flintlock muskets while at sea. Debarked at Staten Island to master the intricacies of tactical drill, both battalions saw heavy action in the south at Savannah and Charles Town. Lt. Col. Duncan MacPherson led the nearly three hundred Highlanders.

The final infantry component of Cornwallis's army was a two-battalion brigade of foot guards. Volunteers were solicited from the three famed British foot guard units, the First Guards, the Coldstream Guards, and the Third Guards, and a composite brigade was formed. Volunteering for American service, the brigade had been sent over in 1776 and divided into two battalions of four companies apiece. A foot guard grenadier company and a guards light infantry company also accompanied the battalion. Each guard battalion now contained about three hundred men while the grenadiers numbered 120 and the light infantry 75. Brig. Gen. Charles O'Hara of the Coldstreams commanded the ad hoc regiment, although the grenadiers and light infantry would fight as separate units.

An artillery section composed of three light guns supported the infantry battalions. Lt. John Macleod of the Royal Artillery, assisted by Lt. John O'Hara and about fifty gunners, served the 3-pound guns. Small but lethal, these weapons were labeled "grasshoppers" for their ungainly appearance. They could either be carried on horseback or hand carried and deployed for action on wooden legs rather than wheeled carriages. Usually a two-horse team pulled the gun tube with limber boxes attached. Their light weight afforded a mobility that permitted their accompanying cavalry or light infantry units, much as civil war horse artillery would perform years hence. Grasshopper projectiles were of two types: solid iron balls or a form of canister whereupon musket balls were packed in a cloth bag, rammed atop the powder charge, and fired, dispersing as they emerged from the gun muzzle. Only effective at short range, Macleod's canister fire would exert a chilling and effective influence on the battle to come.

The two cavalry units accompanying Cornwallis were the Seventeenth Dragoons and the British Legion of Banastre Tarleton. These green-coated dragoons were Loyalists of proven value but tired and worn from extensive campaigning. Lack of cavalry presented Cornwallis with serious tactical disadvantages, as Maj. George Hanger explained: "The militia were all mounted on horseback which made it impossible for us to force them to engage with infantry—if you repulse them you can never inflict material damage."

Cornwallis's army, though diminutive, was well equipped. Veteran infantry units were all armed with the standard Brown Bess flintlock musket. Most troops possessed the 1756 forty-six-inch-barreled Long Land model. This weapon's cylindrical smoothbore barrel was affixed to a walnut stock, the whole measuring four feet, ten inches and weighing nine pounds, eleven ounces and firing a .75-caliber ball. A range of almost three hundred yards was theoretically possible, but the weapon became highly inaccurate past eighty to ninety yards. The heavy lead slug, fired at low muzzle velocity, flattened on contact, producing gruesome wounds. Head and torso shots were usually fatal while a soldier struck in a joint (elbow or knee) faced a dangerous amputation. When struck by a .75-caliber ball, soldiers were often knocked completely off their feet as if struck by a club or iron bar, with shock a common side effect. Theoretically an experienced soldier executing the twelve steps of firing could fire four or five times per minute, but in actual practice two or three shots was usual. Misfires were common, particularly in damp weather.

A rectangular top stud, located behind the muzzle, secured a truly fearsome auxiliary weapon, a sixteen- to nineteen-inch triangular socket bayonet. With the offset blade slipped over the weapon's muzzle, the gun could be loaded and fired with bayonet attached. The German infantrymen were equipped with a similar .80-caliber weapon of German manufacture. Jaeger riflemen carried a three-foot, eight-inch .54-caliber flintlock rifle. These light infantrymen were without bayonets, substituting a twenty-four-inch basket hilted hanger for close fighting. This little force was as professional, spirited, and eager as any force fielded by the British in North America during the revolution. Tactical advances of the style anticipated were costly but effective, usually consisting of a steady advance to the drums to within about forty yards of the enemy's line, absorbing his fire, for the advancing line would halt, dress, and deliver a rolling volley and charge home with the bayonet.

General Nathanael Greene

The American commanding officer in the southern theater was the Rhode Islander Nathanael Greene. Born on August 7, 1742, to a prosperous merchant and part-time Quaker minister also named Nathanael, the youngster displayed a bright and inquiring mind. But Nathanael's academic prospects were curtailed by his stern father's insistence that reading, writing, ciphering, and a strict adherence to the Holy Scriptures were ample education for any child. The youngster went to work in his father's iron foundry at age fourteen, quickly developing a stout physique from hours at the forge. He used his earnings to purchase an impressive array of books with which he attempted to satisfy his yearning for knowledge and education. When he enrolled in the local militia unit his attendance at Quaker meetings declined, and upon the death of his pious father he was suspended from the Society of Friends.

Nathanael courted, fell in love with, and married a local belle, Catharine Littlefield, in July 1774. The orphaned Caty, nineteen years old and thirteen years Greene's junior, was strikingly beautiful, possessed an engaging personality, and was constantly pursued by a bevy of men but seemed always faithful to her adoring Nathanael. Greene gradually assumed a prominent role in the local militia, the Kentish Guards, although a slight lameness in his right knee prevented his participation in drill field activities and curtailed his selection as an officer. He immersed himself in military study, purchasing books on European military leaders through Boston booksellers. In May of 1775 when the Kentish Guards were detailed to join Washington's army at Boston, the Rhode Island Assembly was asked to appoint a brigadier general from the state and unexpectedly the

Maj. Gen. Nathanael Greene. (*National Archives*)

solons named Nathanael Greene for the post. This rapid promotion from private to brigadier general was surely the fastest advancement in rank in American military history.

Greene blossomed rapidly as a troop commander in patriot service, rapidly earning the approval of his peers as well as that of Gen. George Washington. He handled his units well in actions about New York in the fall of 1776, learning some of the realities of militia command. Greene's status within the army grew, as did Washington's reliance on the dependable Rhode Islander. In March 1788, despite his personal objections, the Continental Congress, acting on Washington's recommendation, appointed Greene to the post of quartermaster general of the army, a position he would fill for more than two years. Greene performed near miracles in this new role. His attention to detail, natural intelligence, foresight, and honesty made him a natural for the demanding, unappreciated tasks. Greene worked tirelessly in an attempt to keep the army supplied and equipped without any cash basis. The unpopular system of impressments and receipts was still utilized from the army's earliest organization, contributing greatly to Greene's frustration. Finally, in August of 1780, after serious disagreements with Congress, Greene irrevocably resigned from the office of quartermaster general. Washington, in order to prevent his leaving the service, appointed Greene to the command of the garrison at West Point.

After the American disaster at Camden, Congress requested that Washington appoint a replacement for Horatio Gates, and he immediately recommended that Greene be assigned to his first independent command. In late fall, Greene rode south into absolute chaos, arriving at Gates' headquarters near Charlotte on December 2 to find a dispirited, ragged group of survivors. Restructuring and reorganizing the distressed southern army, Greene attempted to restore morale to the near mutinous troops through better rations and equipment, as well as a reevaluation of officers. His first offensive deployment entailed the dispatching of Daniel Morgan's light troops westward to annoy Tory outposts, an activity that resulted in the significant victory at Cowpens.

During the ensuing campaign and the fight at Guilford Court House, Nathanael Greene conducted his first independent military operation, his personal attributes and positive abilities emerging immediately. Never a gifted battlefield tactician or inspirational captain in the mold of his invalided subordinate, Daniel Morgan, nonetheless, Greene was both mentally and physically tough. He utilized Morgan's tactical advice but relied on his own decision-making abilities to select a battlefield. He demonstrated superb strategic skills in maneuvering his army, and his ability to read Cornwallis's reactions was a remarkable and valuable attribute. Greene's logistical efforts and his keen understanding of geography were unsurpassed in the American army. After the terrific clash of arms at Guilford Court House, Cornwallis went southeast to Wilmington and Greene, disdaining to follow, turned south. The patriot general led his little army into battle at Hobkirk's Hill, Ninety-six, and Eutaw Springs, winning none of these engagements but maintaining the American presence in the south. A British officer observed, "The more he is beaten the further he advances in the end." Following the war, Greene established residence in Georgia, residing at Mulberry Grove, a plantation awarded him by the state of Georgia in recognition of his accomplishments. He lived there with Caty until his untimely death of sunstroke on June 19, 1786. He was forty-four.

The Colonial army that Greene would bring south across the Dan River to fight, although somewhat larger than its British opponent, was primarily composed of undisciplined, short-term militia from the North Carolina and the Virginia Piedmont and contained few regiments of experienced Continentals. The constant flux of arriving and departing units was a great discouragement to Greene. He wrote to Thomas Jefferson, "Every day has filled me with hopes of an augmentation of my force; the militia have flocked in from various quarters, but they come and go in such irregular bodies that I can make no calculation on the strength of my army, or direct any future operation that can insure my success." Resolutely he reorganized his army and on March 10 with forty-four hundred men moved from his Halifax County base into North Carolina, camping near Guilford Court House on the fourteenth.

The backbone of Greene's army was composed of four Continental line regiments. Brig. Gen. Isaac Huger led a brigade of two Virginia line regiments, the Fourth Virginia of Lt. Col. John Green and Lt. Col. Samuel Hawe's Fifth Virginia, while a second brigade composed of Col. John Gunby's First Maryland and Lt. Col. Ben Ford's Second Maryland was under the direction of Col. Otho Williams. The two Maryland units were experienced combat outfits, the two other regiments being recently recruited to strength and containing many green troops. These four Continental regiments totaled slightly more than fifteen hundred effective soldiers.

The majority of Greene's army consisted of nearly twenty-eight hundred militiamen arrayed in six units of brigade size. Two of these brigades, of about five hundred men apiece, were from nearby North Carolina counties and had never seen combat. Brig. Gen. John Butler, a tough old veteran of the regulator movement, led volunteers from Orange, Granville, and Guilford Counties, reinforced by Col. Arthur Forbes' one-hundred-man company from Alamance. Brig. Gen. Thomas Eaton led North Carolinians from Halifax and Warren Counties.

Two brigades of Virginia militia joined Greene as he exited Halifax. Brig. Gen. Robert Lawson brought six hundred men from Pittsylvania, Prince Edward, Cumberland, and Amelia Counties, while Brig. Gen. Edward Stevens' Virginia Brigade, also of about six hundred men, was from the Virginia Valley counties of Rockbridge, Augusta, and Rockingham. These back country units included numerous experienced Indian fighters, many having seen action at Point Pleasant, and most were accurate riflemen. Two late additions added rifle power to Greene's army. Col. Charles Lynch led a Bedford County aggregate of about three hundred long rifle bearers. Also Col. William Campbell, of Kings Mountain command, appeared at the head of sixty southwest Virginia frontiersmen. North Carolina riflemen led by Maj. Joseph Winston and Capt. Martin Armstrong bolstered Campbell's corps. A third unit of Virginians commanded by Col. William Preston, arriving late, was also assigned to Campbell, swelling the rotund Scot's force to a total of three hundred fifty.

Perhaps Greene's greatest troop advantage lay in the quality of his two cavalry units and their commanders, both stronger than Tarleton's now badly worn British cavalry force. Lt. Col. William Washington, an emerging giant of the Cowpens victory, led ninety Continental dragoons augmented by militia horsemen and the intense, ambitious Lt. Col. Harry Lee commanded a second cavalry unit. He arrived in camp at Halifax with seventy-five cavalrymen and eighty-two light infantrymen arrayed in a grandly titled

Lee's Legion. Both officers were tough, experienced leaders of cavalry. A final component was Greene's artillery. Capt. Anthony Singleton and Lt. Samuel Finley directed four brass 6-pound guns of 3.6-inch bore, served by some sixty Virginia artillerymen. Reliable and effective guns with a range of six hundred to eight hundred yards, these weapons utilized either canister or solid shot and more than offset Cornwallis's artillery section.

The Armies Collide

On February 18, Greene dispatched Brig. Gen. Andrew Pickens and his South Carolina partisans, supported by Lt. Col. Harry Lee's cavalry, to cross the Dan River into North Carolina and begin annoying Cornwallis's encampment. The redcoat army was suffering direly for proper provisions, for they were now located nearly 200 miles from their main supply base at Camden and more than 150 miles from Wilmington, where supplies might be obtained by sea. Cornwallis had not been successful in his efforts to gain local supplies and as Sgt. Gideon Lamb of the Thirty-third Regiment of Foot reported, the scarcity of provisions in Hillsborough was such that it was impossible to feed any army, the men eating turnips and Indian corn as a regular portion of their diet. Clearly the British force could not remain in Hillsborough much longer; they must fight or retreat.

As Greene steadily forwarded additional reinforcements for Pickens, the Presbyterian general became bolder, searching for a means to isolate and ambush the hated "scourge" of the Colonial militia, Banastre Tarleton. When that energetic and flamboyant cavalryman led his green-jacketed riders out of Hillsborough and turned west, both

Pickens and Lee followed, seeking an opportunity to attack. Unbeknownst to the Colonial commanders, Tarleton was moving to affect a union with Tory colonel John Pyle, who had recruited a unit of three hundred to four hundred local militia cavalrymen. Tarleton was to escort these badly needed horsemen to Cornwallis's camp. Lee, however, accidentally located Pyle's riders first, with highly controversial results.

A local company of about seventy militia cavalrymen under Capt. Joseph Graham accompanied Lee, riding in a column of twos at the rear of Lee's column. Proceeding carefully west across the Haw River, Lee anticipated a confrontation with Tarleton's British Legion. Suddenly the American column encountered a file of Tory riders who were deceived by the green jackets of Lee's men and thought they were meeting the identically bedecked British Legion. The two columns slowly passed one another, exchanging civilities, until several Tories recognized Maj. Jeremiah Dixon of Graham's Colonial militia and fighting erupted. Lee's cavalrymen were at a decided advantage since they were riding with loaded weapons and drawn swords, expecting a clash with Tarleton, while the Tories carried slung rifles and sheathed swords. The brief, violent encounter was so one-sided that not a single Colonial soldier was slain. Tory dead numbered more than ninety and an additional hundred men were seriously wounded. So sudden and fierce did the fight explode at close range and so heavy were the Tory casualties that the encounter became known in Tory circles as Pyle's Massacre, Lee being accused of retaliating for Tarleton's Waxhaw attack. Many Tories claimed their cries for quarter were ignored, a claim Lee vehemently denied. Extricating his troopers, Lee retreated, realizing that

Tarleton was only a mile or two distant and must hear the din of battle. Cornwallis felt the effects of the ambush in an abrupt reduction of local recruits. Bitterly disappointed, he labeled the lack of Loyalist support about Hillsborough as "dastardly and pusillanimous."

On the twentieth of February light infantry under Gen. Otho Williams crossed the Dan into North Carolina, followed a few days later by Greene with his remaining Continental line regiments and Stevens' Virginia militia. Learning of these movements, Cornwallis abandoned his Hillsborough camps on the twenty-fifth and moved to a position on Stinking Quarter Creek, astride a conflux of roadways that enhanced his flexibility of movement. Greene grew closer, dispatching Williams, Pickens, and Lee to harass the British force. Cornwallis was aware that Greene was located only some twenty miles north, but he was unable to pinpoint his opponent. On March 6, impatient and aggressive, the British commander sent a strong column north in an attempt to flank Williams' annoying light infantry brigade and perhaps separate that unit from Greene's main force and destroy it. He also rationalized that a successful isolation of Williams might cause the patriot commander to face him in a general action. A race for a critical crossroads at Wetzell's Mill ensued as heavy fog hampered troop movements of both armies. Lt. Col. James Webster led a brigade composed of the Twenty-third, Thirty-third, and Seventy-first Regiments. They pounded north despite the intermittent harassing fire from Col. William Campbell's riflemen secreted in the fields and woods. Narrowly beating Webster to the crossroads, Williams, Campbell, and Pickens established a delaying position at Reedy Creek while Lee and Washington aligned their riders on their flanks. After an exchange of rifle fire,

Webster boldly rode forward into the stream, waving his soldiers forward with his hat. Twenty-five Virginia riflemen fired at close range upon the richly uniformed British officer, but all missed their mark. Webster rallied his redcoats, leading the van across the ford and driving Campbell's riflemen rearward for several miles. The screening efforts of Lee and Washington's cavalrymen, however, prevented Webster's gaining any advantage, and he was forced to abandon the advance.

Several days passed during which Greene continued to receive reinforcements. However, one grumbling unit, its term of enlistment expired, decided to leave the army and return home, despite the clear threat of a major clash. These South Carolina and Georgia partisans, displeased with the role of their unit, refused the entreaties of a frustrated Andrew Pickens and started the long ride south, circling the British army. Greene reluctantly permitted the invaluable Pickens to accompany them homeward. Greene restructured his forces again, moving south to Guilford Court House, only twelve miles from Cornwallis's Deep River Meeting House camp. Both commanding generals were now prepared and committed to fight. Cornwallis, upon receiving word of Greene's deployment, began to advance. His need of provisions was so severe that he must achieve victory or abandon the campaign.

Early on the morning of March 15, Cornwallis sent the advance elements of his army forward on the New Garden Road, probing toward Guilford Court House. Banastre Tarleton rode alone in the van, leading his Loyalist cavalry, reinforced by an excellent company of German riflemen, and the light infantry company of the Guards. As the column approached New Garden Church, intermittent carbine and pistol fire interrupted the night's silence. Not one to be caught unawares, Greene had posted Lee with his legion and about one hundred of Campbell's long riflemen in an outpost position on the only serviceable roadway several miles south of his principal encampment. Lee sent a patrol under Capt. Richard Heard to feel farther south toward the British camp. About 2 A.M., Heard reported movement on the road toward Guilford Court House and notified Lee.

Tarleton pressed firmly onward at a trot, driving Heard's vedettes. Reaching a narrow, curved lane encased by high wood fences, his riders hesitated then continued forward, straight into a cunning trap. Lee loosed his dragoons in columns of fours to charge the head of the British advance while Campbell's riflemen sprinted swiftly to the fence lines and opened fire, enveloping the green-jacketed riders. Sharply repulsed, Tarleton's lead elements fell back, their commander wounded by a musket ball through his right hand that would later necessitate amputation of parts of his fore and middle fingers. Lee attempted to follow up his little victory but was checked as Cornwallis dispatched the Welsh Fusiliers forward in support. As Lee closed on the British force, a sudden volley frightened his horse, which reared and threw its rider, leaving him prone and exposed on the battlefield. Fortunately Lee was able to locate another mount and escape under the covering fire of Campbell's riflemen. Lee, now convinced that Cornwallis was advancing with his entire army, withdrew slowly, observing the British van.

Meanwhile, among the low, rolling hills and ravines near Guilford Court House, Greene was coolly and methodically deploying his army. Amid tall hardwoods and heavy undergrowth interspaced with cleared cornfields, he prepared to contest Cornwallis's professionals. Carefully considering the advice of his departed subordinate Daniel Morgan, Greene adopted and modified the Old Waggoner's recommendations. Morgan had written, "Put your riflemen on the flanks, the militia in the center, and picked troops in the rear." However, Greene's army was much larger than Morgan's had been at Cowpens, preventing personal supervision of each line, and the rough woodland limited visibility of the actions, somewhat mitigating the effects of identical deployment. The principal Hillsborough-Salisbury highway ran east to west through the woods and Greene roughly aligned his army astride that roadway, blocking any British advance.

Greene chose his position based on suitability for an in-depth defense, arraying his force in three battle lines. The lines were so far apart as to be out of sight of one another, creating three almost distinctly separate engagements. Greene's first line, situated behind rail fences on the edge of a wood, looked out across cleared fields. A pair of inexperienced North Carolina militia brigades formed the bulk of this first line. Eaton's brigade aligned to the right of the bisecting roadway while Butler's unit, reinforced by Forbes' company, deployed to the left. In the roadway between the militia brigades two 6-pound guns were sited, served by Capt. Anthony Singleton's Virginia gunners. To the right of Eaton's line a light corps was formed to protect the American flank. This flank corps was led by Col. William Washington and included, in addition to his mounted dragoons, a company of Delaware regulars under Kirkwood and Col. John Lynch's rifle battalion. On Butler's left the opposite flank included a similar corps under Colonel Lee that encompassed his legion and a number of small, independent rifle units all consolidated under the direction of Colonel Campbell. Greene awarded considerable responsibility to the cavalry leaders, charging them to "give the enemy all the annoyance in your power." Greene's most unpredictable troops, the North Carolina militiamen, were placed in a carefully selected position: flanks well protected and supported by artillery. As he rode among them, the patriot commander requested two or three volleys of musket fire from each unit, delaying and punishing the British advance, then they could fall back. Greene's flank units were a clever combination of cavalry dragoons, back country riflemen, and musket-bearing, bayonet-wielding infantry. Mutually supportive, this combined arms force could and would fight independently when necessary.

The American commander's second line was some three hundred yards distant, in the rear of the initial line, but due to the dense woods and uneven terrain it was not in visual contact with the first deployment. Two Virginia militia brigades were aligned to defend this deployment in the woods. Lawson's men were stationed on the Colonial right in heavy woods and underbrush while Stevens carefully positioned his brigade on the opposite side of the road. Stevens was a corpulent, dedicated soldier who had experienced the panic of humiliating defeat when his militia brigade fled at Camden, and he had developed his own crude method of preventing another such occurrence. He stationed forty trustworthy sentinels armed with rifles along the rear of his line with orders to shoot the first man who ran. Lawson's unit was the weaker of the two brigades, being depleted by the detachment of Lynch's riflemen, but held a strong position in heavy woods. Stevens' brigade contained a number of ex-Continental soldiers in addition to many Shenandoah Valley Indian fighters, thus his large brigade was considered the best militia force to deploy on that fateful day. The flank corps of Lee and Washington

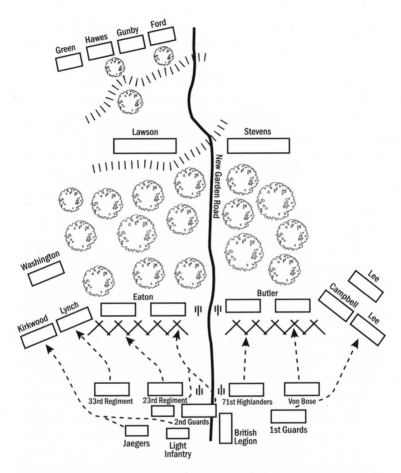

Guilford Court House, March 15, 1781. Cornwallis deployed to assault the first American line but was soon compelled to bring all his infantry on line. Eaton's and Butler's Colonial militia units broke and ran as the British continued forward.

would fall back and secure the flanks of this second line following the completion of their assignment with the North Carolina militia on the initial line. Actual fighting at the second line would prove extremely confusing and difficult. The heavy growth of trees and brush would disrupt formations, breaking down the units of both armies into platoons and squads, an occurrence that would prove beneficial to the rebels.

Almost 500 yards east of the second line, invisible through the trees, Greene arrayed his Continental regiments on the brow of a bowl-like hillside. Due to the unusual configuration of the terrain this line was semicircular and arrayed at an angle to the previous American lines. The Virginia regiments of Green and Hawes were deployed on the left while Gunby's and Ford's Maryland units, alongside, bordered the roadway. Lieutenant Finley's two guns were located between the regiments and the cavalry forces would be expected to cover the flanks. Greene stationed himself with this critical third line, although it was some 850 yards from the battle's opening phase.

This careful placement of the American army maximized the strengths of its various components and the plan succeeded quite well. The militia units were stationed in such a manner that they were forced to fight while the rifle units were sited to generate enfilading fire. The cavalry units were placed so as to allow freedom of movement, and the most experienced infantry regiments anchored the entire position and could protect any withdrawal. While the force was defensively deployed tactically and could not easily convert to offensive action, the army would be difficult to defeat and virtually impervious to a disaster.

Just prior to noon the British column began to file across Little Horseshoe Creek, almost eight hundred yards from Eaton's and Butler's position on the fence line. Singleton opened at once with his 6-pounders and Cornwallis responded by dispatching young Lt. John Macleod's guns forward to counter. A thirty-minute artillery exchange ensued while the British infantry impressively deployed into line of battle. Losses from the gun duel were slight save for the tragic death of Lieutenant O'Hara, Macleod's artillery assistant. This well-liked young officer, the nephew of General O'Hara of the Guards and a favorite of the army, was tragically decapitated by a solid shot. Cornwallis must have pondered over the force and position he faced, for only the militia of the first line were visible, resting their weapons on zigzag fences, while scattered cavalrymen sat quietly on either flank. Boldly, in the tradition of British professional soldiers, he deployed, positioning his regiments for a straightforward attack with which he intended to overwhelm the awed Colonial militia.

Brightly attired British infantry wheeled smartly from marching column into two-deep battle lines, whirling company by company at the double, astounding the onlooking Colonial backwoods militia. Cornwallis arrayed his units on a four-brigade front, two brigades on either side of the roadway, Macleod's guns positioned in the center. MacPherson's Seventy-first Highlanders filed to the right of the road with the von Bose Hessians of Du Puy extending on their right. Maj. Gen. Alexander Leslie, the army's second in command, coordinated the right wing. To the left, the Twenty-third Welsh Fusiliers came on line accompanied by the Thirty-third Regiment of Foot, both ably led by Col. James Webster. Close behind Leslie's wing the First Battalion of Guards under one Lieutenant Colonel Norton formed in reserve, while Webster's reserve consisted of the Second Battalion of Guards under O'Hara and the independent companies of Hessian jaegers, Grenadier Guards, and Light Infantry Guards. Tarleton's dragoons sat astride their horses, idly motionless in the road, their commander almost defenseless, his right arm in a sling, reins in his left.

An expectant silence fell over the field for several minutes following the colorful deployment, even the artillery slowing its exchange. Shortly after 1 P.M., with a sudden throbbing of drums accompanied by the squeal of fifes and the wail of bagpipes, the four brigades moved forward as one, with steadily measured tread. As the bright sunlight gleamed on polished gun barrels and bayonets, faded regimental flags streamed in the cold March wind. The precise lines seemed to move directly at the fence line. There were no supernumeraries, no onlookers; every officer and every man was in his place, a time to die. A magnificent sight unfolded before the uneasy Colonial militia, the formal attack of a disciplined European-style army in the backwoods of North Carolina.

The eminent British historian George Macaulay Trevelyan once remarked, "No man alive could set a battle in array more artistically than Lord Cornwallis." On that bright, cool afternoon this accolade seemed genuine as the well-marshaled British battle line surged forward, moving slightly uphill across muddy fields as diminutive drummers throbbed a lively tattoo of cadence. On either flank, skirmish lines of rebel riflemen obliquely overreaching the British line began a methodical popping fire, aiming for officers or subalterns. The militiamen of Eaton and Butler, crouching behind their fencerow cover, grew nervously quiet, as the swords of the British officers seemed pointed directly at their front. Periodic firing began up and down the militia fence line despite the remonstrations of their officers. As the advance reached about 140 yards' distance the American officers bellowed, "Fire!" and a rippling, sharp volley echoed from the fence line. Redcoats slumped and fell in the mud, but ranks closed and the advance continued without pause. At 40 yards' distance the bright line halted and a long line of Brown Bess muskets fell to the ready. On command, with a clap like rolling thunder, the British regiments fired by volley. Disregarding a weak return fire from the rebels, the redcoats charged bayonets, screaming like banshees. The militia front broke and sprinted rearward. Weapons, ammunition boxes, canteens, and other items were abandoned as nearly one thousand rebels raced rearward, unstoppable.

From this initial clash, a controversy arose that endured for years in the Carolina back country. The furor embraced the performance of Eaton's and Butler's North Carolina militia brigades. These green militia soldiers, most seeing combat for the first time, were placed in the front line of the impending battle and requested by Greene to fire two volleys and retreat back through the second line in a strategy similar to Morgan's use of militia at Cowpens. They observed the spirited deployment and menacing advance of a threatening professional force and without bayonets could not be expected to deter the oncoming array. Greene only intended that they begin the process of attrition dictated by his defense. Many officers derided their performance and General Greene charged that they fired only once at extended range, then threw down their weapons and fled. Likewise, Light Horse Harry Lee claimed their sudden panic endangered the entire army. But Greene was located alongside the third American line, some half mile away through heavy woods, and could not possibly have witnessed the action. Lee, while much closer, was busily involved in organizing his flank corps and could have seen but a small portion of the assault on the fence line. British sources relate a different story. Sgt. Roger Lamb, charging with the Royal Welsh Fusiliers, recalled a line of weapons laying on the fence line when his regiment halted to fire on Eaton's front as well as the havoc created by their discharge. The

Highland regiment attested that they absorbed an unusual number of losses from the fire of Butler's men. Captain Singleton, who commanded the American guns in the road, complimented the efforts of both units of militia on the front rank. However, when the NCOs dressed the redcoat ranks and the Scots came on, stepping over their dead and wounded, no militia unit could be expected to stand.

It is very difficult to reconcile the reports of the various observers in order to gain a true picture of the fight, and we are left with small vignettes of soldiers who glimpsed pieces and parts of the battle through the tall trees and scrub growth. It seems reasonable to assume that the North Carolina militia performed much better than many have claimed. Cognizant of the request that they fire two volleys and retreat, most of the one thousand riflemen fired at 140 yards. Slightly too far for maximum effect, this volley nonetheless caused casualties of note. The speed of the British advance surprised the rookie rebels and dictated that only the fastest and most experienced among them could reload and fire a second time. Some did and the redcoats paid dearly for their persistence. The militia then retreated, an action that quickly became a rout.

From the flanks, the fire of the backwoods riflemen stung the Crown regiments. Lieutenant Colonel Webster, commanding the British left, veered his Thirty-third and Twenty-third Regiments wider to face Lynch's riflemen. General O'Hara was thus obliged to fill his battle line with his Second Battalion of Guards and attached Grenadier company. Webster then ordered the Hessian jaegers and the Guards Light Infantry to march obliquely across the field and attach themselves to his left, extending his line. This maneuver positioned them to confront Lynch's unit and eased the effects of their enfilading fire.

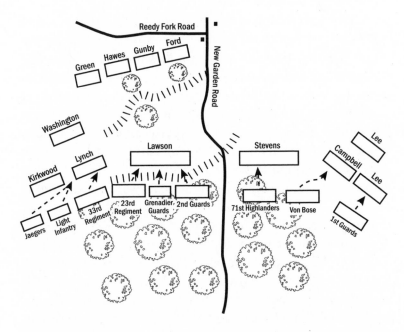

Guilford Court House, second American line. The British regiments
continued through heavy woods to assail the American militia brigades
of Lawson and Stevens. A vicious fight ensued in tangled trees and
undergrowth.

On the British right the von Bose Regiment wheeled
slightly left to face the scalding fire of William Campbell's
consolidated rifle corps. Norton, with the First Battalion of
Guards, was ordered by General Leslie to extend the
British right. When Butler's militiamen broke, Campbell's
riflemen lost contact with the militia save for those several North Carolina units who joined this contingent. A seam
developed in the American line through which Hessians
poured, and assisted by the Guards they pushed Lee's
flank corps some distance from the original battlefield and
into a separate fight. The Seventy-first Highlanders continued forward with an open right flank.

As the initial American battle line disintegrated and its participants sprinted rearward, Cornwallis and his officers faced a perplexing dilemma. Enfilade pressure from the Colonial flank corps had forced the British commander to bring forward all his infantry, presenting his entire army in a single, lengthy, two-deep line with Tarleton's horsemen his only remaining reserve. Directly ahead in the deep woods, the war-whoops of Colonial militia indicated there was more fighting to occur on this bright afternoon, and Cornwallis and his aides vainly rode forward attempting to discover what lay in the trees ahead. As the redcoat brigades regrouped and again started forward, their accustomed shoulder-to-shoulder structure disintegrated. Impenetrable thickets of underbrush, hidden gulleys and ravines, and stout groves of tall hardwoods impeded progress and disrupted military ranks. In their front, groups of Colonials appeared, fired, and fell back as British formations split into platoons and even squads, adapting the bayonet to their own particular woodland fighting.

Two brigades of Virginia militia were scattered in heavy woods astride the road, their task not to defeat their enemy, but to impede the British advance, thereby continuing Greene's strategy of attrition by depth. Lawson's brigade stretched through the trees on the American right while Stevens' tough Indian war veterans were deployed left of the roadway. Col. William Washington's flanking corps smoothly fell back to attach themselves to Lawson's right, Lynch's riflemen peppering Webster's red-coated regiments. On the opposite flank, Lee attempted to perform the identical maneuver, but an unusually large massed column assault by the Highlanders burst through the woods, creating a seam between Stevens and Campbell. Lee's corps was further turned out to the left by the push of the von Bose and First Guards brigades. Stevens' brigade of experienced militiamen met the Highlanders and the close exchange in the woods between these units was furious and bloody. On the British left, the adept Webster coordinated a rapid advance that quickly routed Lawson's brigade save for several pockets continuing to resist in heavy thickets. The Thirty-third Regiment and attached jaegers moved forward, rolling up the American flank units with the remnants of Lawson's troops. The Second Guards continued to advance along the roadway. The Welsh Fusiliers lagged between these two units, becoming entangled in rough ravines. A column of Highlanders penetrated the American lines in such depth that they were cut off, surrounded, and temporarily captured. When the brave, rotund Stevens was shot down his men sullenly began to retreat, carrying their 250-pound chieftain.

Dependable descriptions of this woodland action are few, and all are curtailed by the limited vision of the writers. Samuel Houston, an American militiaman stationed on the left of Stevens' line, recalled a surge of action during which he and his comrades drove the Highlanders in retreat three times, in turn to run from their bayonets a like number. Cornwallis's commissary general, Charles Stedman, described this portion of the action as "of infinite diversity, the British line at times being involved front, flank, and rear." Sgt. Roger Lamb was filling his cartridge box when he observed Lord Cornwallis mounted on a dragoon horse and riding through the woods unattended. Lamb escorted the general to the safety of the Fusilier ranks.

Finally the Virginia militia left the field, covered by Washington's cavalry. As Cornwallis's guns advanced up the roadway and his infantry units regrouped in front of a third Colonial line, the roar of fighting in the woods to the

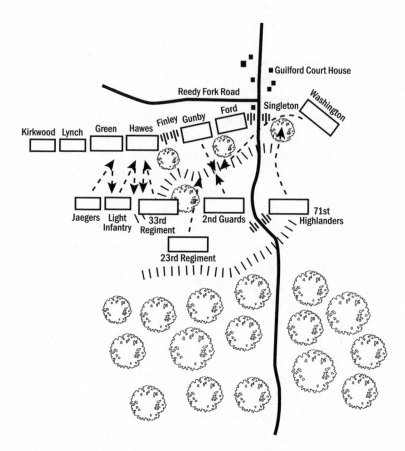

Guilford Court House, third American line. Colonel Webster attacks the well-positioned American Continentals. A hand-to-hand struggle is finally broken by indiscriminate fire of Macleod's guns. Greene withdraws to the Reedy Fork Road, conceding victory to the British.

British right could still be heard. The initial American line had been shattered by the bravery and pluck of his British soldiers, and the second by pure grit, perseverance, and courage, but the third American line, composed of Continental veterans, awaited the redcoats.

As British units emerged from the dark woods into

Guilford Court House, Swale of Decision. Marks the American final line, while the smaller monument is to Col. James Stuart of the Second Guards, slain at that site. (*Photo by Nick Castanes*)

sunlight, they discovered themselves on the lip of an amphitheater, a steep valley, or swale, that had once been cultivated by local farmers but was now covered with weeds, scrub fences, and pine seedlings. Across this ravine, the gleam of gun barrels revealed the location of Continental infantry deployed along a natural crest to the left of the New Garden Road. These units were not aligned parallel to the previous American lines, but slightly askew to follow the terrain. Their position was strong, the best on the field, covering the village of Guilford Court House, located on the opposite side of the road some one hundred yards to their rear. From right to left the American line included Kirkwood's Delaware Company, Lynch's riflemen, Green's Fourth Virginia, Hawes' Fifth Virginia, two artillery pieces, Gunby's First Maryland, and Ford's Second Maryland. The dragoons of William Washington, strengthened by Capt. Thomas Watkins' Virginia cavalry and forty North Carolina militia riders, waited on the right of the road, screening the sleepy village.

The first Crown units to arrive were on the far left and included the jaegers, the Guards Light Infantry, and the Thirty-third Regiment of Foot. Lt. Col. James Webster, bold and confident, led this contingent. Anxious to conclude the day's fighting, he aligned the forward units and led them down into the small valley and up the hillside, charging the troops of Hawes and Gunby. Holding their fire until the redcoats were within fifty yards, the Americans unloosed a punishing volley that stalled the advance, sending the redcoats staggering backward down the hillside. When the advancing soldiers hesitated, Webster rode forward and turned, ordering, "Come on, my brave fusiliers!" But at that very moment Webster was hit, a ball shattering his kneecap. His faithful soldiers ran forward, picked up their commander, and carried him back into the trees on the British side of the valley. The battle now approached its critical moments and a rebel advance possibly could have won the field, but Greene had more conservative responsibilities, the survival of his army.

As Webster's troops retreated, the Second Battalion of Guards swept grandly into the cleared field alongside the roadway. Gen. Charles O'Hara, their commander, already incapacitated with two wounds, had passed command to Lt. Col. James Stuart, who never hesitated, but straightforwardly attacked the Second Maryland with bayonets shining. Ford's Maryland regiment, full of raw recruits, fired a few shots then, surprisingly, threw down their weapons and fled in panic, abandoning Lieutenant Finley and his 6-

pound guns. This sudden retreat enabled Stuart to capture the guns and split the American third line, endangering the entire rebel army. If the Continental regiments could be surrounded, their surrender could signal the final destruction of the American army in the south. Greene, observing the debacle and concluding that he must preserve the core of his army, issued orders for Col. John Green to redirect his Fourth Virginia into a covering position blocking the road and ordered the remainder of his units to withdraw from the field.

Before these orders could be conveyed to the proper officers, the battlefield exploded. Noting the results of the Guards attack, Lt. Col. John Howard, who had replaced the injured Gunby, pivoted the First Maryland to confront the attacking British Guards at point-blank range. Both Colonials and redcoats presented arms and fired in a near simultaneous volley in such close proximity that their muzzle blasts seemed to overlap. As the Guards swung left to confront the Marylanders, Col. William Washington launched his dragoons like a thunderbolt onto the right rear of the Guards, piercing their ranks and slashing guardsmen at will. Alongside Washington rode a giant cavalryman, Peter Francisco, six feet, six inches, 260 pounds, and armed with a five-foot saber. Legend relates that Francisco carved a swath of damage through the British ranks, slaying numerous redcoats before he was wounded. Once Washington's riders cleared the British ranks, he whirled and again led his riders back through the redcoats, recapturing the lost cannon for a time.

As Howard's Marylanders charged in with bayonets, the fight deteriorated into an uncontrollable, swirling melee of dragoons, Marylanders, and guardsmen stabbing, slashing, and striking with bayonets, sabers, gun butts, and fists.

Cavalry monument, Guilford Court House. This column commemorates the charge of William Washington's dragoons into the British Guards Brigade. (*Photo by Nick Castanes*)

Colonel Stuart of the guards and Capt. John Smith of the First Maryland squared off in a private duel, swords in hand. Smith parried Stuart and with a mighty backhanded slice, slew the brave guards officer. A guardsman, in turn, shot down Smith. Cornwallis arrived to witness the brutal exchange. Realizing he must gain control of the melee and reorder his battle line, he ordered young Macleod to bring forward two of his guns and fire grapeshot into the mass of men struggling in the ravine. Macleod hesitated but Cornwallis insisted, despite the weeping protestations of the wounded General O'Hara, lying by the roadside. Macleod opened fire, his guns driving lethal gaps amid the interlocked antagonists, and slowly the combatants separated and withdrew. O'Hara would survive his injuries to die in 1802 as governor of Gibraltar.

As smoke and powder drifted from the ravine, now cluttered with the dead and moaning wounded, both armies reorganized their ranks. Out of the woods the Twenty-third Fusiliers and the Seventy-first Highlanders appeared, tired and bloodied, but able to link alongside the road. A wounded O'Hara rallied the guards. Greene deployed his remaining units in a semicircular formation and began a retrograde movement along the Reedy Fork Road. A limping Colonel Webster realigned his brigades on the left and prepared to advance in concert with guards and Highlanders, but abruptly Greene's Continentals marched away, leaving the bloody field to the victor, a badly battered British army.

Meanwhile a separate and equally desperate fight continued on a range of low hills to the east. Colonel Norton led his First Guards battalion to assist the Hessians in driving Lee's flank corps more than a mile from their original positions. Charge and countercharge, bayonets versus rifles, the combatants raged through the thick woods with first one side then the other seemingly in control. The guards battalion suffered the loss of most of their officers and at one point withdrew to regroup. As the fight in the valley at the third American line grew to a crescendo, Lieutenant Colonel Lee, who could hear the gunfire, determined to elude his British attackers and move in support of Greene's position at Guilford Court House. This left Campbell's riflemen to face the Germans alone. Skillfully disengaging, Lee led his cavalry and infantry in a wide arc through the forest, emerging on Greene's left only to find the battle had concluded.

At almost that instant Cornwallis released his reserves, Tarleton's dragoons, to assist Leslie. Galloping east, the British Legion riders encountered and freed several small groups of Highlanders and Hessians held captive amid the wooded ravines. Upon arriving in Campbell's front, the impetuous Tarleton took immediate command of the action. Spreading his riders on a wide front closely behind the Hessian line, he had the German troops charge and fire a volley then stand aside, allowing his dragoons to charge through their lines, hell for leather out of the gun smoke. Campbell's riflemen were broken and dispersed, racing rearward with Tarleton's saber-wielding riders at their heels. Samuel Houston, who survived this dash for safety through the trees, remarked, "We were obliged to run and many were sorely chased and some cut down." One militia rifle company from Rockbridge County, Virginia, was virtually destroyed. When caught in the rout without cavalry support, few made it back to the Valley of Virginia. Displeased with Lee's abandonment of his riflemen, William Campbell became indignant, vociferously confronting both Greene and Lee. Col. William Preston, who wrote of the bitter feeling created by this incident, recollected that Campbell left camp on the twentieth, returning home to resign his commission in protest.

Greene's Continentals slowly fell back across open fields in orderly fashion until, reaching the Reedy Fork Road, they turned north. The Virginia regiment of Col. John Green, assisted by Washington's remaining riders, covered the withdrawal but little effort was made by the British to pursue, except for a late sortie by Tarleton's dragoons, swiftly repulsed. Lee's Legion followed a different route of retreat, disappearing into the woods and reaching Greene's camp at Speedwell Iron Works the following day. Many of the American militia and rifle companies drifted away through the woods in small groups, some departing for home unannounced while others rallied at Greene's camp.

Cornwallis camped about the buildings at Guilford Court House, his army in possession of the battlefield, the dead, and the wounded. Amid a cold, pelting rain, redcoats searched the fields and woods for wounded comrades. Charles Stedman wrote that "the cries of the wounded and dying, who remained on the field of action during the night, exceeded all descriptions." The melancholy encampment, mourning the loss of so many brave officers and men, could afford scant medical assistance or shelter. A shortage of wagons and teams ensured the further lack of provisions and ammunition. A tired, hungry, injured army lay about the few village buildings, licking its wounds amid the dreary rainfall. Slowly the dead of both forces were collected and buried in great pits.

Two days after the encounter, Cornwallis's army marched east toward Cross Creek, encumbered with many wounded. One of the most revered soldiers in the army, Col. James Webster, was strapped uncomplaining and pale onto a jarring litter borne between two horses. As the column neared Elizabethtown, it was discovered he had expired. Webster was buried with his ornamental sword in a single grave by the roadside, the exact location now lost to memory. The seriously wounded officer, his knee shattered, may have survived had rapid amputation been followed with decent medical care. Cornwallis openly wept, lamenting, "I have lost my scabbard." Tarleton fared better under the care of Dr. Stewart, who amputated a part of his hand.

Losses in the ranks of the veteran British units were irreplaceable. Cornwallis listed 93 killed, 413 wounded, and 26 missing in his report, a total figure of 532 men or 27 percent of his army. In some units, the heavy losses necessitated complete reorganization. The guards battalions absorbed 200 casualties from their 462 effectives, including 11 of their 19 officers. The two units were combined into one battalion, now commanded by Lieutenant Colonel Norton, their lone remaining field officer.

Greene's losses were also substantial but harder to enumerate. He listed 79 killed, 185 wounded, and 1,046 missing, mostly militia. While reported rebel casualties seem smaller, without doubt many of the missing militiamen were wounded or died on their journey home. Such close quarter fighting in difficult terrain produced lengthy casualty lists. Unknown rebels and redcoats lay dying in the woods and ravines.

The American guns were captured intact, as their horses were slain and the guns abandoned. Macleod reported that he accumulated four 6-pounders mounted on traveling carriages from the rebels, shot and powder accompanying. One American source ascribed the origin of two of the four guns in American use with Burgoyne's surrender at

Saratoga, they having been lost and retaken on several occasions since.

The Battle of Guilford Court House was the longest and hardest fought encounter thus far in the south. It was marked by the lengthy, sustained effort of British professionals and a like core contingent of Americans. John Fortescue, a noted British army historian, stated unequivocally, "Never had the prowess of British soldiers been seen to greater advantage than in that bloody and obstinate combat." Cornwallis added that he had "never seen such combat since God made him. . . . the Americans fought like demons." The merits of the Colonial effort can be judged by the quality of their opponents and the absolute razor closeness of the outcome. An exceptional British force performing gallantly and energetically was forced to exert itself to its absolute limit due to rebel efforts. Greene's initial analysis seemed self-serving but proved astute and remarkably accurate when he wrote to Joseph Reed, "We were obliged to give up the ground and lost all our artillery . . . but the enemy was so soundly beaten that they have gained no advantage, on the contrary they are little short of being ruined." By his subsequent actions Cornwallis authenticated Greene's appraisal. Tactically his Lordship had achieved a narrow victory, but strategically he experienced a devastating reversal. British victories of this sort meant nothing in the face of Greene's clever maneuvering and the continued resistance of the partisans.

The British army began a slow, tiresome retreat to Cross Creek (modern Fayetteville); however, provisions for the army could not easily be ferried up the Cape Fear River from the coast. Rebel partisans were too active. Cornwallis moved on east to Wilmington, there to embark his regiments for an appointment with destiny at Yorktown in Virginia.

Afterword

"I have the mortification to inform your excellency that I
have been forced . . . to surrender the troops under my
command."

Lord Cornwallis to Clinton, October 20, 1781

Lord Cornwallis, obstinate and proud, encamped with
his tired, dispirited army for several days following the
battle at Guilford Court House, collecting and tending to
the wounded and dying of both armies, who lay shivering
in a cold, steady rain. Charles Stedman, commissary general of the British force, recalled weeping openly as he listened to the cries of the wounded and remarked, "That
night exceeded all descriptions of misery as near fifty
young soldiers died before dawn." Guards general Charles
O'Hara, despondent over the death of his favorite nephew
and the heavy losses among his guards, lay in agony, suffering from multiple wounds and observing the misery
around him. He commented that the spirit of the army
had been forever destroyed in the woods about Guilford
Court House.

Reluctantly, on March 18, Cornwallis put his troops in
motion and began marching southwest. A pale and quiet

Banastre Tarleton rode alone in the van, his mutilated right arm encased in a sling. Seventeen wagons of groaning wounded too badly injured to endure a lengthy journey followed the cavalryman. They were to be left with the kindly Quakers at New Garden. The army halted there for several days then proceeded farther south to Cross Creek, located on the Cape Fear River. Cornwallis hoped to secure provisions for his starving troops as well as recruits from among the Highland Scots who dominated that area. He was sorely disappointed, for even these usually ardent Loyalists were reluctant to follow the Union Jack. Unable to receive provisions shipped up the Cape Fear due to partisan rebel raiding parties, the British commander was forced to continue downstream to Wilmington, where the Royal Navy could supply provisions and ammunition. On April 7, the tired survivors of the winter campaign reached the safety of the seaport.

Cornwallis had been accustomed to scant direction from superiors since Clinton sailed from Charles Town. He actually preferred this assumed autonomy, but on this occasion he faced strategic decisions that possibly exceeded his personal abilities. He recognized he must either return to Charles Town, a move that implied defeat, or initiate an offensive movement with his depleted regiments, shrunken from disease and battle losses. Refusing to admit failure and searching for the one great victory that would end the war, the British general decided to march north into Virginia and merge forces with those of Gen. Benedict Arnold, camped near Norfolk. The Marquis de Lafayette led a small patriot army in the area but posed no serious threat to a combined forces, and Greene had committed his army to a campaign for the recovery of South Carolina. Cornwallis's decision to strike north seems futile in retrospect for the maintenance of British control in the south. But he could not or did not foresee the coalescence of mitigating factors that were about to occur. The inert, uninspired leadership of the British home office, the absolute incompetence of an assortment of British naval commanders, the good fortune of French admiral Comte de Grasse, and the sudden, aggressive initiation of Washington's strategic plan—all these factors merged to entrap Cornwallis and his army in a capitulation of epic consequences.

A small yet prideful redcoat force emerged from the swamps along the Carolina-Virginia line on May 20 to unite with more than four thousand regulars under Arnold near Petersburg, Virginia. Aggressively moving north to enter Richmond, Cornwallis sent Tarleton with 250 riders west toward Charlottesville in an adventuresome though vain attempt to capture Governor Jefferson and members of the General Assembly. As the solons of Virginia scattered into the mountains, Tarleton turned his column back toward Richmond, where Cornwallis was facing a rebel force under Gen. Anthony Wayne, who had force marched his Pennsylvania line regiments to reinforce Lafayette. Cornwallis slowly withdrew toward Williamsburg as the Colonial force followed. He laid a trap and ambushed the rebel army near Green Spring Plantation but was frustrated when the patriots extricated themselves in the evening twilight without serious losses.

Cornwallis received directions from General Clinton that he was to cease active operations, consolidate his forces, and begin construction of a naval base in the Chesapeake pending the arrival of a large British fleet carrying reinforcements and provisions. After some deliberation he decided to dig in at Yorktown and his men began construction of defensive works about the village.

Meanwhile, American commander George Washington, encamped at West Point on the Hudson, was the recipient of beneficial intelligence. He learned that Cornwallis was fortifying a base, indicating a lengthy stay. He also received information that Comte de Grasse was sailing from Santo Domingo with a French fleet of twenty-eight warships carrying thirty-three hundred French regulars. Washington decided to abandon his ineffective blockade of New York and launch his army alongside French troops quartered in Rhode Island to unite with de Grasse in an attempt to entrap Cornwallis. Through a series of misadventures abetted by incompetent leadership, the English fleet sailed north to protect New York, exposing the mouth of the Chesapeake, an error quickly capitalized upon by de Grasse. The French admiral disembarked his troops on James Island under the Marquis de Saint-Simon and sent his transports up the bay to Point of Elk, where they awaited the hard-marching French and American soldiers.

Washington cleverly feinted a move on New York, then wheeled and marched south. On August 19, French general Jean Baptiste Donatien de Vimeur, Comte de Rochambeau, and four thousand French troops joined him. Uniting at Trenton, New Jersey, the two armies crossed the Delaware and paraded through Philadelphia on September 2 and 3, the smartly attired French troops struggling to maintain pace with the long-striding Colonials. Continuing to Point of Elk the united force completed the four-hundred-mile march, possibly one of the most daring maneuvers of the war. Quickly the allied troops were ferried down the Chesapeake to stiffen the cordon already tightened about Cornwallis's Yorktown defenses.

The village of Yorktown was then located on a bluff scattered along the south side of the York River some two miles from its juncture with the bay. By late September an allied army of eighteen thousand men and ninety guns, including many heavy French siege pieces, surrounded Cornwallis's army. Rochambeau, a noted military engineer, laid out parallels and zigzag approach lines, carefully positioning his prized 24-pound guns. Gradually the siege evolved into an artillery fight, with the allies at distinct advantage. On October 14, two key British redoubts were stormed at heavy cost, but their gain permitted construction of a second parallel only three hundred yards from the British main works. Installation of siege guns in this parallel would expose the redcoats to point-blank fire.

On October 17 a lone drummer boy climbed atop the British earthworks and beat a request for parley. Cornwallis sent out a proposal for terms, a liberal offer instantly rejected by Washington, who insisted on unconditional surrender. After much debate an agreement was reached two days later. Proud Gen. Charles O'Hara of the guards, recovered from his wounds at Guilford Court House, led a long line of dispirited British regiments out of the works, marching to lay down their arms and banners. Regiments of high repute such as the Highlanders, the Welsh Fusiliers, and the Guards Battalion, joined by the von Bose Hessians and three jaeger companies, slowly filed down an approach road toward an open field. Natty French regiments in crimson, pink, blue, and gold facings formed a spectacular sight on one side of the roadway, offsetting the drab, silent Americans aligned opposite. Cornwallis, pleading illness, requested that O'Hara present his sword to Rochambeau but the French general refused to accept, instead pointing to Washington, who angrily deferred O'Hara to General Lincoln, who was so rudely treated at Charles Town.

More than 7,200 British and Hessian troops surrendered

at Yorktown, to be joined by 840 seamen. Battle losses were slight, amounting to 156 killed and 326 wounded while allied casualties were 75 slain and 200 wounded. A second British army had been obliged to surrender to a rebel force now aided by Europeans allies. Truly the greatest strategic coup of the war, this loss of so many prisoners reduced the British army to the occupation of Atlantic seaports. A period of watchful waiting ensued. But in the prison camps at Frederick, Maryland, and Winchester, Virginia, redcoats and Hessians continued to die, succumbing to the disease that so ravaged revolutionary armies. As months and years of arbitration, negotiation, and debate followed, these troops suffered, underfed, under clothed, and unappreciated by the government they had served. In the late summer and fall of 1783, when most sailed for home, large numbers were absent, buried in unknown graves or deserted to start life anew. While the opposition party stirred unrest in England, the loss of so many fine men was at last noticed in the midlands of England and the forests of Hesse.

> *They came three thousand miles and died*
> *To keep the past upon its throne*
> *Unheard, beyond the ocean tide*
> *Their English mother made her moan.*
>   Gravestone Inscription, Redcoat Cemetery

Military operations on the North American continent were virtually concluded with the Yorktown surrender. While Greene continued to maneuver against British and Loyalist strongholds in the south and Indian warfare in the back country sputtered and flared, British forces seemed largely content to retain the comfortable coastal ports. Conflict in other colonial zones around the world occupied British military interest. While the attempt to subdue the revolt in North America could easily have been renewed, a lack of interest by home office officials coupled with the rise to power of the peace party led to recognition that a military victory in North America was unattainable. Great Britain gave up pursuit of a war deemed unwinnable.

The conflict became a diplomatic joust, grinding on until a treaty was ratified in Paris on January 20, 1783, which officially awarded a fragile independence to thirteen widely dissimilar colonies. They were loosely joined by Articles of Confederation whereby each new state enjoyed a certain degree of primacy over Congress and possessed only the rudimentary structure of the British colonial system. It was tenuous and uncertain as to what form of government would emerge in the factionalized country. Fortunate in that the world's major powers were engrossed with one another and possessing enough natural bounty to sustain its citizens, the new country still struggled to form an identity.

Amid this confusion and turmoil, George Washington made his greatest contribution to America. He committed his vast popularity as leader and moral hero, returning from retirement in 1787 to accept the presidency of the Philadelphia Convention and influence the ratification of the Constitution. Adopting a genuine, even strict constitutionalist view, he proclaimed: "This is the moment when the eyes of the world are turned on us and we will establish or ruin our reputation." Even more than his military successes or his presidential precedents, Washington's fervent espousal of a government based on a written constitution molded American character on the world stage. His patience, foresight, and statesmanship, exercised from the pinnacle of military success and public adoration, laid the principles of cooperative government among the peoples of thirteen neophyte local governments.

Though the fledgling nation was taking steps to realize a great potential, not all would benefit in the new America. Unexpected results produced losers beyond those slain or disfigured. Fully twenty-five thousand to thirty thousand colonials who donned the regimentals of Loyalist units found themselves abandoned by a British administration that never really attempted to protect their interests. The Treaty of Paris specifically demanded that Tory properties be restored, but war damages, debts, and economic depression prevented this occurrence. Additionally, in the southern back country, fratricidal violence had created animosities between Whigs and Tories too serious to be alleviated by signatures on a treaty. At war's end large contingents of Tories voted with their feet; they re-immigrated. An estimated ten thousand Loyalists surrendered their properties and moved, along with twenty-five thousand ex-soldiers, many relocating in Nova Scotia, Florida, Bermuda, the Bahamas, or other West Indian islands. While many migrated, those who remained faced persecution, disenfranchisement, and property confiscation.

Native Americans, most of whom were forced into alliances with the redcoats, were confronted with continued aggression, cultural destruction, and compulsory westward migration. British attempts to control their trade had been less encompassing than colonial practices of taking their lands, but both paths could only lead to extinction or flight. A respected Cherokee chief, Old Tassel, spoke artfully and honestly in 1777 when he declared: "Brothers, remember that the difference or reason for war between red coat and buckskin shirt is about our land . . . the very land upon which we stand." He recognized the futility of alliance with either warring party. Active participation by the tribes guaranteed their exclusion from the government

of the new nation while neutrality saw them pushed westward across the Mississippi into the lands of their enemies.
Cherokee passive resistance was attempted but at a terrible price. Their only gain was time, a brief delay until
vengeful American politicians relocated them to
Oklahoma, four thousand or more dying en route. The
seizure of Indian land, illegal before the revolution,
became a patriotic act following the war. Along the Ohio
River, conflict between Indians and whites flared intermit-
tently. Numerous American military expeditions moved
north but with disastrous results, until 1794 when Gen.
Anthony Wayne engineered a significant victory at Fallen
Timbers, driving the tribesmen out onto the plains.

The plight of blacks reached an even more tragic conclusion. Expecting succor from the British military, they
were also abandoned when the fighting ceased. A new
nation espousing freedom and liberty exercised the ultimate hypocrisy by reaffirming its deep-rooted commitment to the institution of chattel slavery. For most slaves
the patriots represented a lack of freedom and opportunity, and support of the redcoats seemed an avenue to eman-
cipation, for England no longer advocated bondage. A
majority of the almost five hundred thousand slaves either
actively or passively favored British victory. For a time the
Continental Army admitted black soldiers, promising freedom to those who fought. But in the south there were concerns over arming and training blacks, for fear of slave
revolt was ever a primary concern. While some protested,
high profitability of the system of slavery crumbled the
moral doubts of legislators and churchmen.

British armies in the south welcomed black volunteers,
first as cooks, teamsters, orderlies, and musicians, then to
fill shrinking ranks. Negro drummers were utilized by

Hessian regiments from their first contact with slaves, the young lads decked out resplendently in reversed regimental dress. British treatment of runaway slaves varied, growing less attentive as the war turned against their effort. Upon the evacuation of Savannah and Charles Town, English vessels transported thousands of former slaves to the West Indies, Jamaica, and freedom. When additional numbers are added from New York and Yorktown, more than thirty thousand blacks found their long-desired freedom. But most of the African Americans in the shining new country did not share in the spoils of independence; instead they were destined to remain in the dark realm of slavery for almost eighty years.

Even those brave back country fighters who had given much to free their land of the British would at first struggle to gain the promises of independence. At the conclusion of the war the southern back country was in a state of flux and chaos. The conflict had produced widespread loss of property and capital, family dislocation, and civilian and military casualties in encounters with partisans and Indians, leaving blood feuds and animosity.

Yet the Treaty of Paris unfolded a broad vista westward. An expanse of territory more than double the size of the rebelling colonies and stretching from the Appalachians to the Mississippi River invited hordes of new settlers. With currency worthless, frontier land was the only resource available to Congress, and thousands of acres were granted in veteran payments or bartered to land speculators for resale. Militant expansionism, hand in hand with nationalism, characterized the rapid occupation of the borderlands. The frontier became an incubator changing the character of those who sought its refuge, creating a "new" American. J. Hector St. John de Crevecoeur in his *Letters from an American Farmer* answered best the query "What is this new American?" He stated that an American was "someone who left behind all his ancient prejudices and manners and adopted new ones from the mode of life he embraced, the new government he obeyed, and the new rank he held. Here, individuals of all nations are melted into a new race of men whose labors and posterity will one-day cause great changes in the world."

A horde of land-seeking adventurers stood poised to sweep in a surging wave west to the Mississippi, ignoring the rights or claims of Indians, the Spanish, or French inhabitants. Hunger for land provided the base for this great migration, for land ownership brought power and status. From the first settlements in this new territory, challenge and opportunity placed maximum value on individual initiative. New leadership styles developed, based on merit and situational needs rather than pedigree or status. Frontier settlers followed those strong enough to lead and whose purposes adjoined their own. Military leaders of innate genius emerged from total obscurity on the borderlands to perform deeds of remarkable significance. Men such as Daniel Morgan, George Rogers Clark, John Sevier, Isaac Shelby, and others would not have surfaced in the staid structure of the Empire. The caste system quickly disappeared in the back country, to be replaced by a cruder society based on energy and ability, not aristocratic right. As this anticipatory mass of immigrant families reached the crest of the Appalachians in Virginia, North Carolina, South Carolina, Georgia, Tennessee, and Kentucky, the first vestiges of the Manifest Destiny of the new nation appeared. Perhaps, dimly sighted, they could glimpse from the mountain peaks the blue waters of the Pacific.

Bibliography

Books

Alden, John Richard. *John Stuart and the Southern Colonial Frontier: 1754-1775*. Ann Arbor: University of Michigan Press, 1944.

———. *The American Revolution*. New York: Harper and Brothers, 1954.

———. *The South in the Revolution*. Baton Rouge: Louisiana State University Press, 1957.

Alderman, Pat. *Nancy Ward and Dragging Canoe*. Johnson City, Tenn.: The Overmountain Press, 1978.

Allaire, Anthony. *Diary of Lt. Allaire of Ferguson's Corps*. New York: New York Times, 1968.

Allen, Garner. *A Naval History of the Revolution*. Vol. II. Boston: Houghton-Mifflin, 1913.

Ambrose, Stephen. *Personal Reflections of an Historian*. New York: Simon and Schuster, 2002.

Anderson, Fred. *Crucible of War: The Seven Years War and the Fate of Empire in British North America, 1754-1766*. New York: Vintage Books, 2001.

Atwood, Rodney. *The Hessians: Mercenaries from Hesse-Kassel in the American Revolution*. New York: Cambridge University Press, 1980.

333

Babits, Lawrence E. *A Devil of a Whipping: The Battle of Cowpens.* Chapel Hill: University of North Carolina Press, 1998.

Bailey, J. D. *Commanders at Kings Mountain.* Gaffney, S.C.: H. DeCamp, 1926.

Bailyn, Bernard, and Morgan, Philip D., eds. *Strangers Within the Realm: Cultural Margins of the First British Empire.* Chapel Hill: University of North Carolina Press, The Institute of Early American History and Culture, 1991.

Baker, Thomas E. *Another Such Victory: The Story of the American Defeat at Guilford Court House That Helped Win the War for Independence.* New York: Eastern Acorn Press, 1981.

Bancroft, George. *History of the United States.* 10 vols. Boston: Little, Brown and Co., 1875.

Bartram, William. *Travels of William Bartram.* Edited by Matt Van Doren. New York: Dover Publications, 1955.

Bass, Robert D. *Gamecock: The Life and Campaigns of General Sumter.* Orangeburg, S.C.: Sandlapper Publishing, 1961.

———. *Swamp Fox: The Life and Campaigns of General Francis Marion.* Orangeburg, S.C.: Sandlapper Publishing, 1959.

———. *The Green Dragoon: The Lives of Banastre Tarleton and Mary Robinson.* Orangeburg, S.C.: Sandlapper Publications, 1957.

Bearss, Edwin C. *Battle of Cowpens: A Documented Narrative and Troop Movement Maps.* Johnson City, Tenn.: The Overmountain Press, 1996.

Biggers, Jeff. *The United States of Appalachia.* New York: Shoemaker and Hoard Publishers, 2006.

Boatner, Mark Mayo III. *Encyclopedia of the American*

Revolution. New York: David McKay Co., 1966.

Borick, Carl P. *A. Gallant Defense: The Siege of Charleston, 1780.* Columbia: University of South Carolina Press, 2003.

Bowler, R. Arthur. *Logistics and the Failure of the British Army in North America.* Princeton, N.J.: Princeton University Press, 1975.

Bruce, Phillip. *The Virginia Plutarch.* Vol. I. New York: Russell and Russell, 1927.

Brunhouse, Robert L. *The Counter Revolution in Pennsylvania.* Harrisburg, Pa.: Pennsylvania Historical and Museum Commission, 1940.

Buchanan, John. *The Road to Guilford Court House: The American Revolution in the Carolinas.* New York: John Wiley and Sons, 1997.

Callahan, North. *Dan Morgan: Ranger of the Revolution.* New York: Holt, Rinehardt, and Winston, 1961.

Calloway, Colin. *The American Revolution in Indian Country.* New York: Cambridge Press, 1995.

Carrillo, Richard F. *The Howser House and the Chronicle of the Grave and Mass Burial.* Research Series # 102. Columbia, S.C.: Kings Mountain Military Park, 1976.

Caruana, Adrian B. *Grasshoppers and Butterflies: The Light 3 Pounders of Pattison and Townshend.* Historical Arms Series, No. 39. Alexandria Bay, N.Y.: Museum Restoration Series, 1999.

Carrington, Henry B. *Battles of the Revolutionary War: 1775-1781.* New York: A.S. Barnes and Co., 1876.

Cash, W. J. *The Mind of the South.* New York: Vintage Books, 1991.

Chesney, Alexander. *The Journal of Alexander Chesney.* London: Alfred Jones, Inc., 1921.

Clark, Adion. "The Colony of Ulster and the Rebellion of 1641." In *The Course of Irish History,* edited by T. W.

Moody and F. X. Martin: Cork, Ireland, 1967.

Clark, Walter, ed. *The State Records of North Carolina*. 3 vols. Raleigh, N.C.: P.M. Hale Co., 1886-1907.

Clinton, Henry. *The American Rebellion: Sir Henry Clinton's Narrative of His Campaigns, 1775-1782*. Edited by William Wilcox. New Haven, Conn.: Yale Press, 1954.

Collins, James. *Autobiography of a Revolutionary Soldier in 60 Years in the Nueas Valley: 1870-1930*. Edited by John Roberts. San Antonio: Naylor Publishing, 1930.

Commanger, Henry S., ed. *Documents of American History*. New York: Appleton-Century-Croft, 1949.

Cornwallis, Charles. *Correspondence of Charles, 1st Marquis of Cornwallis*. Vol. I. Edited by Charles Ross. London: John Murray Inc., 1859.

Cox, Brent Yanusdi. *Heart of the Eagle: Dragging Canoe and the Emergence of the Chickamauga Confederacy*. Milan, Tenn.: Chenanee Publishers, 1999.

Curtis, Edmund. *A History of Ireland*. London: Methusen and Co. Ltd., 1936.

Curtis, Edward E. *The Organization of the British Army in the American Revolution*. Cransbury, N.J.: Scholar's Bookshelf, 2005.

Dallek, Robert T. *Hail to the Chief: The Making and Unmaking of American Presidents*. New York: Hyperion Press, 1996.

Darling, Anthony D. *Red Coats and Brown Bess*. Historical Arms Series, No. 12. Alexandria Bay, N.Y.: Museum Restoration Service, 1971.

Davis, David B. *The Problem of Slavery*. Charlottesville: University of Virginia Press, 2000.

DeCrevecoeur, Hector St. John. *Letters from an American Farmer and Sketches of Eighteenth Century America*. New York: Penguin Books, 1981.

Dohla, Johann Conrad. *A Hessian Diary of the American Revolution.* Edited by Bruce E. Burgoyne. Norman: University of Oklahoma Press, 1990.

Draper, Lyman Copeland. *Action at the Galudoghson, Dec. 14, 1742.* Bowie, Md.: Heritage Books, Inc., 1995.

————. *Kings Mountain and Its Heroes.* Johnson City, Tenn.: The Overmountain Press, 1881.

Duffy, Christopher. *Fire and Storm: The Science of Fortress Warfare.* Newton, Mass.: Arlo Co., 1975.

Duncan, Fannie. *When Kentucky Was Young.* Louisville: Louisville Press, 1928.

Durrett, Reuben T. *Centurian of Louisville.* Louisville, Ky., 1893.

Dykeman, Wilma. *With Fire and Sword: The Battle of Kings Mountain.* Washington, D.C.: National Park Service, 1978.

Edgar, Walter. *Partisans and Redcoats: The Southern Conflict That Turned the Tide of the American Revolution.* New York: Harper-Collins, 2001.

Ellis, Joseph J. *Founding Brothers: The Revolutionary Generation.* New York: Vintage Books, 2002.

Ewald, Johann. *Diary of the American War: A Hessian Journal.* Edited by Joseph T. Tustin. New Haven, Conn.: Yale Press, 1979.

Farager, John Mack. *Daniel Boone: The Life and Legend of an American Pioneer.* New York: Holt Publishers, 1992.

Ferling, John. *Setting the World Ablaze: Washington, Adams, Jefferson and the American Revolution.* New York: Oxford Press, 2000.

Fischer, David Hackett, and James C. Kelly. *Bound Away: Virginia and the Westward Movement.* Charlottesville: The University of Virginia Press, 2000.

Fisher, Sydney George. *The Struggle for American Independence.* Vols. I and II. Cranbury, N.J.: The Scholar's Bookshelf, 2005.

Fleming, Thomas. *Cowpens: Downright Fighting.* Washington, D.C.: National Park Service, 1988.

Fleming, Thomas J. *Now We Are Enemies.* New York: St. Martins Press, 1960.

——— *1776: Year of Illusions.* Edison, N.J.: Castle Books, 1976.

Flexnor, James Thomas. *George Washington and the New Nation.* 4 vols. Boston: Little, Brown and Co., 1965-1972.

Force, Peter, ed. *American Archives.* 5th Series, 3 vols. Washington, D.C.: United States Congress, 1837-1846.

Fortescue, John. *A History of the British Army.* 13 vols. London: AMS Press, 1899-1930.

Fraser, Walter J., Jr. *Charleston! Charleston!* Columbia: University of South Carolina Press, 1989.

Freeman, Douglas Southall. *George Washington.* 6 vols. New York: Scribner's, 1948-1954.

Fuller, J. F. C. *British Light Infantry in the Eighteenth Century.* Bloomfield, Can., 1971.

Garden, James. *Anecdotes of the American Revolution.* Brooklyn, N.Y., 1865.

Gibbs, R. W. *Documentary History of the American Revolution.* Vol. 1. New York: Appleton and Co., 1855.

Gilchrist, M. M. *Patrick Ferguson: A Man of Some Genius.* Edinburgh: NMS Enterprises, 1988.

Grafton, Michael. *A History of the Bahamas.* Ontario: Waterloo Press, 1986.

Graham, James. *The Life of General Daniel Morgan.* New York: Derby and Jackson, 1856.

Graham, Joseph. "Battle of Kings Mountain." In *Kings Mountain and Its Heroes,* edited by Lyman Draper.

Johnson City, Tn.: Overmountain Press, 1996. First published in *Southern Literary Messenger* (September 1845): 1-5.

Graham, William A. *The Battle of Ramsour's Mill, June 20, 1780.* Raleigh, N.C., 1904.

Greene, Francis Vinton. *General Greene.* New York: D. Appleton and Co., 1897.

Greene, Jack P. *Understanding the American Revolution: Issues and Answers.* Charlottesville: The University of Virginia Press, 1995.

Gregorie, Ann King. *Thomas Sumter.* Columbia, S.C.: R.L. Bryan Co., 1931.

Hairr, John. *Guilford Courthouse: Nathanael Greene's Victory in Defeat, March 15, 1781.* Cambridge, Mass.: Dacado Press, 2002.

Haller, Stephen E. *William Washington: Cavalryman of the Revolution.* Bowie, Md.: Heritage Books, 2001.

Hamilton, Edward P. *The French and Indian Wars.* Garden City, N.J.: Doubleday and Co., 1962.

Hammond, Neal O., and Richard Taylor. *Virginia's Western War: 1775-1786.* Mechanicsburg, Pa.: Stackpole Books, 2002.

Hanger, George. *To All Sportsmen and Particularly Farmers and Games Keepers.* London, 1814.

Hart, Freeman H. *The Valley of Virginia in the American Revolution.* Chapel Hill: University of North Carolina Press, 1942.

Harvey, Robert. *A Few Bloody Noses: The Realities and Mythologies of the American Revolution.* New York: Overlook Press, 2002.

Hatley, Tom. *The Dividing Paths: Cherokee and South Carolinians Through the Revolutionary Era.* New York: Oxford Press, 1995.

Henderson, Archibald. *Lord Dunmore's War: 1774.* New York: Century Company, 1920.

———. *The Conquest of the Old Southwest.* Spartanburg, S.C.: The Reprint Company, 1974.

———. *The Transylvania Company.* Chapel Hill: University of North Carolina Press, 1947.

Henry, John. *Journal of the March to Quebec.* New York: Doubleday, 1938.

Hibbert, Christopher. *Redcoats and Rebels: The American Revolution Through British Eyes.* New York: Avon Books, 1991.

Higginbottom, Don. *Daniel Morgan: Revolutionary Rifleman.* Chapel Hill: University of North Carolina Press, 1961.

———, ed. *George Washington Reconsidered.* Charlottesville: The University of Virginia Press, 2001.

Hintzen, William. *The Border Wars of the Upper Ohio Valley: 1769-1794.* Manchester, Conn.: Precision Shooting, 1999.

Hoffman, Ronald, Thad Tate, and Peter Albert, eds. *An Uncivil War: The Southern Backcountry During the American Revolution.* Charlottesville: University of Virginia Press, The United States Capitol Historical Society, 1985.

Hough, Franklin B. *The Siege of Charleston by the British Fleet and Army under Adm. Arbuthnot and Gen. Clinton.* Albany, N.Y.: J. Russell, 1869.

———, ed. *The Siege of Savannah by the Combined Arms of America and France.* Spartanburg, S.C.: Reprint Co., 1975.

Hudson, Charles. *The Juan Pardo Expedition.* No. 23. Washington, D.C.: The Smithsonian Institute Press.

Isaacson, Waltar. *Benjamin Franklin: An American Life.* New York: Simon and Schuster, 2003.

Johnson, Patricia. *General Andrew Lewis of Roanoke and Greenbriar.* Pulaski, Va.: Pulaski Printing Co., 1980.

Johnson, Samuel. *Journey to the Western Isles of Scotland.* Oxford: Oxford University Press, 1924.

Jones, Charles C., ed. *The Siege of Savannah by the Fleet of Count d'Estaing in 1779.* New York: Arno Press, 1968.

Jones, Katharine M. *Port Royal Under Six Flags.* New York: Bobbs-Merrill, 1960.

Jones, Lewis P. *South Carolina: A Synoptic History for Laymen.* Orangeburg, S.C.: Sandlapper Publications, 1971.

Jordan, Laydon W., and Elizabeth H. Stringfellow. *A Place Called John's Island: The Story of John's, Edisto, Kiawah, and Seabrook Islands of South Carolina.* Spartanburg, S.C.: The Reprint Co., 1998.

Kaplan, Sidney, and Emma Kaplan. *The Black Presence in the Era of the American Revolution.* Amherst: University of Massachusetts Press, 1989.

Kauffman, Henry J. *The Pennsylvania-Kentucky Rifle.* Harrisburg, Pa.: Stackpole Publishing, 1960.

Keller, S. Roger. *Isaac Shelby: A Driving Force in the American Struggle for Independence.* Shippensburg, Pa.: Burd Press, 2000.

Kelley, Paul. *Historic Fort Loudon.* Vonore, Tenn.: Fort Loudon Association, 1958.

Kennedy, Billy. *The Scots-Irish in the Carolinas.* Belfast: Ambassador Publications, 1997.

Kennedy, Roger G. *Hidden Cities: The Discovery and Loss of Ancient North American Civilization.* New York: Free Press, 1994.

Kennett, Lee. *The French Armies in the Seven Years War: A Study in Command and Organization.* Durham, N.C.: Duke University Press, 1967.

Kercheval, Samuel. *A History of the Valley of Virginia.* Strasburg, Va.: Shenandoah Publishing, 1928.

Ketchum, Richard M. *Saratoga: Turning Point of America's Revolutionary War.* New York: Henry Holt and Co., 1887.

———. *Victory at Yorktown: The Campaign That Won the Revolution.* New York: Henry Holt and Co., 2004.

Kindig, Joseph Jr. *Thoughts on the Kentucky Rifle in Its Golden Age.* York, Pa.: Trimmer Printing, 1960.

Klett, Guy S. *Presbyterians in Colonial Pennsylvania.* Philadelphia, 1937.

Lacrosse, Richard B. *Revolutionary Rangers.* Bowie, Md.: Heritage Books, 2002.

Lamb, Roger. *An Original and Authentic Journal of Occurrences During the Late American War from Its Commencement to the Year 1783.* Dublin: J. Jones, 1809.

Lambert, Robert S. *South Carolina Loyalists in the American Revolution.* Columbia: University of South Carolina Press, 1987.

———. *A Memoir of His Own Life.* Dublin: J. Jones, 1811.

Lancaster, Bruce. *From Lexington to Liberty.* New York: Doubleday, 1955.

Landers, H. L. *The Virginia Campaign and the Blockade and Siege of Yorktown: 1781.* Canbury, N.J., 1931.

Lawrence, Alexander A. *Storm Over Savannah: Count d'Estaing and the Siege of 1779.* Athens: The University of Georgia Press, 1951.

Lee, Henry. *The American Revolution in the South.* 1869. Reprint, New York: University Press, 1969.

Lewis, Gray. *A History of Agriculture in the South Until 1860.* New York, 1941.

Leyburn, James G. *The Scotch-Irish: A Social History."* Chapel Hill: University of North Carolina Press, 1962.

Lobdell, Jared C. *Further Materials on Lewis Wetzel and the Upper Ohio Frontier.* Bowie, Md.: Heritage Books, 1994.

Lumpkin, Henry. *From Savannah to Yorktown: The American Revolution in the South.* New York: Paragon House, 1981.

MacKenzie, Roderick. *Strictures of Lt. Col. Tarleton's History of the Campaign of 1780 and 1781 in the Southern Provinces of North America: Whereupon Characters and Corps Are Vindicated from Injurious Aspirations and Several Important Transactions Placed in Their Proper Point of View.* London: R. Faulder, 1787.

Maier, Pauline. *The Old Revolutionary.* New York: Norton Co., 1980.

Mansfield, Susan. "An Officer and a Gentleman." In *Patrick Ferguson: A Man of Some Genius,* edited by Dr. M. M. Gilchrist. Edinburgh: Enterprise Limited, National Museum of Scotland, 2003.

Mapp, Alf Johnson. "The Pirate Peer: Lord Dunmore's Operations in the Chesapeake Bay in the American Revolution." In *The Chesapeake Bay in the American Revolution,* edited by Earnest Eller. Centreville, Md.: Tidewater Publishers, 1981.

McCarty, Edward. *South Carolina in the American Revolution, 1775-1780.* New York, 1902.

McRae, Barbara. *Franklin's Ancient Mound: Myths and Histories of Old Nikwasi.* Franklin, N.C.: Teresita Press, 1993.

Meade, Robert D. *Patrick Henry: Patriot in the Making.* Vols. I. New York: J. B. Lippincott, 1957.

———. *Patrick Henry: Practical Revolutionary.* Vol. II. New York: J. B. Lippincott, 1969.

Messick, Hank. *Kings Mountain.* Boston: Little, Brown and Co., 1976.

Meyer, Duane. *The Highland Scots of North Carolina: 1732-1776.* Chapel Hill: University of North Carolina Press, 1961.

Miller, John C. *Origins of the American Revolution.* Boston: Little, Brown and Company, 1943.

Millis, Walter. *Arms and Men: A Study in American Military History.* New Brunswick, N.J.: Rutgers University Press, 1981.

Mitchell, Joseph B. *Decisive Battles of the American Revolution.* Greenwich, Conn.: M. Fawcett Premier Books, 1962.

Mooney, James. *Myths of the Cherokee.* Washington, D.C.: Government Printing Office, 1900.

Monogham, Frank. *Johann Kalb.* New York, 1943.

Moore, M. A. *Life of General Edward Lacey.* Spartanburg, S.C.: Douglas, Evans, and Company, 1859.

Moore, Warren. *Weapons of the American Revolution.* New York: Promontory Press, 1967.

Morgan, Edmund S., and Helen M. Morgan. *The Stamp Act Congress: Prelude to Revolution.* New York: Alfred A. Knopf, 1963.

Morgan, Ted. *Wilderness at Dawn: The Settling of the North American Continent.* New York: Simon and Schuster, 1993.

Moultrie, William. *Memoirs of the American Revolution So Far as It Relates to the States of North Carolina, South Carolina, and Georgia.* New York, 1820.

Nestor, William R. *The Frontier War for American Independence.* Mechanicsburg, Pa.: Stackpole Books, 2004.

O'Connor, Adrian. "Point Pleasant: Forgotten Frontier Clash." In *Southside Revisited.* N.p., 1996.

O'Donnell, James H. III. *Southern Indians in the American Revolution*. Knoxville: University of Tennessee Press, 1973.

Pancake, John S. *This Destructive War: The British Campaign in the Carolinas, 1780-1782*. Tuscaloosa: University of Alabama Press, 1985.

Pauquette, Robert Lewis, and Louis A. Ferleger, eds. *Slavery, Secession, and Southern History*. Charlottesville: The University of Virginia Press, 2000.

Passos, John Dos. *The Head and the Heart of Thomas Jefferson*. Garden City, N.J.: Doubleday Printers, 1954.

Pearfon, Michael. *Those Damned Rebels: The American Revolution as Seen Through British Eyes*. New York: Dapado Press, 1972.

Peterson, Harold. *Arms and Armor in Colonial America*. Harrisburg, Pa., 1956.

Phillips, Kevin. *The Cousin's War: Religion, Politics, and the Triumph of Anglo-America*. New York: Basic Books, 1999.

Posey, John T. *General Thomas Posey: Son of the American Revolution*. East Lansing: Michigan State Press, 1992.

Putnam, A. W. "History of Middle Tennessee: or Life and Times of Gen. James Robertson." In *The First American Frontier*. New York: Arno Press, 1859.

Quarles, Benjamin. *The Negro in the American Revolutionary War*. New York: Norton and Co., 1973.

Ramsay, David. *The History of the Revolution of South Carolina from British Province to an Independent State*. Vol. 1. Trenton, N.J.: Isaac Collins, 1785.

———. *History of South Carolina from Its First Settlement in 1670 to the Year 1808*. Vol. 2. Newberry, S.C.: Duffle Co., 1858. Reprint, Spartanburg, S.C.: Reprint Co., 1959.

Ramsey, J. G. M. *The Annals of Tennessee.* Knoxville: East Tennessee Historical Society, 1967.

Rankin, Hugh F. *The North Carolina Continentals.* Chapel Hill, N.C.: University of North Carolina Press, 1771.

Rankin, Hugh F. *Charles Cornwallis: A Study in Frustration.* New York, 1969.

Robinson, Phillip. *The Plantation of Ulster: British Settlement on an Irish Landscape, 1660-1670.* Dublin: Muesser Co., 1984.

Robinson, Blackwell. *William R. Davie.* Chapel Hill: The University of North Carolina Press, 1959.

Roosevelt, Theodore. *The Winning of the West.* Gloucester, Mass.: Peter Smith Co., 1976.

Salley, A. S., Jr. *Col. William Hill's Memoirs of the Revolution.* Columbia, S.C.: State Co., 1921.

Scheer, George F., and Hugh F. Rankin. *Rebels and Redcoats.* Cleveland, Ohio: World Publishing Company, 1957.

Schenck, David. *North Carolina: A History of the Invasion of the Carolinas by the British Army under Lord Cornwallis in 1780-1781.* Raleigh, N.C.: Edwards and Brought, 1889.

Scotti, Anthony. *Brutal Virtue: The Myth and Reality of Banastre Tarleton.* Bowie, Md.: Heritage Books, 1995.

Scroggins, Michael C. *Huck's Defeat: The Battle of Williamson's Plantation.* York Co. Cultural and Historical Commission, 2002.

Sheehan, Bernard. "The Problem of the Indians in the American Revolution." In *The American Indian Experience,* edited by Philip Weeks. Arlington Heights, Ill.: Forum Press, 1988.

Sheely, Terrence. *Ireland and Her People.* New York: Greenwich House, 1883.

Shelby, Isaac. *Battle of Kings Mountain.* In *Kings Mountain and Its Heroes,* edited by Lyman Draper. Johnson City, Tn.: Overmountain Press, 1996. First published in *American Review* (1945).

Sholes, A. E. *A Chronological History of Savannah.* Savannah, Ga., 1900.

Showman, Richard K., ed. *The Papers of Nathanael Greene, 1766-1781.* 7 vols. Chapel Hill: University of North Carolina Press, 1976-1994.

Skidmore, Warren, and Donna Kaminsky. *Lord Dunmore's Little War of 1774.* Bowie, Md.: Heritage Books, 2002.

Smith, Justin H. *Arnold's March from Cambridge to Quebec.* Bowie, Md.: Heritage Books, 1998.

Smith, William. *Historical Accounts of Bouquet's Expedition Against the Ohio Indians in 1764.* Cincinnati, Ohio: Clarke and Co., 1868.

Snapp, J. Russell. *John Stuart and the Issue of Empire on the Southern Frontier.* Baton Rouge: Louisiana State University Press, 1998.

Sosin, Jack M. *The Revolutionary Frontier: 1763-1783.* Albuquerque: University of New Mexico Press, 1967.

Stedman, Charles. *The History of the Origin, Progress, and Termination of the American War.* 2 vols. London, 1794. Reprint, New York: Arno Press, 1969.

Stemper, Sol. P. *The Bicentenial Guide to the American Revolution.* Vol. III, *War in the South.* New York: E.P. Dutton, 1974.

Stokes, Thomas L. *The Savannah.* Athens: University of Georgia Press, 1951.

Stuart, Charles, ed. *Memoir of the Indian Wars and Other Occurrences: By Col. Stuart of Greenbriar.* New York: Arno Press, 1971.

Tarleton, Banastre. *A History of the Campaigns of 1780 and 1781 in the Southern Provinces of North America.* London: T. Cadell, 1976.

Thaities, Gold, and Louise Kellog. *Documentary History of Dunmore's War: 1774.* Bowie, Md.: Heritage Books, 1989.

Thomas, Sam. *The 1780 Presbyterian Rebellion and the Battle of Huck's Defeat.* York Co. Historical Commission, 1996.

Timberlake, Henry. *The Memoirs of Henry Timberlake, 1765.* New York: Arno Press, Reprint, 1971.

Tracy, M. F. *Prelude to Yorktown: The Southern Campaign of Nathanael Greene, 1780-1781.* Chapel Hill: University of North Carolina Press, 1963.

Tucker, Glenn. *The War of the Revolution.* Harrisburg, Pa.: Stackpole Books, 1973.

———. *Mad Anthony Wayne and the New Nation: The Story of Washinton's Front Line General.* Harrisburg, Pa.: Stackpole Books, 1973.

Turner, Frederick J. *The Frontier in American History.* New York: Dover Press, 1996.

Uhlendorf, Bernard, ed. *The Siege of Charlestown with Diaries of Hessian Officers.* Ann Arbor: University of Michigan Press, 1938.

U.S. Congress. *Report of the Erection of a Monument at Point Pleasant, West Virginia.* 60th Cong., February 1908.

Van Every, Dale. *A Company of Heroes: The American Frontier 1775-1783.* New York: Mentor Books, 1963.

Wallace, Willard M. *Traitorous Hero: The Life and Fortune of Benedict Arnold.* New York: Harper and Brothers, 1954.

Ward, Christopher. *The War of the Revolution.* Edited by John R. Alden. 2 vols. New York: MacMillan Company, 1952.

Weems, Mason L. *The Life of Francis Marion.* Philadelphia, Pa., 1857.

Weigley, Russell. *The American Way of War: A History of United States Military Strategy and Policy.* Bloomington: Indiana University Press, 1977.

————. *The Partisan War: The South Carolina Campaign of 1780-1782.* S.C. Tricentenial Commission, Booklet # 2. Columbia: University of South Carolina Press, 1970.

Weir, Robert M. *Colonial South Carolina.* Columbia: University of South Carolina Press, 1983.

White, Katherine W. *The Kings Mountain Men.* Dayton, Va., 1924.

Wickwire, Franklin, and Mary Wickwire. *Cornwallis: The American Adventure.* Boston: Houghton-Mifflin, 1970.

Wilbur, Marguerite E. *Thomas Jefferson: Apostle of Liberty.* New York: Liveright Publications, 1962.

Wilcox, William B. *The American Experience: Sir Henry Clinton's Narrative of His Campaigns.* New Haven: Yale Press, 1954.

Williams, Otho H. *A Narrative of the Campaign of 1780 by Col. Otho Williams.* Charleston, S.C., 1822.

Wood, Gordon S. *The Americanization of Benjamin Franklin.* New York: Penguin, 2004.

Wood, Gordon, S. *The Greatness of George Washington.* Charlottesville: University of Virginia Press, 2002.

Woodmason, Charles. *The Carolina Backcountry on the Eve of the Revolution: The Journal and Other Writings of Charles Woodmason, Anglican Itinerant.* Edited by Richard J. Hooker. Chapel Hill: University of North Carolina Press, 1953.

Wust, Klaus. *The Virginia Germans.* Charlottesville: The University of Virginia Press, 1969.

Young, Alfred. *The American Revolution: Explorations in*

the History of Radicalism. Dekalb: Northern Illinois University Press, 1976.

Articles

"Battle of Kings Mountain." Compilation from the written reports of Col. William Campbell, Col. Isaac Shelby, and Col. Ben Cleveland. U.S. Congress and *Virginia Gazette.* 18 November 1780.

Burgoyne, John. "A State of the Expedition from Canada." *For the House of Commons.* Reprint. Edited by J. Almond. London: Arno Press, 1969.

Caley, Percy B. "Lord Dunmore and the Pennsylvania-Virginia Border Dispute." *Western Pennsylvania Historical Magazine* 21 (1939): 81-93.

———. "The Life Adventures of Lt. Col. John Connolly: The Story of a Tory." *Western Pennsylvania Historical Magazine* 11 (April 1928): 101-6.

Calloway, Colin G. "We Have Always Been the Frontier: The American Revolution in Shawnee Country. *American Indian Quarterly* 16 (1992): 39-52.

Campbell, Charles. "Introduction to the History of the Colony and Ancient Dominion of Virginia. *Southern Literary Messenger* 14 (1860): 17-26.

Carter, Clarence, ed. "Observations of Superintendent John Stuart and Gov. James Grant of East Florida on the Management of Indian Affairs." *American Historical Society* 20 (1915): 815-31.

Chesney, Alexander. "A South Carolina Loyalist in the Revolution and After." Edited by Alfred Jones. *Ohio State University Bulletin* XXVI, no. 4 (October 1921): 1-149.

Clark, Walter. "The Colony of Transylvania." *North Carolina Historical Society Booklet* III, no. 9 (1926).

Cook, Roy Bird. "Virginia's Frontier Defense." *West Virginia History* 1 (1940): 119-30.

Curry, Richard Orr. "Lord Dunmore and the West." *West Virginia History* 19 (1957-58) 231-43.

Downes, Randolph C. "The Indian War on the Upper Ohio: 1779-1782." *West Virginia Historical Magazine* 17 (1934): 93-115.

———. "Dunmore's War: An Interpretation." *Mississippi Valley Historical Review* 20 (1934): 311-30.

Edwards, William Waller. "Morgan and His Riflemen." *William and Mary Quarterly* XXIII, no. 2 (1914): 73-105.

Evans, Raymond. "The Cherokee." *Journal of Cherokee Studies* II, no. 1 (winter 1977): 24-26.

———. "Notable Persons in Cherokee History: Dragging Canoe." *Journal of Cherokee Studies* 2, no. 1 (1977): 176-89.

Ellison, George. "Cowee Mountain's Wartime History." *The Smoky Mountain News* (December 2001): 1-5.

Fleming, Thomas. "Gentleman Johnny's Wandering Army." *American Heritage Magazine* (December 1972): 82-93.

Foote, W. H. "Cornstalk: The Cherokee Chief." *Southern Literary Messenger* 16, no. 9 (1850): 533-40.

Graham, William A. "The Battle of Ramseur's Mill: June 20, 1780." *Lincoln County Historical Society* 22 (1904): 1-8.

Hedgecoke, Stephanie. "U.S. War Against the Cherokee Nation." *Workers World News* (July 2002): 2.

Howard, Cary. "John Eager Howard: Patriot." *Maryland Historical Magazine* no. 62 (1967): 217-79, 300-17.

Hoyt, William D. "Col. William Fleming in Dunmore's War: 1774." *West Virginia History* 3 (1942): 99-119.

Hudson, Charles M. "The Juan Pardo Expeditions." *Smithsonian Institute Press* (1962): 23, 27-37.

Jones, George F. "The Black Hessians: Negroes Recruited by The Hessians in South Carolina." *South Carolina Historical Magazine* 83, no. 4 (1982): 234-57.

Jones, George F. "A Note on the Victor of Spring Hill Redoubt." *The Georgia Historical Quarterly* LXIV, no. 3 (fall 1979).

Ketchum, Richard M. "England's Vietnam: The American Revolution." *American Heritage* (June 1971).

Kieron, Francis. "The Battle of Guilford Court House." *Journal of American History* VIII (1913): 28-41.

Lambert, Harold. "Cornstalk: King of Rhododendron Country." *West Virginia Historical Magazine* 19 (1957-58): 191-202.

Lewis, Guy Jr. "Norfolk's Worst Nightmare." *Norfolk Historical Society Courier* (spring 2001): 1-4.

Lewis, Virgil. "Manufactured History: Refighting the Battle of Point Pleasant." *West Virginia History* 56 (1902): 76-87.

Lowe, William C. "The Parliamentary Career of Lord Dunmore, 1761-1774." *The Virginia Magazine of History and Biography* 96, no. 1 (January 1988): 3-30.

McAllister, J. T. "The Battle of Point Pleasant." Parts 1 and 2. *The Virginia Magazine of History and Biography* 9 (March 1902): 395-407; 10 (May 1902): 75-92.

McQuire, Odell. "Many Were Sore Chase and Some Cut Down." Parts I-IV. *Rockbridge Advocate* (October–December 1995). Previously Unpublished.

Moomaw, W. Hugh. "The British Leave Colonial Virginia." *The Virginia Magazine of History and Biography* 66 (1958): 147-60.

Murphy, W. S. "The Irish Brigade at the Siege of Savannah, 1779." *The Georgia Historical Quarterly* XXXVIII, no. 4 (December 1954).

Neumann, George C. "The Redcoats' Brown Bess." *American Rifleman* (April 2001): 47-52.

Nichols, John L. "John Stuart: Beloved Father of the Cherokee." *Highlander Magazine* (September/October 1993): 1-9.

Peters, Thelma. "The Loyalists Migrate from Florida to the Bahamas." *Florida Historical Quarterly* 40 (October 1961): 123-41.

Pierce, James P. "Lewis Wetzel: Dark Hero of the Ohio." *The Early American Review* (spring 1997): 37-49.

Posey, John T. "We Appear to Be Very Formidable: Thomas Posey's Revolutionary War Journal, 1776-1777." *Virginia Cavalcade* 44, no.4 (spring 1955): 148-59.

Rankin, Hugh F. "Cowpens: Prelude to Yorktown." *North Carolina Historical Review* XXXI, no. 3 (1954): 336-69.

Reid, Elizabeth. "John Eager Howard." *Magazine of American History* (1881).

Robinson, Blackwell P. "The Revolutionary Sketches of William R. Davie." *North Carolina Division of Archives and History* (1976): 238-48.

Robson, Eric. "The Expedition to the Southern Colonies: 1775-1776." *English Historical Review* LXVI (1951): 535-60.

Rogers, George C., ed. "General O'Hara's Letters." *South Carolina Historical Magazine* 65 (1964): 158-80.

Rogers, Thomas G. "Victory Snatched Away." *Military History Quarterly* (March 1997): 1-10.

Russell, Peter. "The Siege of Charleston: Journal of Capt. Peter Russell." *American Historical Review* 4, no. 3 (1899).

Rye, Isaac. "Evangelical Revolt." *William and Mary Quarterly* 3rd ser., vol. 31 (1974): 345-68.

Simpson-Poffenbarger, Livia. "Point Pleasant: First Battle of the Revolution." *West Virginia History* 36 (October 1974): 40-49.

Sosin, Jack M. "The British Indian Department and Dunmore's War." *The Virginia Magazine of History and Biography* 74 (1966): 34-58.

Swain, D. L. "Indian War of 1778." *Historic Magazine* 1 (1867): 273-75.

Sweet, William W. "The Role of the Anglican Church in the American Revolution." *Huntington Library Quarterly* II (N.d.): 33-70.

Virginia Army account. "Cherokee Expedition of 1776." *Annuals of Southwest Virginia* 2 (1869): 1410.

Wicker, Tom. "Turning Point in the Wilderness: The Clash at Kings Mountain Between Patriots and Tories Began Britain's Long Descent to Yorktown." *Military History Quarterly* (autumn 1998): 1-9.

Wickwire, Franklin B. "Go On and Be Brave: The Battle of Point Pleasant." *Timeline Magazine, the Ohio Historical Society* 4, no. 4 (August-September 1987): 2-15.

Winn, Richard. "General Richard Winn's Notes." *South Carolina Historical and Genealogical Magazine* 43 (1942): 199-206.

Newspapers

Beaufort (S.C.) Gazette, 10 December 1779.

Gazette de Paris, 7 January 1780.

Virginia Gazette, 22 September 1775, 12 and 20 July, 9 August, and 8 September 1776.

South Carolina Gazette, 9 and 11 August 1759.

Pennsylvania Packet, 13 May 1778.

Charleston Courier, 20-21 April 1827.

Charleston Royal Gazette, 23 May 1781.

Papers and Collections

British Headquarters Papers. Colonial Williamsburg, Inc., Williamsburg, Va.

Cornwallis, Charles. Papers. 3 vols., Charles Ross ed. London, England: John Murray Publishers.

Draper, Lyman. Manuscripts. 480 vols. State Historical Society of Wisconsin, Madison, Wisconsin.

Greene, Nathanael. Papers. 7 vols. Howard Showman, ed. Chapel Hill, N.C.: University of North Carolina Press, 1976-1994.

Fleming, William. Papers. Special Collection, Leyburn Library, Washington and Lee University, Lexington, Va.

Jefferson, Thomas. Papers. Julian Boyd ed. 3 vols. Princeton N.J.: Princeton University Press, 1958.

Morgan, Daniel. Papers. Theodorous Myers Collection. New York City Public Library.

Washington, George. Papers. Library of Congress, Washington D.C.

Unpublished Materials

Cheaney, Janie B. "Banastre Tarleton." National Park Service essay, 1998.

———. "Charles Cornwallis." National Park Service essay, 1998.

———. "Daniel Morgan." National Park Service essay, 1998.

Ferguson, Clyde. "General Andre Pickens." Doctoral dissertation, Duke University, 1960.

"Ferguson Rifle." Center for Military History, U.S. Army, Carlisle, Pennsylvania.

National Park Service. "Battle of Cowpens." Parts I-IV. Cowpens Battlefield, South Carolina, and the Center for Military History, U.S. Army, Carlisle, Pennsylvania, 2001.

————. "Battle of Kings Mountain." Parts I-IV. Kings Mountain Battlefield, South Carolina, and the Center for Military History, U.S. Army, Carlisle, Pennsylvania, 2002.

Pettus, Louise. "Battle of Hanging Rock." Paper presented to the York County Cultural and Historic Commission, August 6, 1980.

Russell, Preston A. "Haitans at the Siege of Savannah." Material prepared for inclusion in a booklet for the Coastal Heritage Society, Savannah, Georgia, 2001.

Scoggins, Michael C. "Huck's Defeat, or the Battle of Williamson's Plantation." In York Cultural and Historic Commission booklet, 2002.

Thomas, Sam. "Huck's Defeat, or the 1780 Presbyterian Rebellion." York County Cultral and Historic Commission, 1966.

Watson, S. L. "Expedition Against the Cherokee. Edited by Alfred Fairies. Paper presented to the York County Cultural and Historic Commission, June 1850.

Willard, Kyle. "Culpepper in Dunmore's War." 1955.

Index

Broad Street (in
Charleston), 136
Broughton Street (in
Savannah), 88
Browne, Thomas, 101, 155
Bryan, Morgan, 152, 161,
190
Bryson, Daniel, 72
Buchanan, John, 48
Buck Island, 94
Buckingham Island Ford,
75
Buffalo Ford, 146
Buford, Abraham, 174
Bull, John, 200
Bull Run, Virginia, 215
Bull Street (in Savannah), 88
Bull, William Jr., 61
Bunker Hill, 99
Burgoyne, John, 15, 29,
115, 138, 248, 171, 250,
318
Burnett (American major),
275
Burr's Mill, 245
Butler, John, 292, 299, 302,
304-7
Byrd, William, 61
Byron (British admiral), 90

Calabria, 63
Callasatchee. *See*
Sugartown village

Cambray-Digny, Jean, 126
Cambridge, Massachusetts,
250
Camden, South Carolina,
143-44, 147-48, 150,
153, 155-57, 159, 165-
68, 172, 180, 182, 189,
191, 193-94, 197-200,
210-11, 213, 217, 244,
266, 282, 285, 290, 294,
300
Cameron, Alexander, 69,
75-77
Cameron, Andrew, 64
Cameron, Colin, 88
Campbell, Archibald, 86,
92, 112
Campbell, Arthur, 79
Campbell, Charles, 188,
193, 216
Campbell, William, 29,
79, 83, 212, 215, 218,
222, 224, 227, 230,
233, 237, 293, 296-99,
307-8, 317
Campbell, William Jr., 216
Camp Charlotte, 42, 45, 49
Camp Union, 30-31, 42
Canada, 14-15
Cape Fear River, 177, 319,
322
Cape Hatterras, 117
Carden, John, 190